cultural economy

Culture, Representation and Identities is dedicated to a particular understanding of 'cultural studies' as an inherently interdisciplinary project critically concerned with the analysis of meaning. The series focuses attention on the importance of the contemporary 'cultural turn' in forging a radical re-think of the centrality of 'the cultural' and the articulation between the material and the symbolic in social analysis. One aspect of this shift is the expansion of 'culture' to a much wider, more inclusive range of institutions and practices, including those conventionally termed 'economic' and 'political'.

Paul du Gay is at the Faculty of Social Sciences at The Open University. **Stuart Hall** is Emeritus Professor at the Open University and Visiting Professor at Goldsmiths College, the University of London.

Books in the series:

Representing Black Britain
Black and Asian Images on Television
Sarita Malik

Cultural Economy
Cultural Analysis and Commercial Life
Edited by Paul du Gay and Michael Pryke

cultural economy
cultural analysis and commercial life

edited by paul du gay and
michael pryke

SAGE Publications
London • Thousand Oaks • New Delhi

First published 2002

SAGE Publications Ltd
6 Bonhill Street
London EC2A 4PU

SAGE Publications Inc.
2455 Teller Road
Thousand Oaks, California 91320

SAGE Publications India Pvt Ltd
32, M-Block Market
Greater Kailash - I
New Delhi 110 048

British Library Cataloguing in Publication data

A catalogue record for this book is available
from the British Library

ISBN 0 7619 5992 0
ISBN 0 7619 5993 9 (pbk)

Library of Congress Control Number available

Typeset by Photoprint Typesetters, Torquay
Printed and bound in Great Britain by Athenaeum Press,
Gateshead

contents

Notes on contributors   vii

Acknowledgements   ix

Cultural economy: An introduction   1
Paul du Gay and Michael Pryke

1   Economics as interference   21
        John Law

2   Symbolic economies: the 'culturalization' of economic
        knowledge   39
        John Allen

3   Capturing markets from the economists   59
        Don Slater

4   Work ethics, soft capitalism and the 'turn to life'   78
        Paul Heelas

5   From Holloway to Hollywood: happiness at work in the
        new cultural economy?   97
        Angela McRobbie

6   Identities and industries: the cultural formation of
        aesthetic economies   115
        Keith Negus

7   Re-imagining the ad agency: the cultural connotations
        of economic forms   132
        Sean Nixon

8   Advertising, persuasion and the culture/economy dualism   148
        Liz McFall

9   The unintended political economy   166
        Daniel Miller

10 Production, consumption and 'cultural economy'   185
        Alan Warde

11 Performing cultures in the new economy 201
Nigel Thrift

Index 235

notes on contributors

john allen is Professor and Head of Geography in the Faculty of Social Sciences at the Open University. His recent publications include *Rethinking the Region: Spaces of Neoliberalism* (Routledge, 1998) with Doreen Massey and Alan Cochrane, and *Human Geography Today* (Polity, 1999), edited with Doreen Massey and Phil Satre.

paul du gay is a Senior Lecturer in Sociology and Sub-Dean (Research) in the Faculty of Social Sciences at the Open University. His research is located in the sociology of organizational life. His authored and edited publications include *Consumption and Identity at Work* (Sage, 1996), *Production of Culture/Cultures of Production* (Sage, 1997) and *In Praise of Bureaucracy: Weber, Organization, Ethics* (Sage, 2000).

paul heelas is Professor in Religion and Modernity at Lancaster University. His research interests include religion, spirituality, culture and modern times and amongst his most recent books are *Detraditionalization: Critical Reflections on Authority and Identity* (Blackwell, 1996), edited with Scott Lash and Paul Morris, *The New Age Movement: The Celebration of Self and the Sacralization of Modernity* (Blackwell, 1996) and *Religion in Modern Times* (Blackwell, 2000) edited with Linda Woodhead.

john law is Professor of Technology and Cultural Values in the Department of Sociology and Director of Science Studies at Lancaster University. He has written extensively on the sociology of technology, organizational sociology and actor network theory. His publications include *Actor Network Theory and After* (Blackwell, 1999), edited with John Hassard, and *Organizing Modernity* (Blackwell, 1994).

liz mcfall is a Lecturer in Sociology in the Faculty of Social Sciences at the Open University. Her main research interests are in the sociology and history of economic life. She is currently working on a historical genealogy of advertising practice.

angela mcrobbie is Professor of Media and Cultural Studies in the Department of Media and Communications at Goldsmiths College, University of London. Her research interests include cultural industries (art, fashion, music and magazine), feminist theory, youth and identity. Her books include

British Fashion Design: Rag Trade or Image Industry? (Routledge, 1998) and *In the Culture Society: Art, Fashion and Popular Music* (Routledge, 1999).

daniel miller is Professor of Social Anthropology at University College London. His research centres on consumption. His authored and edited books include *Material Cultures: Why Some Things Matter* (University of Chicago Press, 1998), *A Theory of Shopping* (Polity/Cornell University Press, 1998) and *The Internet: An Ethnographic Approach* (New York University Press, 2000), with Don Slater.

keith negus is a Senior Lecturer in the Department of Media and Communications at Goldsmiths College, University of London. His research focus is creativity and the culture industries with particular reference to the music industry. He is the author of *Music Genres and Corporate Cultures* (Routledge, 1999), *Producing Pop: Culture and Conflict in the Popular Music Industry* (Arnold, 1992) and *Popular Music in Theory* (Polity, 1996).

sean nixon is a Senior Lecturer in Sociology at the University of Essex. His research interests have focused on the relationship between gender and commercial cultures. He is author of *Hard Looks: Masculinities, Spectatorship and Contemporary Consumption* (University of London Press, 1996).

michael pryke is a Lecturer in Geography in the Faculty of Social Sciences at the Open University. His most recent research examines cultures of money and the monetization of space-time. He has recently edited *Unsettling Cities* (Routledge, 1999), with John Allen and Doreen Massey.

don slater is a Reader in Sociology at the London School of Economics. His current research focuses on consumer culture, economic sociology and comparative ethnographies of Internet use. Recent publications include *Consumer Culture and Modernity* (Polity, 1997), *The Internet: An Ethnographic Approach* (Berg, 2000), with Daniel Miller, and *Market Society: Markets and Modern Social Theory* (Polity, 2001), with Fran Tonkiss.

nigel thrift is Professor of Geography in the School of Geographical Sciences at the University of Bristol. His current research includes international business, the nature of consumption, and social and cultural theory. His most recent book is *Spatial Formations* (Sage, 1996).

alan warde is a Professor of Sociology at the University of Manchester and Co-Director of the ESRC Centre for Research on Innovation and Competition (CRIC). His research is in the fields of economic sociology and the sociology of consumption and his recent publications include *Consumption, Food and Taste: Culinary Antimonies and Commodity Culture* (Sage, 1997) and *Eating Out: Social Differentiation, Consumption and Pleasure* (Cambridge University Press, 2000), with Lydia Martens.

acknowledgements

The chapters in this volume derive from a Workshop on Cultural Economy held at the Open University in January 2000. We would like to thank everybody who contributed to the Workshop, especially Richard Sennett and Stuart Hall, who acted as plenary speaker and respondent respectively, and Pamela Walker and Karen Ho, who helped organize the event and ensured its smooth running. Our thanks also to the Geography and Sociology disciplines at the Open University, to Sage Publications, whose financial support enabled the event to take place, and to the Pavis Centre for Social and Cultural Research for playing host.

Finally, a word of gratitude to Julia Hall for commissioning the text and maintaining faith in our capacity to deliver and to the chapter authors who have borne stoically the successive rounds of alterations and amendments.

cultural economy: an introduction

Paul du Gay · Michael Pryke

The sets of processes and relations we have come to know as 'the economy' appear no longer as taken for granted as perhaps once they were. Many of the old certainties – both practical and academic – concerning what makes firms hold together or markets work seem less clear-cut and our knowledge of them feels less secure. Yet among these proliferating uncertainties has emerged – or, better, re-emerged – a belief that something called 'culture' is both somehow critical to understanding what is happening to, as well as to practically intervening in, contemporary economic and organizational life.

This 'cultural turn' takes many different forms depending on context and preferred project. In a number of formal organizational settings – both private and public – for example, senior managers have found themselves turning to 'culture' as a means of attempting to improve organizational per-formance. A central feature of this particular 'cultural turn' is a renewed interest in the production of meaning at work. As Graeme Salaman (1997) has argued, the contemporary interest in 'managing culture' is premised, in large part, upon a belief that so-called 'rationalist', 'mechanistic' or 'bureau-cratic' systems of organization have systematically (sic) destroyed meaning and creativity at work, and that in order to compete effectively in what is conceived of as an increasingly globalized, knowledge-based economy, a foremost necessity is to reverse this process and make new meaning for people at work, thus unleashing their creativity and enterprise. 'Culture' is accorded a privileged position in this endeavour because it is seen to play a crucial role in structuring the way people think, feel and act in organizations. The aim is to produce the sorts of meanings that can enable people to make what senior management consider to be the right and necessary contribution to the success of the organization for which they work. To this end, man-agers are encouraged to view the most effective or 'excellent' organizations as those with the 'right' culture – that ensemble of norms and techniques of conduct that enables the self-actualizing capacities of individuals to become aligned with the goals and objectives of the organization for which they work. As the current head of the British government's Performance and Innovation Unit has argued, solving organizational problems – whether in government or in commerce – is a matter of culture, because it is through culture that people change the way they do things and how they see the world (Mulgan, 1997). One does not have to assume that 'corporate culturalism' unproblematically achieves that which it sets out to accomplish to acknowledge that it constitutes 'a significant part of contemporary organizational life' for an awful lot of people (Thompson and Findley, 1999: 182; see also the contributions by Heelas and McRobbie, this volume).

As in the worlds of formal organization, so too in terms of knowledge, theory and understanding of economic and organizational life within the social sciences. Here, also, culture has assumed an enhanced significance and explanatory weight. This has involved more than academics putting 'cultural' questions closer to the centre of their calculations, alongside economic processes and social and political institutions. Rather, it involves a reversal in the relationship between the vocabularies used to describe things and the things themselves. Instead of viewing a market or firm as existing prior to and hence independently of descriptions of it, the turn to culture instigates a reversal of this perception, by indicating the ways in which objects are constituted through the discourses used to describe them and to act upon them. This is not the same thing as saying that markets and organizations are 'embedded' in a particular socio-cultural context, or that they are 'socially constructed' (Callon, 1999; Crang, 1997: 12). Rather, it is to suggest that economic discourses – not simply or primarily academic 'economics', but those 'hybrid' disciplines such as accounting, marketing, finance, and so forth – format and frame markets and economic and organizational relations, 'making them up' rather than simply observing and describing them from a God's-eye vantage point (Callon, 1998; du Gay and Salaman, 1992; Miller and Rose, 1990).

Thinking for a moment about that object we refer to as 'the economy', it seems obvious that when we seek to manage this entity one of the first things we need to do is build a clear picture of what 'an economy' looks like. We need to ask ourselves: what are its main components, and how do these work, how are they related? In other words, before we can even seek to manage something called an 'economy', it is first necessary to conceptualize or represent a set of processes and relations as an 'economy' which are amenable to management. We need therefore a discourse of the economy, and this discourse, like any other, will depend upon a particular mode of representation: the elaboration of a language and set of techniques for conceiving of and hence constructing an object in a certain way so that object can then be deliberated about and acted upon (Miller and Rose, 1990). Economic discourse here is not simply a matter of beliefs, values and symbols but rather a form of representational and technological (i.e. 'cultural') practice that constitutes the spaces within which economic action is formatted and framed.

And what goes for macro-economic management in this regard also applies to micro-economic management. A crucial feature of many forms of interactive service work, for example, is the more or less direct relationship they involve between one or more service provider and one or more service consumer. The inseparability of the production and consumption of such services makes it difficult for both the manager of the service organization and the service consumer to isolate service quality from the quality of the service provider. In other words, the process of 'disentangling' or 'framing' necessary to the realization of a market transaction is obviously a problem in a context where the interpersonal links, the attachments, are inscribed in the service relation itself (Callon, 1998: 34). A wide range of calculative techniques and technologies have emerged to address this 'problem', each of which is aimed at increasing the ability of producers to 'frame' the service relation and each of which relies upon, albeit in different ways and to different degrees, the subtle imbrication of economic knowledge with other forms of cultural practice (Allen and du Gay, 1994).

Take, for instance, the case of certain forms of retail service work. As the quality of interactive service delivery has been represented as the main determinant of a firm's competitive success or failure, employees involved in such work have found themselves being recruited and trained on the basis of their propensity to exhibit particular capacities and dispositions aimed at winning over the hearts and minds of customers. Through sustained exposure to an often weird and wonderful range of interpersonal and communication management techniques – such as transaction analysis – these service workers have found themselves being trained in how to fashion their conduct – bodily comportment, aural and visual characteristics, and so forth – in order to produce certain meanings for customers and thus a sale for the company. In addition, however, as those training them make clear, they are also being equipped with a set of skills that will stand them in good stead not only inside the workplace but also in the context of other forms of social interaction (du Gay, 1996; Nickson et al., 2001).

Focusing on such forms of service work indicates how difficult it is to disentangle 'economic' from other cultural categories in 'economically relevant practices', to use John Law's term (this volume). This observation holds for work in the marketing, financial and commercial service industries as much as it does for the more direct servicing work found in parts of the retail, hotel and tourist-related trades. The links between economic and other cultural categories in the marketing and advertising industries, where the core task concerns managing, or attempting to manage, the relationship between products and consumers, may be quite readily apparent (see the contributions by Slater, Nixon and McFall, this volume). These links are of equal, if less obvious, significance in other industries. In finance, for example, particularly merchant banking, the elements of communication, display and presentation are not simply restricted to the culture of the 'deal'. Financial networks can be viewed as socio-cultural networks in which 'relationship management' holds the key to economic success (Abolafia, 1998; Thrift, 1994). In so far as international financial centres are effectively characterized by streams of information, each of which is open to interpretation and each with its own contacts, one of the significant skills within international finance is the ability to make and hold contacts, to construct relationships of trust, and to be part of the interpretation of what's really happening. Moreover, the workings of such networks involve more than technical knowledge of financial economists. The pricing models and financial engineering that such experts compose and put in play, for example, are simply surface indications of both the culturally shaped imaginations of space-time and display a collective trust in a monetized future that allow so-called 'new financial instruments', such as derivatives, to work as forms of money (Pryke and Allen, 2000; see also Dodd, 1994: 136). As Thrift (1994) points out, far from a reduction in the need for face-to-face contact in the international financial centres, even allowing for the profusion of 'hard' electronic technologies, there is now greater emphasis on the presentation of self, face work, negotiating skills, and so forth, in large part because of the increasing requirement to be able to read people as well as the increasingly transactional nature of business relationships between firms and clients (see also Allen and Pryke, 1994; Pryke, 1991; Pryke and Lee, 1995). Similarly, the work of Abolafia (1998) shows us traders obsessed with networking, 'multiplying entanglements', as Callon (1998: 40) puts it, the better to calculate economic advantage.

Because contemporary service work involves both economic and other forms of cultural knowledge the identity of services is simply not amenable to representation in terms of a binary divide between 'economics', on the one hand, and 'culture', on the other. Rather than being solely an 'economic' or a 'cultural' phenomenon, service work is a contingent assemblage of practices built up from parts that are economic and non-economic (but always already cultural) and forged together in the pursuit of increased sales and competitive advantage.

But if economics – seen in their broadest sense to include accounting, marketing, and so on – are understood as particular material-cultural or 'discursive' practices, what are the ramifications for the traditional dualism between 'culture' and 'economics' that has structured so much debate in the social sciences? The first thing to note is that this 'discursive' conception of 'culture' effectively overturns, or, at the very least, side-steps, the criticial representation of 'culture' as always already on one side of a presumed opposition – between 'culture' and 'politics', 'culture' and 'economics', and so on. As long as debate is structured around such distinctions – between, say, a cultural logic that pertains to human inwardness (and intrinsic meaning) and an economic logic that does not (i.e. Sayer, 1997) – then we will continue to miss the point; namely, that 'culture' is not a logic, sphere, value or 'life-order' at all (Turner, 1992: 43). As Weber (1948: 323–59), for example, argued long ago, we are cultural beings precisely because we are not natural, living, social, religious, poltical or economic beings. This particular understanding of economics as 'culture' focuses attention on the practical ways in which 'economically relevant activity' is performed and enacted. It serves to show, in other words, the ways in which the 'making up' or 'construction' of economic realities is undertaken and achieved; how those activities, objects and persons we categorize as 'economic' are built up or assembled from a number of parts, many of them supplied by the disciplines of economics but many drawn from other sources, including, of course, forms of ostensibly non-economic cultural practice (Miller, 2000; Slater, this volume).

To highlight the contingent 'assemblage' of the 'economic' in this way is not to endorse a politics, as some advocates of the 'cultural turn' can appear to imply. For the latter, the discovery of 'contingency' serves to free up ideologically frozen relations of dependence and domination in the name of human possibility and inventiveness. As Charles Turner (1992: 3) for example has argued, the declaration that particular forms of (economic) conduct and practice are not 'natural' is 'no longer made in order to contrast them with a "really" natural mode waiting to be uncovered, nor is it founded on a belief that the attainment of the truly "natural mode" is the task of politics'. Rather, the politics that is presumed to follow from the discovery of 'contingency' is 'that declaration, that predicative activity, the asssertion that a state of affairs could have been and can be otherwise' (Turner, 1992: 3). This turns out to be a bit of a canard, though, for it seems very difficult, if not impossible, to make contingency a matter of either celebration or suspicion, as opposed to a brute fact that has to be dealt with. This is a difficult lesson for some proponents of the 'cultural turn' to learn; they appear to believe that what they take to be their epistemological sophistication gives them a political advantage over those who, for example, maintain a belief in objectivity. But this, as Stanley Fish has indicated, is a 'flat-out misreading of the lesson that anti-foundationalism preaches' (1994: 20). If all arguments, for example, are contingent and therefore challengeable at some basic level, then no argument, including the argument that all arguments are contingent and therefore challengeable, can claim an epistemological (or political) superiority that would give its advocates any sort of advantage 'independent of the hard work of presenting evidence, elaborating analogies, marshalling authorities, and so on' (Fish, 1994: 20). It is because all arguments owe their force to contingency at some level that no meta-argument can claim contingency for itself alone or bestow a progressive politics upon it. 'Contingency', as Fish indicates, 'is a given and can count neither for nor against an argument; any argument must still make its way by the same routes that were available before contingency was recognized' (1994: 20).

This in turn suggests that, while one can profess a cultural or discursive view of economics and continue to make strong economic assertions, one cannot necesarily do economics in a way that follows on from one's convictions concerning its cultural constitution. This is because doing economics and doing, what we might term, 'cultural economy' are two rather different sorts of practice. As Callon (1998: 50) has suggested, the objects of economics are made up by ignoring or forgetting their cultural or social constitution. Doing economics means acting on the assumption of a determinate nature waiting to be described and calculated about by a neutral observation language; doing 'cultural economy' means acting on the assumption that economics are performed and enacted by the very discourses of which they are supposedly the cause. Any attempt by social scientists to enrich practically what Callon (1998: 34) describes as the 'cold and disincarnated' objects of economics may be on a hiding to nothing precisely because it risks confusing two distinct practices, with a subsequent loss of focus (and purpose) for them both.

increasing 'culturalization'?   Exploring and assessing the explanatory reach of this 'economics as culture' or 'cultural economy ' perspective provides one of the central themes of this volume, as a brief examination of the individual chapters makes clear. It does not, however, provide the sole focus. For our term 'cultural economy' is also designed to carry another register of meaning or signify another set of debates. This second strand refers to certain epochal claims – often associated with terms such as 'economies of signs', 'the network society', ' the knowledge economy', and so on and so forth – that we are living through an era in which economic and organizational life has become increasingly 'culturalized' (Castells, 2000; Lash and Urry, 1994; Leadbeater, 1999). So what does it mean to talk about 'cultural economy' in this latter sense?

Well, one of the most sustained attempts to make this argument is contained in work of Scott Lash and John Urry. In their book *Economies of Signs and Space*, they argue that

> Economic and symbolic processes are more than ever interlaced and interarticulated; that is . . . the economy is increasingly culturally inflected and . . . culture is more and more economically inflected. Thus the boundaries between the two become more and more blurred and the economy and culture no longer function in regard to one another as system and environment.
>
> (Lash and Urry, 1994: 64)

In attempting to back up their claim that the economy is now more than ever 'culturalized' they point to a number of developments. For example, they argue that organizations whose business involves the production and distribution of cultural hardware and software have become amongst the most innovative and creative economic actors in the world. Today, the 'culture' industries broadly defined and other so-called 'soft' knowledge intensive industries not only represent some of the most important economic growth sectors but also offer paradigmatic instances of the de-differentiation of 'culture' and 'economy' in terms of their own business practices (Lash and Urry, 1994: 108–9).

Second, Lash and Urry argue that more and more of the goods and services produced for consumers across a range of sectors can be conceived of as 'cultural' goods, in that they are deliberately and instrumentally inscribed with particular meanings and associations as they are produced and circulated in a conscious attempt to generate desire for them amongst end-users. They maintain that there is a growing aestheticization or 'fashioning' of seemingly banal products whereby these are marketed to consumers in terms of particular clusters of meaning, often linked to 'lifestyles', and this is taken as an indication of the increased importance of 'culture' to the production and circulation of a multitude of goods and services. This process, they argue, has been accompanied by the increased influence of what are often termed the 'cultural intermediary occupations' of advertising, design and marketing; those practitioners who play a pivotal role in articulating production with consumption by attempting to associate goods and services with particular cultural meanings and to address those values to prospective buyers (Lash and Urry, 1994: 222).

Finally, Lash and Urry suggest that the growing importance accorded to signifying practices in doing business is evident not only in the production, design and marketing of goods and services, but also in the internal life of organizations as well. Indeed, as we have seen, there has a been a distinct 'turn to culture' within the world of business and organization in recent years that is premised, in part, on the belief that in order to compete effectively in the turbulent, increasingly internationalized markets of the present, a foremost necessity for organizations is to change the way they conduct their business and the ways that people conduct themselves in organizations (Lash and Urry, 1994: 108)

Now it is important to note that the empirical significance of these epochal claims of 'increased culturalization' needs careful consideration. Authors working in fields as diverse as the social anthropology of economic life and the history of advertising practice, for example, have indicated just how empiricially insubstantial are the exemplary oppositions – between a more 'use'-value-centred past and a more 'sign'-value-centred present – that run through epochalist accounts such as these (Douglas and Isherwood,

1979; McFall, 2000 and this volume; Miller, 1995; Nixon, 1997; Sahlins, 1976). Much of the hyperbole surrounding claims of increased 'culturaliza-tion' can be explained, perhaps, by the fact that those taking the 'cultural turn' in the field of economic and organizational analysis are busy finding 'culture' where previously none was thought to exist. However, they also tend, perhaps, to work against the grain of 'cultural economic' analysis, as an emergent form of inquiry concerned with the practical material-cultural ways in which 'economic' objects and persons are put together from dis-parate parts, by setting up their co-ordinates too far in advance and thus leaving no 'way out' from their terms of reference. This has the effect of rendering certain potentially important, if (seen from the heights of grand 'theory') often seemingly banal, contextual details insignificant or even in-visible. As we argued earlier, techniques of 'economic management' do not come ready-made. They have to be invented, stabilized, refined and repro-duced; they have to be disseminated and implanted in practices of various kinds in a range of different locales. This involves much hard, tedious work whose success and effects cannot be taken for granted 'in advance'. Thus, the emergence and development of such techniques are probably not best expli-cated in terms of the large-scale transformative processes – transitions from Fordism to post-Fordism or from organized to disorganized capitalism, for example – beloved of much epochal theorizing, but rather cry out for the 'grey, meticulous and patiently documentary' genealogical methods recom-mended by Foucault (1986: 76), among many others (see also the contribu-tions of Law and McFall, this volume). This should not be taken to imply an out-and-out rejection of all claims of contemporary 'culturalization'. Quite obviously there are many substantive developments in economic and orga-nizational relations – such as the obsession amongst senior managers of large enterprises with changing 'corporate culture', which we mentioned earlier – that might conceivably be explicable in terms of some sort suitably situated 'culturalization' hypothesis[1] (see the contributions by Allen, Heelas, McRobbie and Warde, this volume). However, it is important that such claims be assessed with care and on more of a case-by-case basis rather than simply being assumed or asserted. As Paul di Maggio, for example, has argued in relationship to the current upsurge of interest in all things 'cultur-al' in the field of economic and organizational analysis, 'the price of the insights and explanatory power that a cultural perspective can generate is an enduring scepticism toward "culturalist" accounts that claim too much or generalize too broadly' (1994: 27).

As di Maggio suggests, an attitude of scepticism towards culturalist accounts that would over-reach themselves is not the same thing as outright hostility to culturalist approaches *per se*. Ray and Sayer, however, come per-ilously close to making such a categorial error in their discussion of 'culture'/ 'economy' relations, in general, and epochalist representations of cultural-

economic implosion, in particular. According to them, epochalist representations are actually dependent upon a general distinction between 'cultural'
and 'economic' logics which they are incapable of acknowledging (Ray and
Sayer, 1999: 4). Although epochal theorists continually trade on the contemporary dissolution of 'the culture–economy distinction', they 'are unable
to stop referring to the cultural and the economic separately, which suggests
that we actually need it' (Ray and Sayer, 1999: 4). The problem centres on
the nature of the 'it' that Ray and Sayer suggest we still need. They argue
that '"culture" and "economy" are not synonyms' (1999: 4) for, if they were,
cultural studies could be renamed economic studies with no loss of meaning
or intellectual purpose. Yet, few, if any, proponents of the contemporary cultural turn, including those we might reasonably categorize as 'epochally' oriented, would suggest they were synonymous. Ray and Sayer then proceed to
argue that 'culture' and 'economy' are not 'antonyms, and neither do they
refer to separable "spheres" of social life'. Furthermore, since the basic terms
have several meanings, there may well be more than one culture–economy
distinction' (1999: 4). This seems all very plausible. As we have already seen,
it is practically quite difficult to institute *a general, prior, analytic distinction*
between 'culture' and 'economy' when, on the one hand, as Sayer himself
elsewhere acknowledges, the 'economy has always been as much a cultural
site as any other part of society, such as the family, community or school'
(1997: 7), and, on the other, a range of non-reducible and non-transferrable
culture–economy distinctions are continually emerging and re-emerging in
specific sites and contexts – in ongoing processes of generating social distinctions between different classes of person (Bourdieu, 1984), for example.
The point here is that actual cultural interests and capacities – and the distinctions they might give rise to – can only be formulated and assessed in the
context of definite normative and technical regimes (such as those provided
by educational, aesthetic, legal, economic, political, sexual or familial institutions). There is no reason to assume that these regimes are founded on any
prior, general analytic distinction or opposition between 'culture' and something else – 'economy', for instance – rather than such a distinction emerging historically as a contingent feature, say, of particular relations between
such regimes.

Yet, having indicated how difficult it is to maintain a general analytic
distinction between 'culture' and 'economy', Ray and Sayer (1999: 4) proceed to argue for one on the grounds of political and theoretical necessity.
The distinction they formulate, though, is a remarkably familiar one. They
argue that it is possible to distinguish between an economic logic that is concerned with the calculation of means/ends relations and a cultural logic that
is concerned with ends in themselves. As Sayer puts it, an analytic distinction
between 'culture' and 'economy' needs to be maintained in terms of 'a difference between intrinsically meaningful activities, artefacts and relationships

whose value is primarily internal, and instrumental activities directed towards the external goal of the reproduction of social life' (1997: 8). As Ian Hunter (1994: 149) has indicated, it was Kant who 'posited the existence of a universal moral imperative in terms of the pursuit of the good "for its own sake" – rather than because one was inclined to pursue it as the result of social training and practice, or because it served a worldly purpose'. Even Max Weber's discussion of value-rational behaviour – the case of a person who pursues an ultimate end even in the face of great social and personal cost – is a Kantian example (and this from possibly *the* supreme cultural economist [Hennis, 1988: 135]). However, Kant's 'identification of ultimate ends with the existance of a unified moral personality governed by a universal sense of moral duty' (Hunter 1994: 149) is very different from Weber's more historical and anthropological programme. For Weber, as we saw earlier, cultural interests and capacities are not the expression of a universal moral personality; they are the plural creation of historically specific ethics or 'life orders' (du Gay, 2000; Hunter, 1988; Turner, 1992). The ends of value-rational action are therefore 'multiple and specific to particular regimes: religious, legal, economic, aesthetic, and so on', as Hunter indicates. For Weber 'the "ultimate" character of such action merely refers to the zeal with which a particular end is adhered to in one of these domains'.

This in turns suggests that Weber's historical and anthropological programme cannot sustain a general analytic distinction between formal and substantive rational action (or between 'intrinsically' and 'instrumentally' oriented activity, as Ray and Sayer prefer it), and this for two reasons. First, because the pursuit of ends in a substantively rational manner is itself dependent upon a certain formalization or disciplining of ethical life. In other words, it is the product of socio-cultural relations of training and practice within specific spaces and contexts. Second, the 'formal' rationality of economic management, for example, itself gives rise to substantive ethical goals. In *Economy and Society* (1978: II, 956–1005), Weber points to the 'formalistic impersonality' of bureaucratic organization – its refusal to acknowledge inherited differences in status and prestige – as a source of social levelling and democratic equalization: '[C]onsistent bureaucratic domination means the levelling of "status honor" . . . [T]he dominant norms are concepts of straightforward duty. Everyone is subject to formal equality of treatment' (1978: II, 975).

Similar complexity can be discerned in Weber's discussions of substantively rational activity. In *Economy and Society* (1978: II, 812–13), he describes the workings of a theocratically oriented, substantively rationalized legal system, where decisions based upon the ultimate imperatives of religion hold sway over the formal rationality produced by adherence to positive legal procedure. In so doing, he points to the manner in which legal formalism is capable of developing and sustaining a substantive defence against the arbitrary exercise of power precisely because of its procedural imperviousness to ultimate moral imperatives.

> Formal justice is thus repugnant to all authoritarian powers, theocratic as well as patriarchic, because it diminishes the dependency of the individual upon the grace and power of the authorities. To democracy, however, it has been repugnant because it decreases the dependency of the legal practice and therewith of the individuals upon the decisions of their fellow citizens. . . . In all these cases formal justice, due to its necessarily abstract character, infringes upon the ideals of substantive justice. It is precisely this abstract character which constitutes the decisive merit of formal justice . . . to those who on ideological grounds attempt to break down authoritarian control or to restrain irrational mass emotions for the purposes of opening up individual opportunities and liberating capacities.
>
> (Weber, 1978: II, 812–13)

As Weber's work suggests, any attempt to instigate categorical distinctions between 'intrinsically' and 'instrumentally' oriented activity in order to support a general normative analysis of economic and cultural life will quickly come up against brute empirical realities that it will not be able to account for or make much reasonable sense of. And this for two reasons. First, as Ian Hunter has argued, 'value-oriented or substantive rationality do not [sic] constitute a single universal Kantian moral imperative capable of functioning as a moral yardstick for all other forms of rationality' (1994: 150). Second, as Weber's examples clearly indicate, formally and substantively oriented conducts are too contextually specific and historically contingent to allow them to function as a general 'means–ends' moral discriminator in the manner implied by Ray and Sayer's theoretical distinction. Albert Hirschman (1977: 133), for example, has shown how formally rational economic conduct or 'self-interest' became regarded, in the early modern period, as a vehicle for exorcizing those disastrous 'passions' (associated with the 'full human personality') that had fuelled the European wars of religion.

Ray and Sayer (1999) seem bemused to find that, despite their insistence on the contemporary implosion of 'economy' and 'culture' or the dematerialization of the economic into a plethora of signs, scapes and networks, some proponents of the 'cultural turn' continue to deploy the terms 'culture' and 'economy' in distinct and meaningful ways. This, they argue, is a contradiction. It is not necessarily so. As we have already seen, to do cultural economy is not the same thing as doing technical economics; but, equally, to profess a culturalist view of economic and organizational life does not preclude one from making strong economic assertions – concerning the ways in which markets are formed, the ways in which the marketing of goods and services takes place, or the ways different accounting technologies transform the meaning and reality of organizational management. One can continue to use the terms 'economy' and 'culture' in doing 'cultural economy' without one's practice falling apart. What one should, perhaps, avoid trying to do is to impose a general analytic distinction between 'economy' and 'culture' on one's material prior to examining, anthropologically, its practical constitution.

the structure of the book　　The chapters in this book are organized around these two particular notions of 'cultural economy'. In other words, they approach 'cultural economy' either as a means of exploring the ways in which economic and organizational life is built up, or assembled from, a range of disparate, but inherently cultural, parts, or as a series of claims concerning the extent to which economic and organizational relations in the present are more thoroughly 'culturalized' than their historical predecessors. More often than not they end up, either explicitly or implicitly, developing both strands at the same time.

The text is divided into four broad parts. Part One (Chapters 1–3), is concerned predominantly with 'cultural economy' in the first sense of this term, as a means of analysing the construction of disparate forms of economic knowledge and the constitution of economically relevant activity. In Chapter 1, John Law seeks to develop a set of conceptual tools that help to make sense of material practices that are both economic and cultural and to draw attention to the complexity of practices that run through the 'economic' . He does this by drawing on developments derived from semiotics, post-structuralism and Science and Technology Studies and provides a fascinating exploration of the material orderings of a case study laboratory which reflect and perform enterprise, administration and science as 'vocation'. The account he relates makes central some of the major issues at the heart of cultural economy.

Law argues, first, that practices, subjects and cultures, including forms of economic calculation, such as accounting, should be understood as materially heterogeneous relations. Second, in line with Callon and with others in this volume, he argues that these relations are performed and the style of the performances should be attended to; that, in other words, economic subjectivities are the outcome of interference. For as Callon (1998: 23) points out, highlighting the work of Peter Miller (1998), accounting tools (to which both Law and Daniel Miller in this volume make explicit reference) do not simply aid the measurement of economic activity, they shape the reality they measure and thereby contribute to the performance of calculative agencies and modes of calculation in much the same way that economics 'perform the economy' (Callon 1998: 26). Furthermore, caught in such dynamics, the management of such an organization, for example Law's case study Daresbury, find themselves accounting for their action in a discourse shaped to a growing extent by agents – accountants and management consultants – who have recently entered the frame. Lastly, Law argues that the calculative agent required of economics is always in the making, is never complete. This leads him to conclude that, rather than economic culture, the idea of 'economically relevant activity' captures the 'complexities and the heterogeneous materials that produce and are produced within those practices'.

In Chapter 2 John Allen draws attention to the sidelining of expressive forms of economic knowledge as interest focuses on the elision of culture and the economy. While the emphasis on the creative and the cultural has grown, particularly as creative skills are now associated with the profitability and future of the so-called 'new culturalized economy', so the need to recognize aesthetic and more affective forms of knowledge has also gained ground. Invoking the work of Ernst Cassirer and with echoes of Simmel, who long ago insisted 'that the whole human being is involved in the acquisition of knowledge' and drew attention to the 'importance of humans' "inner life" (feelings, affects, will, motivations, etc.) and the role it plays in the acquisition of knowledge' (Kaern, 1990: 76), Allen makes a case for more affective forms of knowledge to be recognized in cultural economy. For, as his chapter argues, even in the most recent approaches to economic knowledge, such as those written by John Urry, Scott Lash and Robert Reich, and even the likes of Charles Leadbeater, the cognitive is prioritized over the expressive forms of economic know-how. Both culture and economy, for Allen, run together in all economic sectors, combining in different strengths the abstract, the expressive, the affective and the aesthetic, making each distinctive while not making any combination, such as the material and the symbolic, exclusive to any one sector.

As Callon has argued, 'The market is not a two-step process with a competition phase followed by an exchange phase. The type of representation puts the creation process of products and demand for these products in parenthesis, a process which involves a web of close connections between designers, producers, distributors and consumers' (Callon, 1998: 43; see also Callon, 2000). In the same spirit, in Chapter 3, Don Slater unearths the networking involved in 'capturing the the customer'. Slater adopts an angle to the fusion of culture and economy that more or less belongs within the cultural turn. Through reporting an ethnography of cultural intermediaries, advertising agents, Slater argues forcefully that 'cultural' and 'economic' action in markets and market relations can never meaningfully be separated out; they are entangled and interdependent within the social practices of making markets (see also Crang, 1997; Slater and Tonkiss, 2001: 195). He argues further that lessons drawn from studies of consumption and material culture might usefully be adopted in an approach to cultural economy which treats such categories as *lived processes* rather than formal categories. Moreover, in line with a cultural economy approach outlined earlier in this introduction, he repeats Callon's insistence that economic theory is brought into this analysis of the economic processes: economic theory is an active participant in the making of economic realities.

Part Two (Chapters 4–5) focuses on the issue of work ethics in the present and the question of their increasing 'culturalization'. In Chapter 4, Paul Heelas suggests that a useful way of arguing against those who conceive of the economic realm as impervious to culture is to examine the role played in economic and organizational life by work ethics. Having established the 'cultural-economic' character of work ethics, Heelas proceeds to discuss the extent to which contemporary work ethics might be considered more 'culturalized' than their historical predecessors by focusing on what he terms the contemporary 'self-work ethics' of 'soft capitalism'. For Heelas, the development of this soft self-work ethic is in large part due to the perceived failure of other forms of work ethics. He identifies, in particular, the inability of certain traditional forms of work ethics adequately to grasp or deal with what he considers to be the cultural 'turn to life' – 'life' as that 'inner' realm that is regarded as ultimately belonging to the individual alone – among those better educated, more expressivistic members of Western societies.

This 'turn to life' and its related 'self-work ethics' also forms the central focus of Chapter 5. Here, Angela McRobbie charts the growing importance of a particular ideal of self-expressive work in the so-called 'creative industries' (see also McRobbie, 1998). As she argues, these industries are continually represented – by management gurus, academics and politicians, for example – as leading-edge exemplars of an emerging 'talent-led economy' populated by youthful individuals who demonstrate a perpetual capacity for energy, creativity, resourcefulness, resilience and enterprise, and, as such, are continually mined for ethical models of economic and personal conduct for all members of the population to emulate. In considering the discursive construction of this ethic of self-expressive work in the creative industries and in charting some of the inequities it generates, McRobbie has cause to engage with, and offer critiques of, recent, influential general analyses of the changing cultures of work proffered by Richard Sennett (1998), Ulrich Beck (2000) and Charles Leadbeater (1999).

McRobbie's chapter provides a useful framing device for and bridge to the concerns of Part Three (Chapters 6–8). Here the focus is on the historical and contemporary cultural-economic constitution of aesthetic and creative economies. In Chapter 6, Keith Negus draws attention to an important shift that has occurred in the study of the production of popular music. He charts a move way from approaches that attempt to understand the impact of specific forms of industrial production on aesthetic artefacts (by applying notions of 'industry' to 'culture') towards a perspective which approaches aesthetic production as an assemblage of cultural-economic activities (by applying theories of culture to industry). Focusing on the activities of staff working in the recording industry, Negus indicates how this shift of emphasis enables a more complex understanding of the dynamics of aesthetic production within this and other so-called 'culture industries'. In particular, he shows how different occupational groupings within the recording industry are infused by particular norms and techniques of conduct – what he terms a 'culture of production' – and how the latter contribute to the construction and maintenance of highly distinct boundaries within the industry.

In Chapter 7, Sean Nixon explores one particular aspect of the service relation in advertising – the contract of agreement between client and agency – as a means of analysing the cultural economy of contemporary advertising practice. He indicates the ways in which financial arrangements – specifically forms of remuneration – established in these contracts both reflect and enact particular assumptions about the identity of advertising agents as certain sorts of service provider. He argues that the symbolic signficance of these financial forms is as great as, if not greater than, their economic or commercial significance. He shows how recent attempts by advertisers to 're-imagine' the nature of their business, as a response to perceived changes in their commercial environment, have at their core a reconceptualization of the forms of financial compensation which agencies receive from clients. The focus on remuneration is so important to advertising's 'cultural change' agenda, he argues, precisely because of the powerful meanings it carries about the nature of the client/agency relationship.

Nixon's empirical focus helps to provide a more nuanced account of the cultural economy of advertising than those more epochalist accounts that have dominated cultural analysis in this area (Wernick, 1991). In Chapter 8, Liz McFall ploughs a similar furrow, indicating how detailed, historical genealogical work on advertising practice issues a distinct challenge to purveyors of the 'increased culturalization' hypothesis. Focusing on the issue of 'persuasiveness' as a means of analysing claims about advertising's 'culturalizing' role, she argues that historically theorized accounts have tended to be weakly historically empiricized. Evidence of 'increased persuasiveness', she suggests, is drawn primarily from textual work. The latter suffer from a lack of contextualization that prevents them from offering grounded analyses of the significance of advertising at any given time. She concludes that a contextualized historical study of advertising as cultural-economic practice provides a useful antidote to the over-dramatic assertions inherent in epochal accounts of increasing culturalization.

The final part of the book (Chapters 9–11) is concerned with exploring the relationship between cultural economy and political economy. In

Chapter 9, Daniel Miller distinguishes between two aspects of the contemporary 'cultural turn' and indicates why he finds one compelling and the other far less so when it comes to understanding the political economy of modern capitalism. He argues that the 'cultural turn' as a particular approach to the study of economic institutions within the social sciences (cultural economy in our first sense of the term) has provided some important explanatory advances which it would be foolish for political economists to ignore. However, he is far less sanguine about claims of 'increasing cultutralization', which imply a change in the object of analysis rather than in the style of analysis. For Miller, this sort of 'cultural turn' can offer no insights into the political economy of modern capitalism. Rather it imposes a remarkably abstract self-referential model on material whose constitution it never bothers to investigate empirically but simply assumes in advance. For Miller this aspect of the 'cultural turn' possesses an elective affinity with what he considers to be the dominant development in contemporary market and non-market institutions and processes, the rise of 'virtualism' – hyperabstract, fetishistic modelling that effectively creates that which it purports to describe.

In Chapter 10, Alan Warde chooses to work with what he calls a 'more operational definition of culture' in addressing what for him, and for other authors in this volume, has become a central question: the degree to which 'contemporary economic relations are more or less culturalized than their historical predecessors'. He takes as his starting point Raymond Williams' three uses of the term 'culture' – a general process of intellectual, spiritual and aesthetic development; a particular way of life; and the works and activities of intellectual and especially artistic life – and inserts each into the claim that the economy, to include industrial activities, consumption and advertising, has become more culturalized. While Warde's chapter works towards an affirmation of the claim that today's economic relations are 'more or less' culturalized, his approval is not without qualification. Such qualification draws upon his detailed empirical studies of economic practices, work experiences and the functioning of economic organizations. In the end, it seems to him that the 'logic of economizing' has not been as thoroughly culturalized as some proponents might have us believe. For while consumer culture and the outputs of the culture industry, with the associated multiplication of mediatization, advertising and sophisticated selling techniques, have certainly moved on apace, the implication simply does not hold that the outcome is the cultural saturation of everyday life and the weakening of the logic of economic practice.

The issue of the growing significance of the manipulation of organizational cultures touched upon by Warde, and earlier by Law, becomes the central focus of the last chapter. Here Nigel Thrift raises issues related to the emergence of what he refers to as 'fast' managerial subjects. He explores some of the significant related pressures – such as those stemming from drives towards short-term performance and the desire for a faster pace of business life – which inform today's business spaces which are the breeding places, as it were, of his fast managerial subjects. Management subjects, he argues, are being produced through three types of active and performative space through which, Callon (1998) would suggest, ideas and material practices are being circulated. Together, these entangled spaces constitute what Thrift calls a *new geographical machine* able to make new qualities and quantities visible and therefore available to be worked upon. This new machine draws on a number of influences to produce three spatialities, each of which is infused with the new business cultures. The increasing influence of business magazines shapes new *spaces of visualization*; the employment of performative techniques in the practices of management work on subjects to produce new *spaces of embodiment*; and the increasing mobility of management represents *new spaces of circulation*. Taken together these spatialities are the chief inspiration for his claim that the cultural economy of significant business markets heralds a new phase of 'caring imperialism'.

note

1. Take the way that the economy today is being talked about. Technical economic know-how sometimes seems to be giving way to a set of interlinking appeals that draws upon a range of disciplines and images. What has been called the 'therapeutization of the economic' sees an 'economic' issue such as unemployment approached not in terms of the need to tinker with aggregate demand, but as a socio-cultural-economic issue revolving around the 'attitude' of the unemployed: 'They need conselling and advice on how to represent themselves for employment' (Thompson, 1999: 609). Similarly, national and international competitiveness calls for economic agents and organizations to respond to the demands of what Callon (2000), amongst many others, terms 'highly self-reflexive markets'. And by acting out and through the images conjured up by cultural dispatches calling for economic actors to be (more) innovative, efficient and better performers, and by adapting to the recent and profound shifts that have taken place about how markets should work, the 'economy' is made to be more self-reflexive and hence more competitive.

references

Abolafia, M. (1998) 'Markets as cultures', in M. Callon (ed.), *The Laws of the Markets*. Oxford and Keele: Blackwell and the Sociological Review.

Allen, J. and du Gay, P. (1994) 'Industry and the rest: the economic identity of services', *Work, Employment & Society*, 8 (2): 255–71.

Allen, J. and Pryke, M. (1994) 'The production of service space', *Environment and Planning D. Society and Space*, 12 (4): 453–76.

Beck, U. (2000) *The Brave New World of Work*. Cambridge: Polity.

Bourdieu, P. (1984) *Distinction*. London: Routledge.

Callon, M. (1998) 'Introduction: the embeddedness of economic markets in economics', in M. Callon (ed.), *The Laws of the Markets*. Oxford and Keele: Blackwell and the Sociological Review.

Callon, M. (1999) 'Actor network theory – the market test', in J. Law and J. Hassard (eds), *Actor Network Theory and After*. Oxford and Keele: Blackwell and the Sociological Review.

Callon, M. (2000) 'The Economy of Qualities'. Paper presented to Culture & Economy Seminar, Goldsmiths College, University of London, December.

Castells, M. (2000) *The Rise of the Network Society* (2nd edn). Oxford: Blackwell.

Crang, P. (1997) 'Cultural turns and the (re)constitution of economic geography', in R. Lee and J. Wills (eds), *Geographies of Economies*. London: Edward Arnold.

Dodd, N. (1994) *The Sociology of Money*. Cambridge: Polity.

Douglas, M. and Isherwood, B. (1979) *The World of Goods: Towards an Anthropology of Consumption*. Harmondsworth: Penguin.

di Maggio, P. (1994) 'Culture and economy', in N. Smelster and R. Swedberg (eds), *The Handbook of Economic Sociology*. Princeton: Princeton University Press.

du Gay, P. (1996) *Consumption and Identity at Work*. London: Sage.

du Gay, P. (2000) *In Praise of Bureaucracy: Weber, Organization, Ethics*. London: Sage.

du Gay, P. and Salaman, G. (1992) 'The cult[ure] of the customer', *Journal of Management Studies*, 29(4) 616–33.

Fish, S. (1994) *There's No Such Thing as Free Speech . . . And It's a Good Thing Too*. Oxford: Oxford University Press.

Foucault, M. (1986) 'Nietzsche, genealogy, history', in P. Rabinow (ed.), *The Foucault Reader*. Harmondsworth: Penguin.

Hennis, W. (1988) *Max Weber: Essays in Reconstruction*. London: Allen & Unwin.

Hirschmann, A. (1977) *The Passions and the Interests*. Princeton, NJ: Princeton University Press.

Hunter, I. (1988) *Culture and Government*. Basingstoke: Macmillan.

Hunter, I. (1994) *Re-thinking the School*. Sydney: Allen & Unwin.

Kaern, M. (1990) 'The world as human construction', in M. Kaern, B.S. Phillips and R.S. Cohen (eds), *Georg Simmel and Contemporary Sociology*. Boston: Kluwer Academic Press.

Lash, S. and Urry, J. (1994) *Economies of Signs and Space*. London: Sage.

Leadbeater, C. (1999) *Living on Thin Air: The New Economy*. Harmondsworth: Viking.

McFall, E. (2000) 'A mediating institution? Using an historical study of advertising practice to rethink culture and economy', *Cultural Values*, 4 (3): 314–38.

McRobbie, A. (1998) *British Fashion Design: Rag Trade or Image Industry?* London: Routledge.

Miller, D. (1995) 'Consumption as the vanguard of history', in D. Miller (ed.), *Acknowledging Consumption*. London: Routledge.

Miller, D. (2000) 'Turning Callon the right way up'. Unpublished paper.

Miller, P. (1998) 'The margins of accounting', in M. Callon (ed.), *The Laws of the Markets*. Oxford and Keele: Blackwell and the Sociological Review.

Miller, P. and Rose, N. (1990) 'Governing economic life', *Economy & Society*, 19 (1): 1–31.

Mulgan, G. (ed.) (1997) *Life After Politics*. London: Fontana.

Nickson, D. et al (2001) 'The importance of being aesthetic', in A. Sturdy, I. Grugulis and H. Wilmott (eds), *Customer Service*. Basingstoke: Palgrave.

Nixon, S. (1997) 'Circulating culture', in P. du Gay (ed.), *Production of Culture/Cultures of Production*. London: Sage.

Pryke, M. (1991) 'An international city going "global"', *Society & Space*, 9: 197–222.

Pryke, M. and Lee, R. (1995) 'Place your bets: towards an understanding of globalization, socio-financial engineering and competition within a financial centre', *Urban Studies*, 32 (2): 329–44.

Pryke, M. and Allen, J. (2000) 'Monetized time-space: derivatives – money's "new imaginary"?', *Economy and Society*, 29 (2): 264–84.

Ray, L. and Sayer, A. (1999) 'Introduction', in L. Ray and A. Sayer (eds), *Culture and Economy After the Cultural Turn*. London: Sage.

Sahlins, M. (1976) *Culture and Practical Reason*. Chicago: University of Chicago Press.

Salaman, G. (1997) 'Culturing production', in P. du Gay (ed.), *Production of Culture/Cultures of Production*. London: Sage.

Sayer, A. (1997) 'The dialectic of culture and economy', in R. Lee and J. Wills (eds), *Geographies of Economies*. London: Edward Arnold.

Sennett, R. (1998) *The Corrosion of Character*. New York: W.W. Norton.

Slater, D. and Tonkiss, F. (2001) *Market Society: Markets and Modern Social Theory*. Cambridge: Polity.

Thompson, G. (1999) 'Situating globalization', *International Social Science Journal*, June: 139–52.

Thompson, P. and Findley, P. (1999) 'Changing the people: social engineering in the contemporary workplace', in L. Ray and A. Sayer (eds), *Economy and Culture After the Cultural Turn*. London: Sage.

Thrift, N. (1994) 'On the social and cultural determinants of international financial centres: the case of the City of London', in S. Corbridge, R. Martin and N. Thrift (eds), *Money, Space and Power*. Oxford: Blackwell.

Turner, C. (1992) *Modernity and Politics in the Work of Max Weber*. London: Routledge.

Weber, M. (1948) 'Religious rejections of the world and their directions', in H.H. Gerth and C. Wright Mills (eds), *From Max Weber*. London: Routledge.

Weber, M. (1978) *Economy and Society* (2 vols). Berkeley: University of California Press.

Wernick, A. (1991) *Promotional Culture*. London: Sage.

economics as interference

John Law

The range of chapters in this book suggests that there are many ways of thinking of cultural economy. Perhaps it has to do with the growth of the culture industries. Perhaps it has to so with what is taken to be the 'cultur-alization' of activities that might previously have been more 'economic' in character. And/or perhaps it has to do with the so-called 'cultural turn' in social science – the increasing preoccupation with the analysis of culture that has grown up with a parallel growth in the sense that culture is every-where, and that what was previously taken to be economic was always, in addition, essentially cultural in character.

These three possibilities are not necessarily mutually exclusive. However, this chapter belongs more or less uneasily to the third approach, the so-called 'cultural turn', because it has nothing to say about culturaliza-tion, and still less about the culture industries. Indeed, it has relatively little to say about any form of change in the character of economic activity. Instead, it proposes an analysis of economically relevant activity which is cultural, at least in a broad sense. The assumption I work from, then, is that culture is everywhere and that little has changed in this respect. I assume that economically relevant activity has always been cultural and that the tools of cultural analysis may be applied to what one might imagine to be 'strictly economic' activity.

Nevertheless, though it fits with the cultural turn, the approach that I develop belongs only more or less uneasily to it. This is because it is first and foremost an analysis of material practices, and of certain practices, orderings or discourses which produce economically relevant activity. Though in some loose sense practice is no doubt broadly 'cultural', the extent to which the term 'culture' is appropriate to an analysis of practice is uncertain. I take this to be the case for several reasons. First, to be sure, 'culture' is a term which covers such a multitude of sins – or approaches. Its initial significance is unclear. Second, in many of its more classic uses the term implies homo-geneity in the meanings or beliefs held by a group of people. This, to put it no higher, is distinctly uncomfortable, tending to reflect what one might think of as a 'bias to continuity' by seeking out similarities rather than differences or tensions.[1] Third, it exists, at least classically, as one of the terms in a series of unfortunate dualisms in which it is relegated to a more or less idealist world of beliefs, ideas and symbols. Culture as opposed to economy, that is one version of this division. Culture versus structure is another. Culture versus practice (where culture has to do with beliefs) is a third. Culture versus technical or practical efficacy (as in the analysis of ritual behaviour that cannot be explained in terms of its practical outcomes) is a fourth. And culture versus the material world, this is a fifth variant.

As is obvious, it is possible to use the term in other ways, and I entirely accept that it is indeed widely used in ways that break down these dualisms. The increasing popularity of the analysis of 'material culture' bears witness to this, as does the general attempt, reflected in several of the other chapters in this book, to understand the economy in a cultural mode. So, though it largely avoids the term, the argument of this chapter should not be read as an objection to the possibility of a cultural analysis of economy. Instead, it should be understood in two ways. First, as an attempt to develop a toolkit for making sense of certain material practices that might be understood both as 'economic' and as 'cultural'. As will become clear, it is a toolkit that derives from semiotics and post-structuralism, and in particular a version of these approaches from within the discipline of Science, Technology and Society (STS). And, second, it should be understood as an argument about complexity: practices, it is suggested, carry and enact complex interferences between orders or discourses, and if we are to understand economically relevant practice it is important to investigate those interferences.

office   I've got an image in my mind from about 1990. It's the office of the Director of the Daresbury SERC Laboratory near Warrington in Cheshire.[2] Picture this office. It's got a nice oiled-wood desk with a comfy working chair. It's got a conference table, again in a better class of wood, with about half a dozen well-upholstered upright chairs. It's got three low easy chairs and a coffee table. This is where the Director – I'll call him Andrew – meets with distinguished visitors. It's also where the ethnographer sits, the fly on the wall, when he listens in to the meetings of the Daresbury management board. And the room as a whole, without being luxurious – the director of a public establishment does not equip his office in the style of the better-heeled reaches of the private sector – speaks of comfort, privilege and command.[3]

Part of the apparatus of command lies on the desk. It is interesting how the materials of discretionary power change as the generations pass. Gold pens and silver ink-stands like those on my grandfather's respectable middle-class businessman's desk? No. Instead there is a telephone, a dictaphone and a personal computer. The personal computer is networked. And it is, as we know, a versatile tool. For communication. For instance, Andrew has just told the other men who make up the senior management that if they don't check their electronic diaries then he's not responsible if they miss out on crucial meetings – because that's how they'll be told about them from now on. He reads his email here too. In principle he can send and receive faxes – though his secretaries in the next room, the gendered buffer room that surrounds many of the sites of power, send and receive most of them. For communication but also for word-processing, treating texts. And of course, for building spreadsheets, of which more in a moment.

Andrew is a powerful man. He is also a calculative agent. There are important differences between calculative agency, on the one hand, and economic agency, on the other. Yet, as is obvious, they are also closely related. In this chapter I explore the character and some of the limits of calculative (and therefore of economic) agency and its practices by using STS tools and drawing primarily, though not exclusively, on empirical material derived from Daresbury.

First, I argue that practices, subjects and 'cultures' (including those of calculation and economics) may be understood as materially heterogeneous relations. This is a particular claim of STS, though it resonates with other – for instance, Foucauldian and feminist – traditions

Second, I suggest that these relations, subjects and cultures are enacted or performed, and that it is important to explore the strategies or styles of those enactments and performances. This is a claim which is again more or less consistent with a Foucauldian approach, though the turn to performance (and the exploration of its implications) take us far beyond Foucault. One of its implications is that performances are somewhat unpredictable, and that the relations, subjects and cultures are thus in some measure variable between different performances.[4]

Third, I suggest that if we are to understand economic practices in their different and multiple specificities, then it becomes important to understand how these interfere in different and specific performances with other, alternative strategies and styles. This, then, is a second form of heterogeneity. Economic subjectivities, while impeded by their Others in interference, are also constituted with and by those Others.

Finally, I argue that the calculative and discretionary agent required in economics is always incomplete. More precisely, I argue that in practice the logic of economic liberalism lives within and alongside other logics or discourses, and cannot survive without this irreducible excess.

materiality   No doubt, over ten years on, and caught in the eye of a storm about the future of synchrotron radiation research in the United

Kingdom, the office that I remember at Daresbury has changed. Certainly the Director whom I knew has gone as the generations of top managers replace themselves. And it would be astonishing if a Pentium IV computer didn't grace the desk of Andrew's successor instead of, what, a 386, a 486? But the details don't matter because my first point is not about change but about stability. It is that if we are to talk about culture at all, then it certainly doesn't exist in the abstract. It doesn't even simply exist as a set of discourses programmed into bodies – although bodies are, to be sure, crucial in the performances of culture. Instead, or in addition, it is located and performed in human and non-human material practices. And these are material practices which extend beyond human beings, subjects and their meanings, and implicate also technical, architectural, geographical and corporeal arrangements.

This is – or it ought to be – old news. Perhaps Marx told us this. Certainly Michel Foucault and a series of feminist and non-feminist partial successors have done so.[5] Many anthropologists and social geographers too[6] – though from my uneasy hybrid location somewhere between sociology and STS it seems to me that it still remains quite difficult to avoid the kinds of dualisms I touched on in the introduction. But what have STS and STS-influenced approaches to say about this? The answer is that in the recent past there have been a number of studies of economically relevant practice, and in particular of the constitution of markets.[7]

One of the nicest, simplest, earliest and most straightforward studies is by French sociologist Marie-France Garcia (1986). Written in the tradition of Pierre Bourdieu, this describes the way in which a market for the wholesale buying and selling of strawberries was set up physically and socially (though Garcia's argument is precisely that the two cannot be levered apart). Physically, because a building was constructed where transactions were brought together, transactions previously distributed here and there around the countryside in specific negotiations between buyers and growers. A building where the strawberries to be sold were brought together, arrayed, made visible for inspection. A building with an electronic display to make the bidding visible to all concerned. A building where, though all could see the scoreboard and the auctioneer, the buyers could not see the sellers, or vice versa. Indeed a kind of panopticon. Physically, then, the new market was a place, a set of socio-technologies, and a set of practices. But socially it was also a set of rules. 'Bring the strawberries here, to the market. Do not sell them on the side to wholesalers.' 'Grow recognized brands of strawberries – or they won't be accepted into the market.' 'Label them properly and pack them in an appropriate manner.' And so on, and so on.

In his edited book *The Laws of the Markets* (1998c), Michel Callon has extended and developed this argument. He argues that markets aren't given but constructed. Which means, among other things, that there is not 'a market', or 'the perfect market', with various deviations from this natural state of grace in the non-platonic realities of the world. Instead he's saying that there are markets, and markets, and then there are more markets. Different forms, different material forms. His particular additional twist is that economic theory – for instance neo-classical theory – has been vitally important, indeed performative, for the formation of particular markets. Beware, he is saying. The old idea that social sciences are an ornament that freewheels around in mid-air is quite wrong: they do make a difference. And this is a lesson that has been also been drawn by those who point (for instance) to the social engineering that has produced the 'single unified market' of the EU, or to the discourses enacted to produce the possibility of the massive exchange of commodities and currencies that constitutes the globalization of economic activity (e.g. Massey, 1997; Thrift, 1996). Or, for the case of the strawberries in the Sologne in France, the activities of a particular, economically proselytizing Enarchiste fresh from his Paris training about the necessities and benefits of economic liberalization, on his first stint out in the real world to bring the benefits of marketization to the French provinces. As if preposterously, somehow, liberalization meant less rather than more.

Markets, then, or economics (note, as does Callon, that both appear in English in the plural), involve performing calculations, monetary interchanges, transactions and relations of all kinds. But what does this take in practice? Any answer to this question becomes an investigation of practice. It becomes an investigation of the ordering of materially heterogeneous socio-technical economically relevant relations, their enactment and performance. It also becomes an investigation of the constitution of relevant forms of agency and subjectivity. To explore this further I am now going to return to the Daresbury SERC Laboratory.

manpower   Andrew is sitting at his desk. He's about to call an emergency meeting of the management board. He's bothered because the 'second Wiggler project', the so-called 'flagship project' for the laboratory, is starting to fall seriously behind schedule. But what is there to see of this second Wiggler project? Does it look as if it is behind schedule? The answer is, it doesn't. Not really. Not in any way that you or I could see. For as he sits fretting in his office, it is nothing more than a hole in the ground, and a bunch of construction workers pouring concrete. There's no particular sign that anything is wrong. It's a mess all right, but only a mess in the way that all construction sites are a mess: hard hats, hard shoes and mud everywhere.

So what does Andrew see of this project? The answer is that he sees something that no-one else sees, at least not easily: he sees some figures in a spreadsheet. And the spreadsheet tells him (forgive my use of the laboratory vernacular) that about 11 'man-years' have been devoted to the project, whereas at this stage the figure should have been 18. This is what he sees: that the project is not getting the effort that it needs. It is falling behind schedule. In fact, though this is invisible, so to speak, on the ground, the project has already used up all the contingency time built into the original schedule.

How does Andrew know about the inadequate manpower? To answer this question we need to follow the materialities of socio-technologies – and in the present context, two of these, though they are intimately related.

First, courtesy of the Microsoft Corporation, there is a spreadsheet. Obviously the spreadsheet is not some kind of accident. As with every calculative system from the invention of double-entry book-keeping on, it works in certain ways, tending to create some possibilities and delete others.[8] Without ignoring the possibilities of subversion and misuse (we have moved a long way from technological determinism in STS and there is a large literature on the subversion and reappropriation of technologies[9]), to a fair extent it works in ways that reflect and perform the logics of power. But, at the same time, it constitutes, reproduces, remakes, the needs of powerful actors, collective or individual. Locally, then, Andrew becomes some kind of visionary, someone who has seen the future and knows that it does not work. A particular kind of manager in a particular kind of organization.

Second, where do the figures come from, the 'raw material' for this virtual panopticon? The matter-of-fact answer is that the figures are put together in an organizational and textual apparatus which the laboratory (again forgive the vernacular) calls the 'manpower booking system'. Every month laboratory employees are supposed to fill in and return a form describing in half-day chunks how they spent their time in the previous month. There are permissible categories – for instance, a series of projects, a number of administrative tasks, local or more general management – which means that there are impermissible categories too, activities that don't fit very well, not to mention the difficulty of what to do with those fragmented half-days which feature so importantly in most organizations.

In fact the figures are collected with some difficulty. A small but significant percentage of the employees forget to return them – some as an act of resistance. Others enter codes which make no sense – again sometimes as an act of resistance. The forms are returned to the accounting department, where they are checked and entered into the laboratory administrative computer. At which point they become arithmetically tractable, and produce the entries in the spreadsheet that I've already mentioned, and with this a particular form of visibility – the discovery, for instance, that the second Wiggler project is seriously behind schedule.

performance   That's the empirical story. But what to make of it?

There are, I guess, two ways of thinking about an apparatus like the manpower booking system and the spreadsheet. One is to treat them – and perhaps particularly the latter – as passive tools deployed by active agents. They may, of course, be interested tools, ideologies, but tools they are, enabling and constraining but essentially passive. The other is to imagine, in some version of a material semiotics, that we're dealing with a set of heterogeneous elements all of which are performing to produce relations – including managerial (and quasi-economic) subjectivities, organizations and culture. As in other parts of social theory, the fault-line in STS around this issue is deep.[10] As I implied earlier, I want to press the latter, semiotic, line. I want to say that a pattern, a micro-physics, a non-intentional strategy of calculative and quasi-economic power, is recursively performing itself in these heterogeneous relations.[11] This means that it is useful not to distinguish between humans and non-humans.[12] Instead I will deploy a semiotics of materiality to try to work out how they all perform together to produce the set of relations which gives them their shape, their style or their mode of ordering.

Think, then, of the spreadsheet. If this is a 'thing', or a fairly stable set of relations (what people in STS sometimes call a 'black-box'), it is also, at least in relation to its use, a performance. Together with the person using it, it acts to produce effects. The argument is that it is an actor in its own right. This becomes most visible when it crashes (which it may do without the intervention of a user at all). But its effects are just as important – indeed arguably more so – when it is actually running, when it doesn't crash. What, then, can we say about the style of relations performed in a spreadsheet?

One answer, the quick answer, is that it embodies and enacts a series of relations which tend to reflect and reproduce specific social and technical agendas. But what is going on here? What is that style? And how does it tend to (re)make economically relevant relations?

Any preliminary response to these questions would include the following. First, the spreadsheet is an agent of homogenization. Thus in the first instance, what one might think of as a 'spreadsheet world' is created, which takes the form of a set of cells bearing no particular relation to one another.[13] That is what one sees when one opens a program like Excel: a bunch of empty cells. But any particular spreadsheet involves two further additional conditions. First, some of those cells are specified as operators which relate other particular cells to one another in specific ways. That is, the program generates a set of similarities and differences between specific cells (or groups of cells), sets of possible relations. Second, it includes other cells (those to which the operators refer) which are given values derived either from outside the spreadsheet (e.g. in the form of manpower booking figures) or as a result of the actions of the operators. To enter the spreadsheet-world at all, both operators and values have to take symbolic form. Indeed, they have to take definite symbolic form.[14] There is no room for that which cannot be expressed or treated either in terms of symbolic logic, or in terms of arithmetical, statistical or other mathematical operations.

Second, since the kind of spreadsheet-world we're most interested in here is statistical and arithmetical, economically relevant, we can specify this homogenization further. The spreadsheet is also enacting quantitative relations: there is no space in the spreadsheet for that which cannot be counted or rendered into symbolic form (perhaps as the form of labels for particular figures to indicate their significance or meaning).

Third, the spreadsheet is a major socio-technology of simplification. As we have seen, there are heroic simplifications which go into the production of the figures in the first place. But the tide of simplification also runs strong after the values have been allocated to the input cells. Much is being turned into rather a little. Much is, of course, being deleted. (Though much, as I'll note in a moment, is also being created.)

Fourth, the spreadsheet is a major socio-technology for centring. It is a strategy for producing a figure, or more likely a series of figures, which can be assimilated by a single person reading the spreadsheet in a more or less single scan. A spreadsheet that fails to do this is of no use in the construction of calculative agency.[15] Technically, then, a spreadsheet performs a more or less complex series of relations which juxtapose values and perform operations to produce a centre. To use Bruno Latour's phrase, it draws things together, though, to be sure, it draws them together in a particular way – in a particular style – and there are, of course, many other ways of drawing things together.[16] Or, if one prefers to put it like this, there are many other modes of calculative agency.

Fifth, but as I noted above, this is not simply a matter of simplification. It is also one of creation. I need to press this point. The spreadsheet is making new realities, performing them into being. The loss of predicted man-years – this was not a figure, or even a reality, that existed outside the apparatus of the spreadsheet itself. Even the notion of a 'delay' is dependent on a socio-technology of projects, project timekeeping, and all the rest. The straightforward and common-sense way of putting it – for instance, that the spreadsheet offers an 'overview' of the distribution of effort between projects – while not wrong, is therefore also dangerously misleading. Overviews, simplifications, the mastery of time and space, are not given in the order of things. Rather, they are artfully performed into being. If Andrew sits in the tower of this particular panopticon, then this is an effect of a set of performing relations, and not because he sees further by himself. What I earlier referred to as the 'style' of the spreadsheet-world is one which generates a homogeneous, unambiguous, probably quantitative, summary form of visibility. It creates, or, more precisely, performs, the project in a particular way.[17]

Sixth and finally, in creating this reality the spreadsheet performs a subject position that is potentially discretionary. Discretion, to be sure, exists in the possibility of selecting between alternative courses of action, and is usually seen as being intimately linked to social power.[18] But how does discretion get generated? One part of an answer is that, as has been widely noted, it is definitionally linked to a capacity for action. In the case in point, Andrew is able to act in certain ways with some degree of probability that his actions will indeed get carried on through other people. Again, then, this is a relational matter. But another part of an answer is that the construction of options is also important – for unless options can actually be generated and explored, then there is, indeed, little possibility of discretion: there is only one future possible course of action. And here the spreadsheet takes part in the action because the values and the operators can be readily manipulated. It is a simple matter of changing figures and formulae. In effect, then, the spreadsheet is a set of relations which can easily be used to perform 'what happens if . . . ' possibilities.[19] The creation of (im)possible futures. The performance of calculative subjectivities in a socio-technology of simulation.

real costs   So far I've sketched an outline of some of the materialities and practices involved in the production of a particular form of economically relevant subjectivity. This is a subjectivity that homogenizes or quantifies, simplifies, centres, and generates new realities and (as a part of this) discretionary simulations. The apparatus which produces this is performative – there is nothing natural about this calculative subjectivity. And it is also materially heterogeneous. But, as I also noted above, it is not the only mode of calculative subjectivity. Neither is it the only economically relevant version of calculative subjectivity. So what additions or alternatives might one imagine? What else is embedded in the practices of calculation? Again, I want to tackle these questions empirically.

At the time I was finishing my ethnography the managers and administrators at Daresbury were working on an important socio-technical innovation: they were seeking to integrate the regular laboratory accounting system with the manpower booking system that I have described above. What was the purpose of this exercise? The answer is that they were trying to create a socio-technology which would tell them about the 'real' cost of labour. But what does 'real' mean in this context? The health warnings that I issued above in the context of the manpower booking system are equally in order here. The 'real cost of labour' is a construction, something enacted in the practices of a heterogeneous socio-technical apparatus. In this chapter I'm not going to describe in detail the reality-producing strategy embedded in this putative apparatus. But in outline what happened is that 'the project' had become the most important administratively relevant category.

Why was this? The answer is that 'the project' had become relevant because the laboratory was starting to sell its services to outside, often commercial, users. And as the managers frequently said to one another, 'We don't know the real cost of the services that we offer.' Indeed, more strongly, there was a widespread view that the laboratory had entered into a number of important projects at a bargain-basement price, and that it was actually taking a loss on these. The idea, then, was that if the manpower booking figures discussed above could be converted into money, then it would become possible to calculate the 'real cost' of projects by adding the labour that they absorbed to the cost of materials and all the rest. Then it would, as a result, become possible to budget for services offered, and write contracts which reflected those 'real costs' rather than some 'imaginary', and possibly over-modest, estimate.

It would, of course, be possible to write an essay about the circumstances which made it important to create a full-blown cost accounting system. That essay would ring bells with any British public-sector employee who lived through and enjoyed the benefits of Thatcherism in the 1980s as it spread through the state apparatus. Thus by 1990 Daresbury Laboratory was caught in the grip of a government-driven public-sector zeal for markets and enterprise. Like the universities, the laboratory had been originally conceived outside a market system. It was established and funded by the then Science Research Council (SRC), not coincidentally close to the Huyton constituency of the then Prime Minister, Harold Wilson. Again like the universities, it received a recurrent grant to cover its running costs. But with the advent of the Thatcher administration, circumstances began to change. First, SRC/SERC funding tended to become less generous. Second, Daresbury was encouraged to find alternative sources of funding – several of the experimental stations were, for instance, co-funded with the NWO, the Dutch research funding body. And third, the laboratory was encouraged to sell its services to the private sector. Thus a number of high-tech companies – for instance, ICI, which had major research facilities at neighbouring Runcorn – started to use the facilities, and became progressively more involved in aspects of the work of the laboratory.

It was in this context that the need for an apparatus for calculating 'real costs' started to become important. This version of 'real costs' had simply not been relevant under the previous administrative regime. Most of the time the laboratory wasn't selling anything in commercial terms, so it didn't need to think that way. Instead, it received a grant from one of the boards of the SERC. It was then responsible for making sure that it didn't routinely overspend that grant (though it was also considered very bad form to underspend too since this would send the wrong signals to the SERC). The result was that in general, budgeting was an aggregate matter.[20] If there was a projected surplus, recurrent or non-recurrent expenditure would be bumped up – employees would be taken on or new equipment purchased. If there was a projected deficit, then the hirings would stop, and there would be a moratorium on purchases of all but the most essential supplies or equipment.

The lesson to be drawn from this is that the notion of 'real costs' only makes sense in the context of a particular purpose or aim. It is a strategic matter, or, better, a reflection of particular strategic concerns. The pre-Thatcher orderings performed in the laboratory indeed produced 'real costs' – but these were real in a form that was different to those that came later. They related to different concerns. On the one hand, they generated costs in relation to the laboratory as a whole. And on the other hand, they produced figures in relation to individual items, purchases, wage bills and all the rest. With the advent of economic liberalism and the need to sell services and bid 'realistically' for the supply of particular projects, the definition of 'real costs' shifted to the level of the project – that is to say, they came into being somewhere between the level of the individual items, on the one hand, and the overall cost of the laboratory, on the other. And, as I have noted, this is what the managers were working on at the time I completed my study. They were attempting to create a socio-technical apparatus which would perform this version of real costs, first by linking the cost of specific non-pay items to projects, and second (again as I have noted) by trying to find a way of linking the salary and wage costs of particular individuals to the time spent by those individuals on particular projects. The conclusion we need to draw from this is that they were re-creating 'the project' as an economic entity, as well as one performed on the floor of the laboratory, and in the work of engineers and scientists.

How did this look from the point of view of project managers? The answer will again not be unfamiliar to those versed in recent changes in the education system – or indeed, more generally, the public sector – in the United Kingdom. Analytically, the answer is that a fairly dramatic shift in subjectivities was under way. Junior managers were starting to be told that they were responsible for managing budgets – and also for staying within those budgets. They were being told that they were responsible for producing appropriate services (sometimes, but only sometimes, to outside paying customers) without exceeding their budgets. And they were (though to a variable extent) being told that they were also responsible for going out and seeking sources of income. For generally being co-effective.

This, then, was the creation of a new regime of subjectivity and responsibility. In effect, junior managers were being asked to calculate and perform as mini-entrepreneurs. But (this was acknowledged by all concerned) the practices of the socio-technical apparatus that would allow them to perform in this way were lagging behind. For instance, as I have mentioned above, the integration of the manpower booking system with the cost-accounting apparatus was only starting to come into effect at the moment of my departure. Costs were not yet being drawn together, or centred. But there were other difficulties too. For instance at the time I was in the laboratory budget holders and project managers found that they were being issued with printouts, sometimes several inches thick, on a monthly basis, detailing the purchases relevant to their projects. The complaints were endless: how, the junior managers wanted to know, could they plough through two inches of a printout where every box of screws was itemized? This was a complete waste of time. Here too, then, costs were not yet being drawn together and centred. Following the analysis of the spreadsheet offered earlier, one might suggest that the homogenization performed in the printout had not been matched by an appropriate simplification. There was, as yet, no centre to the panopticon. Indeed no panopticon. And the desire for an entrepreneurial subject had not been matched by its practice in a heterogeneous socio-technical apparatus.

forms of calculation   I noted above that quantified, centred and discretionary calculation is only one possible strategy of calculation. Indeed, it is only one possible strategy of *economic* calculation. It is now possible to add further substance to this suggestion. For, if we observe the administrative and management struggles to define and perform the new and project-relevant version of real costs at the Daresbury Laboratory, it becomes clear that we are dealing not with one but with two forms of accountancy.

The first we might call standard administrative accounting. This was long-established in the laboratory. So how did it work? The answer is that though it was (as I have noted) a set of practices for drawing figures together to calculate income and outgoings for the organization as a whole, administrative accounting was a socio-technology that primarily embodied and performed a strategy of detailed legally relevant surveillance. As in other organizations, it was intended to ensure that the right items were purchased – or at least that the right price was paid for them – and that those who supplied them were indeed paid. It ensured, correspondingly, that employees were paid what they were owed and no more. Again, it was a socio-technology which worked to ensure that at least some fingers were kept out of at least some tills. It allowed and performed a procedural, administrative, as Max Weber might have suggested, legal-rational form of economically relevant calculation, and the subjectivities which go with this. Such, then, was the performance of a set of relations that produced printouts that were two inches thick. This was because the competent administrative accountant, the competent calculator, the competent subject in this form of ordering, is precisely someone who needs to check the detail, to make sure that the bills have been paid, and all the rest of it. There is no need to draw things together in a discretionary manner. Indeed, to do so would defeat the entire object of the legal-rational subjectivity performed in this strategy for ordering.

All of which is quite at variance with the second project-relevant performance of accounting. This, as is obvious, is a version of management accounting, and enacts a quite different strategy, affording a quite different kind of subjectivity. We need not discuss this in detail again. However, in general, where administrative strategy demands detail, management accounting precisely effaces detail in its performance of necessary discretionary centring: the centring which, as we have seen, the managers were struggling to create as they sought to graft a new management accounting system on to the existing administrative accounts – and link these with the manpower booking system discussed earlier.

conclusion   I have described two forms of accountancy, two forms of (economically relevant) calculation, two strategies, and two forms of economic subjectivity which interfere with one another. Indeed, they exclude one another (for detail is, in an important sense, the Other to the overview), but are, at the same time, also dependent on one another – because, at the very least, the strategy of management accounting includes the products of administrative accounting, products which become the values entered into some of the cells of a management accounting spreadsheet. The argument I'm making, then, is that the material practices and apparatuses of economic life and the subjectivities that they generate perform as a complex multiplicity that is neither entirely coherent, nor completely incoherent. Following an argument developed by Annemarie Mol in the quite different context of medical activities, I am saying that economically relevant activity is more than one and less than many.[21]

One way of making the argument is to say that we are in the presence of two discourses of economics, two discourses of economically relevant calculation. Mini-discourses. But if we build it in this way, the story does not stop here. For if we might name the two that we have uncovered as 'enterprise' and 'administration', there are others as well. What, for instance, of 'vocation'? This, marginal and Other to both enterprise and administration, is also necessary to them. For, if we think of the Daresbury Laboratory, what is it all about? What is its rationale? I haven't explained this in detail – this is not relevant for the present argument – but the general answer is that it is about doing (what we might think of as) vocational science. The material orderings of the laboratory reflect and perform enterprise and administration, but they also, and perhaps predominantly, reflect and perform a particular version of the vocation of scientific puzzle solving.[22] So an ordering mode of vocation is essential to the working of the laboratory. Without the conduct of science there would be no administration, and no customers either. And it is possible to find other discourses of science, for instance 'charisma'. But perhaps, for the present purposes, three will do. And this is the bottom line. For the study of Daresbury was motivated in part by the hubris of Thatcherite 'enterprise', but the conclusion, which I have tried to work through here for the formation of economically relevant and calculative subjectivities, suggests that the organization, its management and its economically relevant actions were (no doubt are) all constituted in a complex set of balances, oscillations, power-plays, tensions, deferrals and displacements between practices carrying different economically relevant strategies. The corollary is that reduction to any one (in this case enterprise) is (and would be) impossible. Or, if one prefers to put it this way, that economic/managerial/organizational performances are irreducible to a single logic, but dependent on the non-conformability of Others. That, for instance, enterprise needs vocation and administration even though it cannot assimilate or know these in its own terms.

Clearly the relations between different ordering styles or logics are different in different economically relevant performances. The attempted hegemony of enterprise (including administratively imposed enterprise) was and is novel, at least in the public sector. There is no question but that it has reshaped the character of economically relevant practice in public-sector organizations – and that it continues to do so. What is colloquially known as the 'Thatcher revolution' has, in most respects, been pursued by subsequent administrations of either political hue. In the UK we live, as Michael Power (1997) puts it, in an audit society which seeks to mimic via administrative means certain paradigmatic conceptions of appropriate market-based relations and subjectivities.

But there are limits, limits to the extent to which the balance can be pushed in the direction of enterprise – or indeed towards any single vision of ordering. Practice is larger, more complex, more messy, than can be grasped within any particular logic. To be sure, the limits to discourses or narrative forms have been well rehearsed in the literatures on modernity. Reduction is not simply dangerous – as Zygmunt Bauman has so eloquently shown.[23] It also, in the long run, experiences its limits. In the present context, then, the conclusion is both that it is hubris to imagine that 'enterprise' could order all of economically relevant activity, and also, and more generally, that 'economics' are well named. This is because as well as depending on and reflecting non-economic strategies, economics themselves are also multiple, intersecting, supporting, but also undermining – or interfering with – one another. Which is why a notion of 'economic culture' doesn't work so well.

And why I prefer, as we think of economically relevant activity, to talk in terms of the complexities of practices and the heterogeneous materials that produce and are produced within those practices.

notes

A number of friends and colleagues have helped me to think about the complexities of organizationally relevant economic calculation. These include Michel Callon, Ivan da Costa Marques, Annemarie Mol, Ingunn Moser and Vicky Singleton. I am grateful to them, to the managers of Daresbury Laboratory, who explored so much of their thinking with me, and also to the ESRC, which funded the study which made possible the management ethnography on which this is based. Finally, I am grateful to members of the 'Cultural Economy' symposium held at the Open University, UK, in January 2000, and in particular to Paul du Gay and Michael Pryke, for their comments on an earlier version of this chapter.

1. See the argument developed in Chapter 6 of Law (2002).
2. SERC is the acronym for the Science and Engineering Research Council, which was the major UK state funding body for academic research in the natural sciences at the time.
3. The study of the Daresbury SERC Laboratory is more fully described in Law (1994).
4. This is an argument that has been carefully developed in the context of medical practice by Annemarie Mol (2002a).
5. Though most would avoid the term 'culture' for the reasons sketched out above. References here include Foucault for his work on medicine (1976) and discipline (1979), Judith Butler (1990), and the so-called 'English Foucauldians' (see, e.g., Michael Power [1991, 1994] and Graham Burchell [Burchell et al., 1991]).
6. This work is to be found, for instance, in the *Journal of Material Culture* and *Society and Space*, and is represented in this volume by the chapters by Daniel Miller and Nigel Thrift.
7. I will consider some of these below, but they include work by Michel Callon (1998a, 1998b, 1998c, 1999, 2002), Marie-France Garcia (1986), Donald MacKenzie (1999), Karin Knorr-Cetina and, in the context of STS-informed debate within geography, Nigel Thrift (1996).
8. On this see, for instance, the magisterial work by Elizabeth Eisenstein (1980).
9. My favourite example derives from the electricity supply industry. See the writing of Madeleine Akrich (1992) on this.
10. It turns around the distinction in STS between the social construction of technology (SCOT), which tends to the former view, and various semiotically influenced approaches, which reflect some of the concerns of post-structuralism. These include actor network theory, which rigorously takes the latter view, insisting that action (and subjectivity) are better understood as effects of ramifying relations rather than as originating in particular (e.g. human) locations. The difference is neatly summed up in de Vries (1995), and somewhat acrimoniously in an exchange between Michel Callon and Bruno Latour (1992), on the one hand, and Harry Collins and Steven Yearley (1992), on the other. For a recent account of actor network theory and some of its successor projects, see Law and Hassard (1999).

11. I use Foucauldian language here, but a vocabulary that does a similar job has been developed in actor network theory, for instance in identifying strategies which produce large-scale effects (Latour, 1983), or in talk about modes of ordering (Law, 1994).

12. The argument is pressed at length in Latour (1987), but is also carefully developed by Michel Callon in his important paper on the fishermen and the scallops of Saint Brieuc Bay (1986).

13. In talking of a 'spreadsheet world', I'm adapting the notion of the 'actor-world' developed by Michel Callon (1980, 1986). Arguably the actor network model here developed is Leibnizian, and actor networks may be understood as monads. On this see Latour (1988) and Law (2000).

14. Though this is not always the case, the values are likely to be arithmetical. And the operators are either of the form 'if x, then y, else z', or, probably more common, they perform arithmetical or other mathematical relations, deriving new cell values from old.

15. We will see shortly that in the context of Daresbury management, some of the paperwork signally failed to draw matters together, simplify, and render itself tractable.

16. This argument is beautifully developed in Latour (1990).

17. There are various other vocabularies for making this point. For instance, feminist technoscience student Donna Haraway (1991) talks of the impossibility of the God trick, the view from nowhere. The idea that 'the project' is a performed reality is explored at some length in Law (2001).

18. For an introduction to the literatures on power, see Barnes (1988) and Lukes (1974). For further discussion in the context of Daresbury and actor network theory, see Law (1991).

19. Formally, since every value and operator can be manipulated, there are indefinitely many possibilities. In practice, however, the freedom for manoeuvre is more restricted. Some data values entered cannot be so easily changed (e.g., the number of man-years thus far devoted to the project - though this was indeed 'corrected' in the course of discussions on the management board). Again, some symbolic operators are more or less fixed (conversion of half-days into man-years).

20. With some exceptions. For instance, particular large capital projects might be identified, as was indeed the case with the publicly funded second Wiggler project mentioned above.

21. This has been developed in a series of papers and at book length. See, in particular, Mol (1998, 1999, 2002a, 2002b; Mol and Berg, 1994).

22. The argument is developed more fully in Law (1994) and Law and Moser (1999).

23. The classic case is his study of the Holocaust (See Bauman, 1989).

references

Akrich, M. (1992) 'The de-scription of technical objects', in W. Bijker and J. Law (eds), *Shaping Technology, Building Society: Studies in Sociotechnical Change.* Cambridge, MA: MIT Press.

Barnes, B. (1988) *The Nature of Power.* Cambridge: Polity Press.

Bauman, Z. (1989) *Modernity and the Holocaust.* Cambridge: Polity.

Burchell, G., Gordon, C. and Miller, P. (eds) (1991) *The Foucault Effect: Studies in Governmentality*. Hemel Hempstead: Harvester Wheatsheaf.

Butler, J. (1990) *Gender Trouble: Feminism and the Subversion of Identity*. New York and London: Routledge.

Callon, M. (1980) 'Struggles and negotiations to define what is problematic and what is not: the sociology of translation', in K.D. Knorr, R. Krohn, and R.D. Whitley (eds), *The Social Process of Scientific Investigation: Sociology of the Sciences Yearbook, 4*. Dordrecht and Boston: Reidel.

Callon, M. (1986) 'Some elements of a sociology of translation: domestication of the scallops and the fishermen of Saint Brieuc Bay', in J. Law (ed.), *Power, Action and Belief: A New Sociology of Knowledge? Sociological Review Monograph, 32*. London: Routledge and Kegan Paul.

Callon, M. (1998a) 'An essay on framing and overflowing: economic externalities revisited by sociology', in M. Callon (ed.), *The Laws of the Markets*. Oxford and Keele: Blackwell and the Sociological Review.

Callon, M. (1998b) 'Introduction: the embeddedness of economic markets in economics', in M. Callon (ed.), *The Laws of the Markets*. Oxford and Keele: Blackwell and the Sociological Review.

Callon, M. (ed.) (1998c) *The Laws of the Markets*. Oxford: Blackwell and the Sociological Review.

Callon, M. (1999) 'Actor network theory: the market test', in J. Law and J. Hassard (eds), *Actor Network Theory and After*. Oxford and Keele: Blackwell and the Sociological Review.

Callon, M. (2002) 'Writing and (re)writing devices as tools for managing complexity', in J. Law and A. Mol (eds), *Complexities in Science, Technology and Medicine*. Durham, NC: Duke University Press.

Callon, M. and Latour, B. (1992) 'Don't throw the baby out with the bath school! A reply to Collins and Yearley', in A. Pickering (ed.), *Science as Practice and Culture*. Chicago: University of Chicago Press.

Collins, H.M. and Yearley, S. (1992) 'Epistemological chicken', in A. Pickering (ed.), *Science as Practice and Culture*. Chicago: University of Chicago Press.

de Vries, G. (1995) 'Should we send Collins and Latour to Dayton, Ohio?', *EASST Review*, 14: 3–10.

Eisenstein, E.L. (1980) *The Printing Press as an Agent of Cultural Change: Communications and Transformations in Early-Modern Europe*. Cambridge: Cambridge University Press.

Foucault, M. (1976) *The Birth of the Clinic: an Archaeology of Medical Perception*. London: Tavistock.

Foucault, M. (1979) *Discipline and Punish: the Birth of the Prison*. Harmondsworth: Penguin.

Garcia, M.-F. (1986) 'La construction sociale d'un marché parfait: le marché au cadran de Fontaines en Sologne', *Actes de la Recherche en Sciences Sociales*, 65: 2–13.

Haraway, D. (1991) 'Situated knowledges: the science question in feminism and the privilege of partial perspective', in D. Haraway (ed.), *Simians, Cyborgs and Women: the Reinvention of Nature*. London: Free Association Books.

Latour, B. (1983) 'Give me a laboratory and I will raise the world', in K.D. Knorr-Cetina and M.J. Mulkay (eds), *Science Observed*. Beverly Hills, CA: Sage.

Latour, B. (1987) *Science in Action: How to Follow Scientists and Engineers Through Society*. Milton Keynes: Open University Press.

Latour, B. (1988) *Irréductions,* published with *The Pasteurization of France.* Cambridge MA: Harvard University Press.

Latour, B. (1990) 'Drawing things together', in M. Lynch and S. Woolgar (eds), *Representation in Scientific Practice.* Cambridge, MA: MIT Press.

Law, J. (1991) 'Power, discretion and strategy', in J. Law (ed.), *A Sociology of Monsters? Essays on Power, Technology and Domination, Sociological Review Monograph, 38.* London: Routledge.

Law, J. (1994) *Organizing Modernity.* Oxford: Blackwell.

Law, J. (1999) 'After ANT: topology, naming and complexity', in J. Law and J. Hassard (eds), *Actor Network Theory and After.* Oxford and Keele: Blackwell and the Sociological Review.

Law, J. (2000) 'Comment on Suchman, and Gherardi and Nicolini: knowing as displacing', *Organization,* 7: 349–54.

Law, J. (2002) *Aircraft Stories: Decentering the Object in Technoscience.* Durham, NC: Duke University Press.

Law, J. and Hassard, J. (1999) *Actor Network Theory and After.* Keele and Oxford: Sociological Review and Blackwell.

Law, J. and Moser, I. (1999) 'Managing, subjectivities and desires', *Concepts and Transformation: International Journal of Action Research and Organizational Renewal,* 4: 249–79.

Lukes, S. (1974) *Power: a Radical View.* London: Macmillan.

MacKenzie, D. (1999) 'Physics and finance: s-terms and modern finance as a Topic for Science Studies', Edinburgh: Department of Sociology, University of Edinburgh.

Massey, D. (1997) Paper presented to the Keele University Geography Department.

Mol, A. (1998) 'Missing links, making links: the performance of some artheroscleroses', in A. Mol and M. Berg (eds), *Differences in Medicine: Unravelling Practices, Techniques and Bodies.* Durham, NC, and London: Duke University Press.

Mol, A. (2002a) 'Cutting surgeons, walking patients: some complexities involved in comparing', in J. Law and A. Mol (eds), *Complexities in Science, Technology and Medicine.* Durham, NC: Duke University Press.

Mol, A. (1999) 'Ontological politics: a word and some questions', in J. Law and J. Hassard (eds), *Actor Network Theory and After.* Oxford and Keele: Blackwell and the Sociological Review.

Mol, A. (2002b) *The Body Multiple: Ontology in Medical Practice.* Durham, NC, and London: Duke University Press.

Mol, A. and Berg, M. (1994) 'Principles and practices of medicine: the coexistence of various anaemias', *Culture, Medicine and Psychiatry,* 18: 247–65.

Power, M. (1991) 'Auditing and environmental expertise: between protest and professionalisation', *Accounting, Auditing and Accountability Journal,* 3: 30–42.

Power, M. (1994) *The Audit Explosion.* London: Demos.

Power, M. (1997) *The Audit Society: Rituals of Verification.* Oxford: Oxford University Press.

Thrift, N. (1996) *Spatial Formations.* London, Thousand Oaks, CA and New Delhi: Sage.

symbolic economies: the 'culturalization' of economic knowledge

John Allen

There is much to be said for the *rapprochement* of culture and the economy, especially as recognition dawns that the much valued, yet somewhat elusive, creative know-how which drives economies is tied up with the relationship. The move to the centre of the economic stage of all things cultural and creative has brought forth an understanding that knowledge and know-how need not only be entertained through the language of science, judgement and technological innovation. There is room for an appreciation of the 'softer' symbolic, aesthetic, more affective forms of knowledge alongside, or even entangled within, the resolutely cognitive. Or so it would seem.

In this chapter, I wish to argue that although in everyday practice such entanglements may be present, many insightful accounts of economic knowledge remain trapped within a formal, codified script of knowledge that, often unintentionally, marginalizes the expressive and prioritizes the cognitive. This is as true of recent work on the 'knowledge economy', such as Charles Leadbeater's popular text *Living on Thin Air: The New Economy* (1999), as it is of more culturally attuned writers on economic know-how and ingenuity such as John Urry, Scott Lash and Robert Reich.

Moreover, it is perhaps something of a paradox that writers, such as Sharon Zukin, who have sidestepped the cognitive realm of patented reason and technology by going out of their way to stress the symbolic significance of certain sectors of the economy have unwittingly skewed our sense of economic knowledge by failing to acknowledge the symbolic basis to *all* forms of economic knowledge. It is simply misleading to equate the symbolic with the cultural, as some writers do, and then proceed to speak about a range of sectors – from the fine arts and the music industries to multimedia and broadcasting – as if they exercised a monopoly over the creative deployment and extension of symbolic forms.

In what follows, I hope to be able to show that 'cultural' and other industries, be they service or manufacture, have more in common in terms of symbolic function and know-how than that which divides them. There is a symbolic form to the kinds of economic knowledge to be found in the finance and information-based services such as banking, insurance, accountancy and law, as much as there is in those industries which wear 'culture' on their sector label. Equally, in the much vaunted technologically innovative sectors of telecommunications, engineering and computing, economic knowledge rests upon a combination of symbolic functions and uses which shares much with the symbolic schemas that routinely shape the practices of the recognized 'cultural' industries. The point, quite simply, is that different economic activities play across a variety of symbolic registers – abstract, expressive, affective and aesthetic – and *combine* them in ways that render sectors distinctive. As such, any simple binary understanding of economic knowledge between, say, the cognitive and the aesthetic, or between the material and the symbolic, fails to apprehend the richness of knowledge in each and every area of the economy. There is no one symbolic sector to the contemporary economy, only economies which display a dexterity of symbolic knowledges in a variety of combinations, with certain sectors distinguished by one particular combination rather than another.

Before exploring the different symbolic registers upon which knowledge rests in today's advanced culturally coded economies, I first want to highlight why it is that expressive or affective forms of knowledge are often unintentionally marginalized in favour of cognitive reason, despite a willingness to do otherwise.

codifying the uncodable   A willingness to do otherwise, to resist a simplistic cognitive interpretation of economic knowledge which only values formal, abstract, patented reason, is present in the work of Lash and Urry, most notably in their *Economies of Signs and Space* (1994) and relatedly in Lash's *Another Modernity: A Different Rationality* (1999), as well as in Reich's popular study *The Work of Nations* (1993). Each of these writers, however, notwithstanding his intentions, seems to hand back economic knowledge to cognitive reason by default.

Ceding the high ground   In *Economies of Signs and Space*, for instance, Lash and Urry stress the contemporary importance of the sign or symbolic content of commodities over their material content. This, by now, well-rehearsed argument, which asserts that economic value currently owes less to the tangible nature of production and rather more to its semiotic character, despite its contentious nature, has the advantage of drawing attention to the proliferation of sign values in the production and circulation of commodities.[1] According to Lash and Urry, this production of signs has predominantly taken two forms: a cognitive form, which is exemplified through the flow of information, digital codes and other abstract symbols; and an aesthetic form, which in the broadest of genres engages the expressive side to economic life. The latter is directed at the world of affects, although widely interpreted to include much of what conventionally falls under the play of representation – the mix of images in advertising, the sign value of material objects, the semiotic work of branding, and so forth. Overall, this symbolic activity adds up to an aestheticization of the economic, which takes place within the sphere of production as well as in the circuits of exchange and consumption.

Significantly, Lash and Urry do not restrict symbolic work to a particular sector of the economy. They recognize, for example, that the design process is as much an integral part of manufacturing as it is of fashion or any number of consumer services. Yet they do make a strong case for considering cognitive signs separately from aesthetic signs, in so far as the process of manipulation involves two distinct forms of reflexivity and knowledge. Knowledge on the basis of cognitive reflexivity operates on the understanding that the analytic principles – be they concerned with legal principles, financial calculations or forms of insurance risk assessment – are themselves open to question and subject to renegotiation. Knowledge via aesthetic reflexivity meanwhile operates on a hermeneutic basis whereby subjects – say in the sphere of consumption, retail and fashion – are actively involved in the construction of their own identities through their engagement with lifestyle and consumer choices. The symbolic interplay that constructs consumer codes is thus not something that is handed down through a marketing tradition but is itself open to manipulation by active consumers.

Now we do not have to agree wholeheartedly with these examples of reflexivity to admit that the cognitive and the aesthetic, the realm of analysis and abstraction and that of imagination and affect, are two different ways of apprehending and knowing the world. Even though the aesthetic is defined by Lash and Urry in an excessively broad fashion to cover much more than the expressive side to economic meaning, the difference in symbolic function performed by the cognitive and the aesthetic are deemed sufficient to warrant separate epistemological treatment. Whilst the cognitive and the aesthetic are conceived as separate domains of symbolic activity, each with its own specific mode of operation, that does not mean that Lash and Urry consider them to be on an equivalent epistemological footing, however.

Only the former, it seems, the cognitive stream of codes and abstract symbols which make up what is taken to be the 'new economy', are subject to protocols of judgement designed to sift out knowledge from bits of data and information that form the background hum to a digital economy. Cognitive reflexivity, Lash and Urry argue, presupposes judgement, whereas aesthetic reflexivity is grounded in conventions of taste and the everyday.

> Aesthetic reflexivity is instantiated in an increasing number of spheres of everyday life. . . . If knowledge-intensive production of goods and services is embodied in the utility of the latter, design-intensivity is embodied in the 'expressive' component of goods and services, a component having significance from the goods of the culture industries to the 'managed heart' of flight attendants. . . . Aesthetic or hermeneutic reflexivity is embodied in the background assumptions, in the unarticulated practices in which meaning is routinely created in 'new' communities – in subcultures, in imagined communities and in the 'invented communities' of, for example, ecological and other late twentieth-century movements.
>
> (1994: 6)

Habit and convention, what we routinely agree as members of taste communities, thus become the means by which 'knowledge' is accessed in the aesthetic realm. There is no specific operation of judgement involved whereby some appeal to a kind of universality is made which draws a line, however vague and ambiguous, between knowledge and cultural convention (or a 'universal subjectivity', as Kant would have it[2]). The predispositions of a taste community, those who on a day-to-day basis 'know' the codes and conventions which inform cultural-economic activities and use them to shape collective practices, thus become the arbiters of the aesthetic domain. Aesthetic knowledge shades into culture generally, and any specificity that may have arisen from the exercise of judgement is lost. Almost by default, therefore, cognitive knowledge of the analytical and abstract sort comes to stand in for economic knowledge proper.

This disavowal of judgement from the aesthetic realm, however, is not without consequences; the most significant of which is that it effectively hands back economic knowledge to codification. Scott Lash in *Another Modernity: A Different Rationality* and elsewhere compounds this division when he counterposes two modernities, one based upon the 'hard' knowledge and cognition of the Enlightenment tradition and the other based upon the 'soft' expressiveness of modernism as cultural experience. In what he heralds as the fusion of these qualities in a new order of technological culture (the techno-scientists and techno-artists of the digital cultural economy), the outcome reads less like the hybrid economy that he envisages and more like the evacuation of epistemology from the domain of the economic. The celebration of the fusion of commodities and capital, on the one hand, with signs and symbols, on the other, so that a global information culture is produced which simply *is*, which stands in for nothing in particular, merely abandons the ground of economic knowledge to those who feel less uncomfortable with tying down meaning or embracing the certainty offered by patented reason. Certainly those understanding that expressive forms of meaning defy explicit codification, such as the ability to recognize and to react to works of art and design without being able to articulate their reasoning, or the ability to judge the mood of a film or other visual composition without being entirely aware of the cues involved, will not deter others with less understanding from trying to encode the uncodable.

Serving abstractions   Reich, for instance, falls into the latter camp. In *The Work of Nations* he asserts that the manipulation of symbols, the analysis of data, words, oral and visual representations, forms a critical part of what most professions do to add value to goods and services. The manipulation of symbols is the process by which new knowledge comes into play, leading, for example, to the introduction of new software technologies, inventive legal arguments, innovative financial instruments, new advertising techniques or a breakthrough in architectural design. Whilst the output of such activities is by no means always radical in departure, the work with numbers, sounds, words and images presupposes an appreciation of the various symbolic codes which make meaning and innovation possible.

Reich refers to those who perform this kind of work as symbolic analysts.

> Symbolic analysts solve, identify, and broker problems by manipulating symbols. They simplify reality into abstract images that can be rearranged, juggled, experimented with, communicated to other specialists, and then, eventually, transformed back into reality. The manipulations are done with analytic tools, sharpened by experience. The tools may be mathematical algorithms, legal arguments, financial gimmicks, scientific principles, psychological insights about how to persuade or to amuse, systems of induction or deduction, or any other set of techniques for doing conceptual puzzles.
>
> (1993: 178)

As the foregoing indicates, the creative play of symbolic work is not limited to a particular sector of the economy; symbolic analysis is a practice which cuts across industries involving engineers as much as financiers, production designers as well as marketing strategists. Interestingly, though, the process of manipulation seems to be remarkably similar regardless of the symbolic form in question. Abstraction and analysis, reason and conceptualization, remain the mainstay of the cerebral activities involved, with little or no attention paid to what it might mean to work with symbols that are not overtly cognitive or ambiguous in style.

In this respect, Reich's understanding of symbolic function bears all the hallmarks of Lash's Enlightenment stream of rationality. The stress placed upon the systematic manipulation of abstract symbols involving the exercise of judgement on the basis of reason rather than representation or expression amounts to a form of knowledge that would not be out of place in an R & D centre where the abstract coupling of knowledge and innovation is fêted.

To be fair to Reich, his is one of the few attempts within the economic domain seriously to entertain the relationship between symbolic activity and creative play. Yet his seeming unawareness of the different symbolic registers upon which knowledge may rest leads him to impose a broadly cognitive yardstick upon the sensuous, the meaningful and the expressive regardless of their phenomenological specificity. In many ways it is akin to thinking that because there is such a phenomenon as 'creative' accountants whose task it is is to manipulate numbers, then any kind of symbolic juggling and creative inventiveness in the economy naturally follows the same pattern. This will certainly come as something of a surprise to fashion designers, composers, and the like, who focus on the affective side to economic activity and whose task is often to work without the aid of any explicit codification. Indeed, their very creativity may be dependent upon their ability to work *through the ambiguity* of their symbolic materials to reach an altogether different point from that conceived by Reich.

Detachable knowledges   Reich's argument effectively loses its way, but the rather myopic view of economic knowledge which underpins it is perhaps best exemplified by more recent accounts of the dynamics of the 'new economy', where the celebration of tacit, unstated knowledges is quickly transformed into a recognizable process of codifiable returns which allows for their reproduction and ubiquitous use.[3] Diane Coyle's enthusiasm for the 'weightless' economy is at one extreme, albeit the unthinking end, of this trend. In her book *The Weightless World: Thriving in the Digital Age* (1999) she moves swiftly from a concern to understand the intangible sources of value embodied within the creative content of a film, piece of music or software to a position which reduces everything to its costless reproduction and widespread dissemination through the latest in telecommunications technologies. Any sense that there might be something more to the increasingly immaterial, creative side to economic production and circulation which escapes systematic formalization simply fails to register.

Towards the more considered end of the spectrum is Leadbeater's *Living on Thin Air: The New Economy*, which sets out a case for accepting knowledge as *the* critical driving force of a modern economy. It is a more considered text because, first, it acknowledges that knowledge within the economy is not something that is easily spread or transferred between corporate actors, rather 'it can only be enacted through a process of understanding, through which people interpret information and make judgements on the basis of it' (1999: 29). Thus it is recognized that creativity is not merely about the formalization of previously unstated ways of doing things, but involves an interplay between tacit and explicit knowledges. And secondly, it is noteworthy for its recognition that all things innovative in the 'new economy' do not revolve solely around science and technology.

> The knowledge-driven economy is not made up by a set of knowledge-intensive industries fed by science. This new economy is driven by new factors of production and sources of competitive advantage – innovation, design, branding, know-how – which are at work in all industries from retailing and agriculture to banking and software.
>
> (1999: 10)

Yet for all this sensitivity to contextual, unstated and aesthetic forms of economic knowledge across a range of industries, when pressed to make a general case for knowledge capitalism all too quickly Leadbeater falls back upon the language of explicit codification: licensing, intellectual property rights and patented reason. In a wittily entitled chapter, 'Delia Smith not Adam Smith', which likens the process of knowledge creation and exploitation to that of licensed recipe distribution, where knowledge is spread by purchasing the right to use rather than own something, we are left with a formal model of know-how based on replication (see also Chapter 5, this volume). Any fuzziness associated with the process of tacit interpretation or interest in the non-graspable side to intangible production disappears once the need for *explicit* codification moves centre-stage. The need to communicate ideas and practices in a replicable fashion, to tie down knowledge in people's heads or in the way that they do things, simply overshadows any concern that the main source of added value may actually *elude* a formal process of encoding.

It is not difficult to follow where this pressure for codification may lead in respect of which kinds of economic activity are represented as value-laden and which are not. Among the most valued occupations are likely to be those that produce 'knowledges' which are detachable and replicable, and lend themselves to analysis and judgement. Today's software engineers as well as latter-day civil engineers, financial 'rocket' scientists as well as laboratory-based scientists, would all fit within the frame, as would most if not all the activities considered by Reich. Certainly, the technologically driven sectors of telecommunication and computing or the information-based services, from law, consulting and finance on, would figure prominently among the knowledge-intensive industries, whereas those whose symbolic schemes are poorly shared by comparison would not. The more replete, ambiguous nature of expressive knowledges, those more open to negotiation than manipulation, which are to be found across and within economic sectors, arguably would fail to show.

In that sense, the 'thin-air business', the prioritization of ideas, ingenuity and know-how, is essentially one of manipulation. It is a cognitive story which, often unwittingly, loses the expressive or affective side to economic action principally because the quest for creativity and knowledge favours intangibilities that can be codified and reproduced. Thus where the aesthetic enters into the economy through branding or design, or the expressive becomes evident through an image-driven product, it is an instrumental logic which quickly prevails, not the affective dimension in all its replete and ambiguous moments. To do otherwise, it would seem, is to invite misunderstanding and incomprehension about what knowledge generation – as a process – is deemed to be all about. After all, Delia Smith, the cookery writer, advocates mixing already available ingredients to a precise formula, but that does not mean to say that there is nothing sensuous about food production. It's merely that this dimension defies codification and therefore receives scant attention in Leadbeater's work.

Whereas Leadbeater's focus, for all its worth, fails to engage with the fuzziness of economic knowledge, at least the likes of Lash and Urry do grasp its central relevance to economic practice. Although the ambiguity of non-cognitive knowledges is acknowledged in their work, however, their insistence on placing them outside of the ambit of judgement cedes the high ground of economic knowledge to the 'hard'-edged exponents of manipulation and reason.

registering the symbolic   There is an implicit danger in the foregoing that any discussion of what is more or less codifiable simply reproduces the dichotomies of the material versus the symbolic or the cognitive versus the aesthetic or expressive. Of equal concern is that such dichotomies may then be used to map out the economy along exclusively material and symbolic lines and thus overstate the differences between economic activities in terms of their knowledge content. Thus, if we were to follow Sharon Zukin's line of thought in *The Culture of Cities* (1995) and elsewhere,[4] we could be forgiven for thinking that the finance, information, and arts and entertainment industries, loosely described, are the only areas of the economy engaged in symbolic activity. Thus in all mature urban centres she argues that it is possible to discern

> a symbolic economy based on such abstract products as financial instruments, information and 'culture', i.e. art, food, fashion, music and tourism. The symbolic economy is based on the interrelated production of such cultural symbols as these and the spaces in which they are created and consumed – including offices, housing, restaurants, museums and even the streets.
>
> (1998: 826)

Symbolism here, then, encompasses both visual representation and cultural meaning, and takes in the branding of cityspaces, the sale of images, as well as the aestheticization of economic production and consumption more broadly. Whilst the range of symbolic manipulation described by Zukin is extensive, taking us beyond simplistic aesthetic or image-driven versions, the overarching impression gained from her work is that of an economy where the symbolic is restricted to certain sectors and does not include, for instance, the work of design engineers within manufacturing, or less obviously the work of biotechnology consultants or agro-chemical specialists! Of course, the intent of her work was not to produce the definitive or comprehensive account of symbolism and economy, yet my seemingly rather absurd conjecture that we also consider bio-symbolism is to remind us that economic symbolism is not a post-1960s/1970s phenomenon. The symbolic basis of economic knowledge is pervasive and it does not stop at the boundaries of the downtown area and its industries.

This is not to suggest, however, that there is nothing specific to the symbolic arrangement that characterizes, say, the fashion industry or the film industry. Rather, what distinguishes such industries in terms of their know-how and imagination is the distinctive *combination* of various kinds of symbolic dexterities and knowledges. Different industries, and the economic activities therein, play across a variety of symbolic registers – abstract, expressive, affective and aesthetic – and combine them in ways which stress certain kinds of symbolic usage at the expense of others.

Thus it is not the case that fashion and film occupy the symbolic realm of the expressive and the aesthetic, whereas finance and engineering are confined to the abstract and the cognitive realms of industry and output. On the contrary, in the case of film, for instance, an assessment of the industry's output would include an appreciation of its aesthetic qualities, in respect of both its visual impact and narrative construction, *and* a technical assessment of its sound, lighting and editing quality, *as well as* judgement on how well the products are marketed and promoted imaginatively. Various forms of symbolic production are thus combined *within* a particular industry, although each would blend and weight the different symbolic functions according to their overall nature and specificity. Even something as hard-nosed and rational as the business of credit, and the use of money more generally, has an expressive meaning, the knowledge of which cannot be deciphered solely through a series of cognitive manipulations.

Perhaps the best way to shed light on the different kinds of symbolic knowledges in play within the economy is to work through the different registers in a more systematic fashion. To do this, I want to draw upon the work of the German philosopher of culture Ernst Cassirer, who, in the first half of the twentieth century, became convinced early on that a cognitive, science-based view of knowledge was unjustifiably limited. Whilst his work on symbolic knowledges did not concern itself with things economic, his identification of different symbolic functions as the means through which we 'access' the world arguably has much to offer at a time when the non-material, creative side to production relies heavily upon the input of signs and symbols to differentiate products and make them meaningful.

Cultural modes of knowing   As someone interested in the cultural sciences of the time as much as the natural sciences, Cassirer's work reflected to some extent the heady intellectual and cultural atmosphere of Berlin at the beginning of the twentieth century filtered through his more formal grounding in matters of logic, metaphysics and the 'exact' sciences (Verene, 1979). In particular, his interrogation of the mathematically minded, 'exact' sciences like physics led him to question the privileged position that such thinking occupied at that time as the benchmark of knowledge (Krois, 1987). Above all, it led him to consider the various ways – conceptual, perceptual, affective – in which it is possible to 'know' the world and how it is rendered *meaningful.*[5]

The nub of the issue for Cassirer was that the formal reasoning of natural scientific knowledge, and the abstract judgements of mathematics in particular, whilst valid as a form of theoretical meaning, did not amount to a prototype for all knowledge. It was only *one* form of meaning amongst others; *one* conceptual system of meaning embedded within a shared cultural framework of signs and symbols. Other ways of symbolically apprehending the world which do not coincide with abstract conceptual signs, such as the expressive qualities of art or the referential qualities of language, also invoke meaning, although within quite different frameworks of knowledge and knowing. On this view, it is simply misleading to reserve the accolade 'knowledge' for one kind of symbolic formation when others of a different nature open up a quite different type of understanding and access to the world.[6]

We should be clear about what is meant by 'access' here, as the term gives us a clue as to the nature of Cassirer's symbolic knowledges. Symbolic knowledges, for Cassirer, do not simply reflect a world 'out there'; rather they provide a means of apprehending and comprehending it (Krois, 1987). The validity of a symbolic formation does not rest upon its ability to provide a copy of the material world. On the contrary, it derives its validity from within; that is, from within an organized system of relations between signs which produce meaning that are fixed by convention. The numerical symbols of mathematics are one such system, the aesthetic symbols of light and shade and harmony are another, and so on. The relationship between symbolic knowledges and the material world is a mediated one, therefore, in which meaning is dependent not upon particular numbers, musical sounds, specific images or the marks we place on a piece of paper, but upon their *symbolic function*: what they express, represent or signify.

Much of this argument is conducted in Cassirer's three-volume *The Philosophy of Symbolic Forms*, although it is the final volume, published in 1929 and subtitled 'The Phenomenology of Knowledge', which develops the broad standpoint that sensation alongside imagination and understanding may all be placed on an equivalent epistemological footing. With a nod in the direction of Hegel's first major philosophical work, the reference to a 'phenomenology' of knowledge was intended to convey the point that 'knowledge must convey the totality of cultural forms' (1957 [1929]: III, xiv), not just those of abstract cognition. Whilst, today, the rigorous systematic thinking of Cassirer and his allusion to totalities would draw breath in some quarters as well as looks of disdain, the reference to *cultural* modes of knowing and experience would not be out of place in most social science circles.

Knowing through affect   The third volume of Cassirer's cultural philosophy is given over to the exposition of three symbolic functions: those of expression, representation and signification.[7] Broadly speaking, the first of these functions, symbolic expression, has close affinities to contemporary concerns with embodied or experiential forms of knowledge which stress their non-representational nature (see Shusterman, 1997; Thrift, 1999). As a kind of practical theory, the mode of understanding sought has less to do with abstract notions of discovery and more to do with what Nigel Thrift refers to as 'different possible ways in which we might relate ourselves to our surroundings' (1999: 304). The stress here is upon an immediate, non-discursive mode of experience which, according to Shusterman (1997), has bodily feeling as its locus. The intense, often visceral, nature of immediate experience recalled by Shusterman, and its significance for somatic aesthetics, runs in parallel to Cassirer's observation that expressive meaning is related directly to sense perception and bodily awareness. As John Krois summarizes, 'insofar as perceived phenomena appear to us as agitating, soothing, gloomy, joyful, pacifying or otherwise exhibiting a mood, they exemplify what Cassirer calls expressive symbolism' (1987: 86).

Expressive symbolism is perhaps best understood as a structure of feeling where, for example, a stylish piece of fashion or the lyrics of a new musical composition 'move' us in some way that is unrelated to, say, the latest 'language' of fashion or the technical competence by which the music is reproduced. For Cassirer, what stimulates us in relation to design or lyrical composition is not only their respective popular or linguistic appeal; it is, in the case of the former, the harmony of the design, its colour and form, or in relation to music, the unison of sounds, the specific rhythm, tone and pitch which brings a certain satisfaction to the ear. In common with all forms of aesthetic knowledge, an appreciation of film, art, design, music, display and others rests upon their sensuous form – the feelings they express – not simply upon their technical or analytical excellence. In short, there is a creative content to such affects that cannot readily be measured by any cognitive yardstick.

The novel point here, as developed by Cassirer, is that whilst such aesthetic appreciation may be viewed as the result of a series of unformed feelings, the process of understanding involved is far from passive. On the contrary, the very production of expressive meaning is itself dependent upon the symbolic codes which make the experience an objective cultural moment. As Cassirer argues in relation to aesthetic experience:

> Art is expression, but it is an active, not a passive mode of expression. It is imagination, but it is productive, not merely reproductive imagination. Artistic emotion is creative emotion; it is that emotion which we feel when we live the life of a form. Every form has not only a static being; it has a dynamic force and a dynamic life of its own. Light, colour, mass, weight are not experienced in the same way in a work of art as in our common experience. . . . [For the cultural producer] the words, the colours, the lines, the spatial forms and designs, the musical sounds are not only technical means of reproduction; they are the very conditions, they are the essential moments of the productive artistic process itself.
>
> (1979 [1942]: 160–1)

In other words, when formulating aesthetic judgements there are specific operations of knowledge involved which take place on the basis of a constitutive symbolic domain. It is this domain, where words, sounds, and images function as an expressive system of signs, which makes possible cultural understanding, regardless of whether such features can be fully articulated by those involved in the appreciation of a particular art form like film or music. More to the point, it makes it possible to consider the expressive as a form of symbolization which is not subjective or psychological in nature, but integral to the cultural meaning of objects and practices.

Thus in relation to the range of activities associated with, say, the law, entertainment or engineering design, practices which 'move' people or are evocative in style may be viewed as part of an objective cultural schema, the symbolism of which may be replete and full-bodied but none the less communicable. In relation to an artful piece of legal reasoning or a demonstrative concert performance, for example, or a novel piece of service R & D, where meaning may come through affect rather than signification, the cues may form part of a more ambiguous symbolic order, yet still approximate to something that we can call expressive knowledge.

Knowing through codes　In contrast, the second of Cassirer's symbolic functions, representation, is perhaps the most familiar means by which shared cultural meanings become established. Once a word or image stands in for or depicts something else, the expressive or sensual side diminishes and the referential dimension takes centre-stage. Language is the most obvious system of representation, although in the broad semiological approach of Roland Barthes any object or activity can function 'like a language' in the production of cultural meanings.[8] In his classic text *Mythologies* (1973), Barthes opened up a rich symbolic seam which, for example, made it possible to talk of a 'language' of fashion where clothes function as identity codes for particular social and cultural groupings. Provided that dress codes are understood and that the difference between items of fashion are marked symbolically, a wider realm of signs is communicated that is open to manipulation through advertising, styling, branding and marketing.

This takes us closer to what it is about representational systems such as language that enables Cassirer to speak about their 'mythical' or imaginative properties. At the core of this understanding is the now widely accepted view that language is fundamentally ambiguous in its relation to the material world. In fact, it is this very ambiguity which reveals the extent to which representation, as a form of knowledge, may stand for little that is actually deemed the 'real' world. Or as Cassirer succinctly expressed it, language '*begins* only where our immediate relation to sensory impression and sensory affectivity *ceases*' (1953 [1923]: I, 189). In this sense, anything that functions like a language, as a system or representation, may involve an imaginative play of signs which none the less provide 'access' to a particular 'world', be it cultural, political or economic. This is perhaps where most of Lash and Urry's stress on the symbolically saturated nature of economic goods is in evidence. As the site of playful representation, the semiotic work of advertising, branding, and the like, involves the skilful deployment of symbols, regardless of whether or not the signs themselves represent anything in particular. While Lash and Urry place such playful work of representation under the term 'aesthetic', it is perhaps more useful to treat their fascination with 'postmodern goods' as the result of a contrived exercise in the formation of judgements around taste and distinction.

Finally, the third of Cassirer's symbolic functions, signification, amounts to what was for him the most developed knowledge accomplishment: the systematic manipulation of abstract symbols. This takes us back firmly to the ground of formal reasoning, cognition and abstract judgement. If symbolic expression is at one end of the knowledge spectrum, then symbolic abstraction is to be found at the other. This, for Cassirer, was principally the world of mathematics, geometry and physics, where reason has progressed far beyond representation with the introduction of numerical concepts and notations that corresponded to earlier, non-numerical forms. According to Krois,

A purely symbolic conception of number regards it neither in terms of psychological activity nor in reference to things, but as a specific form of symbolic interpretation with a validity of its own. In the philosophy of mathematics the series of natural numbers is regarded as a relational 'order in progression' without reference to the counting subject. The validity of mathematics is thereby enclosed in the medium of mathematics itself. The full development of mathematics disregards the question of how well it copies the world; rather, mathematics is perceived as a way of having or understanding a world. The same holds for all symbolic forms. The symbolic interpretation does not copy a given world; it makes a world accessible.

(1982: 84–5)

Having access to such an abstract world, for Cassirer, having the ability to simplify reality in this way, to analyse and extend reasoning, so that, for example, the world may be grasped by fewer axioms and principles, held out the prospect of being able to think about new possibilities which have yet to be encountered. The more that one is able to articulate a set of possibilities, say, in biotechnology or software development, in abstract terms, the greater the ability to manipulate them symbolically and thus conceive of alternatives and variations which give rise to fresh understandings. This, unmistakenly, is the landscape of 'scientific' innovation, where cognitive frontiers are pushed back and knowledge extended through experimentation and 'pure' thought.

If this sounds familiar, then that is because Leadbeater's account of a knowledge-based economy, where physical assets represent something of an encumbrance in the new economy, is not so far removed from this frontier land.[9] The raw materials of know-how and ingenuity which take a 'pure' knowledge (not information) form in this landscape feed on a sense of intangible innovation and thus promote a sense of worth that is less material, more abstractly honed. And of course, this kind of manipulation is also the most amenable to replication and reproduction in simple form. Whilst Cassirer's account of formal knowledge undoubtedly over-emphasizes the significance of numerical symbols within a small range of sciences, for example by neglecting the role of other notational devices in conceptual advancement (most notably models, diagrams, graphs and maps of whatever kind), the stress overall remains one of reason's advancement through abstract judgement.

Entangled knowledges   It is important to recall at this point that, for Cassirer, the three symbolic domains of knowledge each operate under specific epistemological conditions, none of which may simply be reduced to habit or scientific convention. If that were the case, the foregoing would amount to little more than detailed descriptions over how one type of knowledge differs from another. As defined symbolic formations, however, their judgemental schemas provide the context within which 'new' knowledge, or, more accurately, symbolic innovation, may be considered and judged. Rather than viewing aesthetic innovation, for example, as the result of established cultural group recognition, developments, say, in visual design or computer-generated imagery would be subject to judgement within specific symbolic schemas.

This position, although somewhat questionable given the contemporary stress placed upon the relative nature of judgement, does serve to broaden the basis upon which economic knowledge and the manipulation of symbols may be assessed. In a variety of ways, the position outlined resonates with that argued by the pragmatist philosopher Nelson Goodman in his *Ways of Worldmaking* (1978) and later works, which posit a multiplicity of worlds, each known in different ways, and impossible to combine into a single frame of symbolic reference.[10] Perhaps more than Cassirer, however, Goodman insists on the absolute inseparability of symbolic forms, acknowledging the embodied nature of cognition and the cognitive role of feeling, which perhaps should alert us to the inseparability of different forms of symbolic knowledge in each and every area of the economy.

As we have seen in the case of the film industry, the technical and the aesthetic co-exist and combine in ways which give the sector its distinctive blend of symbolic knowledges. It is neither possible nor desirable to draw a clear line between 'hard' and 'soft' knowledge options, in so far as they combine to produce the kinds of aesthetic innovation which have long characterized the industry's practices. The same may be said of finance and the new forms of money and their associated risk instruments, which make it possible to combine rational, calculative practices with more imaginative representations of what money can do in a fast-fleeting world that are far removed from conventional monetary routines.[11] Symbolic innovation in this context works across the symbolic registers in a particular way, echoing Cassirer's argument that meaning, or rather economic meaning, is dependent not upon any specific notation or image, but upon what they express, represent or signify. In short, economic knowledge and meaning is dependent upon symbolic function and it is their entangled nature which differentiates one set of economic activities, one industry, from another.

At the very least, Cassirer and Goodman's thinking should make us suspicious of any singular attempts to divide up economic activity along cognitive or aesthetic lines, and forces us to acknowledge the entangled nature of economic knowledges which shape much of what we take to be creative know-how.

conclusion In a chapter that started with the *rapprochement* of culture and the economy, I have spent a significant amount of time and effort trying to show how easy it is to slip into codified scripts of economic knowledge which, often unreflectively, sideline the expressive. I have also attempted to show that where such slippage is avoided, the outcome is often to fall back into simple binaries around the material and the symbolic, the cognitive and the aesthetic, as ways of dividing up economic activity. By this, I do not mean that day-to-day business is executed along these lines, merely that the kinds of visceral messiness that makes up economic practice somehow do not seem to register as part of the knowledge dynamic of so-called 'weightless' or 'thin-air' economies. The fact that particular industries *combine* various symbolic practices in *specific* ways and that this is what gives them their *distinctive* knowledge-producing character seems somehow too difficult to translate or, indeed, apprehend.

Perhaps the key word, here, is translation. Despite an obvious willingness to embrace the cultural, the expressive and the affective as part of what goes on in economic life, writers as different as Scott Lash and Charles Leadbeater seem unable to translate aural, visual or expressive works without recourse to some form of explicit codification. For Lash, in his hybrid domain of techno-culture, the tactile and the ambiguous become the 'ground' for the new information age, refigured by the digital networks to become something recognizably formal in cultural terms. And for Leadbeater, for all his concern with intangible assets and implicit knowledges, the excess that is creativity still somehow becomes subject to the business of replication and reproduction in codifiable forms.

The translation of poorly shared, ambiguous forms of economic meaning that work through affect rather than signification may defy explicit coding, but that does not mean to say that they are not recognized, reacted to and judged by the cues available as part of something creative and knowledgeable. The fact that the economic contexts in which many people work out their lives may strike them as obvious does not imply that sense and meaning are clear for all to see. The practise of negotiating unformed feelings as part of a fuzzy worklife is not something that captures the attention, but it is none the less a key dimension of economic know-how today. To think otherwise is to cede the economic landscape of the symbolic and the affective to the encoders, whether in the fields of finance, service, manufacturing or indeed agro-chemicals.

notes

I would like to thank Paul du Gay, David Hesmondhalgh and Michael Pryke for their insight and comments on an earlier draft of this chapter.

1. This familiar argument takes its cue from the work of Jean Baudrillard (1983, 1993), which argues that, given the fundamental ambiguity of representational systems, we no longer expect signs to represent anything in particular. The arbitrary nature of the sign has itself become the site of playful representation to such an extent that inauthenticity is not only anticipated but, so the argument goes, understood as well.

2. In the *Critique of Judgement* (1987 [1790]), Kant wrestles with the fact that aesthetic judgements, if they are to be considered as something more than subjective preference, must claim some kind of universal status. Yet, clearly, judgements of taste in relation to art or music or design rely largely on a subject's 'feeling' for what is in harmony. To avoid an unmediated subjectivism, Kant moves closer to the idea of a universal convention and the possibility of individuals transcending their own particular needs and desires. As Terry Eagleton outlines it, for Kant,

> Aesthetic judgements are thus, as it were, impersonally personal, a kind of subjectivity without a subject or, as Kant has it, a 'universal subjectivity'. To judge aesthetically is implicitly to declare that a wholly subjective response is of the kind that every individual must necessarily experience, one that must elicit spontaneous agreement from all.
>
> (1990: 93)

This view runs into difficulty, however, once the possibility of radically different artistic appropriations is entertained.

3. See, for example, the work of Nonaka (1994) and Nonaka and Takeuchi (1995), which has been influential in relation to organizational 'knowledge' creation of a detachable form.

4. See also Zukin (1996, 1998), for example.

5. The stress placed upon *cultural meaning* by Cassirer in his work on symbolic forms is intended to convey the objective rather than the subjective or psychological nature of cultural forms. Each of the three symbolic functions

– expression, representation and signification – outlined below conveys different 'dimensions of meaning' (Cassirer, 1957 [1929]: III, 448–9). See also Krois (1987).

6. This position is outlined fully by Cassirer in his introduction to Volume III of *The Philosophy of Symbolic Forms* (1957 [1929]).

7. Krois (1987) prefers to use the term 'significance', probably to avoid misunderstanding over the general use of signifying practices, following Saussure (1974 [1916]). For Cassirer, the use of the term 'signification' is restricted largely to abstract symbolism and the 'world' beyond reference.

8. It should be noted, however, that Barthes was somewhat ambiguous about representing art or music 'as a text', as if meaning in these activities could simply be articulated in a coded form. For example, he asks:

> Then what is music? Panzéra's art answers: a *quality of language*. But this quality of language in no way derives from the sciences of language (poetics, rhetoric, semiology), for in becoming a quality, what is promoted in language is what it does not say, does not articulate. In the unspoken appears pleasure, tenderness, delicacy, fulfillment, all the values of the most delicate image-repertoire. Music is both what is expressed and what is implicit in the text: what is pronounced (submitted to inflections) but is not articulated: what is at once outside meaning and non-meaning, fulfilled in that *signifying [signifiance]*, which the theory of the text today seeks to postulate and to situate. Music, like signifying, derives from no metalanguage but only from a discourse of value, of praise: from a lover's discourse: every 'successful' relation – successful in that it manages to say the implicit without articulating it, to pass over articulation without falling into the censorship of desire or the sublimation of the unspeakable – such a relation can rightly be called *musical*.
>
> (Barthes, 1985: 284–5)

9. Interestingly, Daniel Bell (1973), that other pioneer of a knowledge-driven economy, based his understanding of a post-industrial economy on an 'abstract system of symbols' which shape the practices of innovation in science, technology and related fields. More to the point, he actually drew upon Cassirer's work in *The Cultural Contradictions of Capitalism* (1976) to justify a clear separation between the 'economic' and the 'cultural', pointing to the fact that only abstract symbolism and not expressive symbolism produced *economic* knowledge.

> I mean by culture – and here I follow Ernst Cassirer – the realm of symbolic forms and, in the context of the argument of this book, more narrowly the arena of *expressive symbolism*: those efforts, in painting, poetry, and fiction, or within the religious forms of litany, liturgy, and ritual, which seek to explore and express the meanings of human existence in some imaginative form.
>
> (1976: 12)

10. It is not, I should stress, my intention to give Goodman the last word on symbolism. His reliance on perception and the pictorial tends to bias his understanding towards the visual and away from, say, the aural worlds outlined so vividly by Jonathan Ree in *I See a Voice* (2000). Where Goodman is insightful, however, is over the relevance of non-verbal forms of cognition generally. See his *Of Mind and Other Matters* (1985) and the section entitled 'Art in Action' which addresses the cognitive and the aesthetic in art.

11. See Pryke and Allen (2000) for an account of representation and calculation in new forms of money such as derivatives.

references

Barthes, R. (1973) *Mythologies*. St Albans: Paladin.

Barthes, R. (1985) *The Responsibility of Forms: Critical Essays in Music, Art and Representation*. Berkeley and Los Angeles: University of California Press.

Baudrillard, J. (1983) *Simulations*. New York: Semiotext(e).

Baudrillard, J. (1993) *Symbolic Exchange and Death*. London and New Delhi: Sage.

Bell, D. (1973) *The Coming of Post-industrial Society*. New York: Basic Books.

Bell, D. (1976) *The Cultural Contradictions of Capitalism*. New York: Basic Books.

Cassirer, E. (1953) [1923] *The Philosophy of Symbolic Forms* (Vol. I). New Haven, CT, and London: Yale University Press.

Cassirer, E. (1955) [1925] *The Philosophy of Symbolic Forms* (Vol. II). New Haven, CT, and London: Yale University Press.

Cassirer, E. (1957) [1929] *The Philosophy of Symbolic Forms* (Vols I–III). New Haven, CT, and London: Yale University Press.

Cassirer, E. (1979) [1942] 'Language and art', in D.P. Verene (ed.), *Symbol, Myth and Culture: Essays and Lectures of Ernst Cassirer, 1935–45*. New Haven, CT, and London: Yale University Press.

Coyle, D. (1999) *The Weightless World: Thriving in the Digital Age*. Oxford: Capstone.

Eagleton, T. (1990) *The Ideology of the Aesthetic*. Oxford: Blackwell.

Goodman, N. (1978) *Ways of Worldmaking*. Hassocks: Harvester.

Goodman, N. (1984) *Of Mind and Other Matters*. Cambridge, MA: Harvard University Press.

Kant, I. (1987) [1790] *Critique of Judgement*. Indianapolis and Cambridge: Hackett.

Krois, J.M. (1987) *Cassirer: Symbolic Forms and History*. New Haven, CT and London: Yale University Press.

Lash, S. (1999) *Another Modernity: A Different Rationality*. Oxford: Blackwell.

Lash, S. and Urry, J. (1994) *Economies of Signs and Space*. London: Sage.

Leadbeater, C. (1999) *Living on Thin Air: The New Economy*. Harmondsworth: Viking.

Nonaka, I. (1994) 'A dynamic theory of organizational knowledge', *Organizational Science*, 5 (1): 14–37.

Nonaka, I. and Takeuchi, H. (1995) *The Knowledge-Creating Company*. Oxford: Oxford University Press.

Pryke, M. and Allen, J. (2000) 'Monetized time-space: derivatives – money's "new imaginary"?', *Economy and Society*, 29 (2): 239–64.

Ree, J. (2000) *I See a Voice: A Philisophical History*. London: HarperCollins.

Reich, R. (1993) *The Work of Nations*. London and New York: Simon and Schuster.

Saussure, F. de (1974) [1915] *Course in General Linguistics*. London: Fontana.

Shusterman, R. (1997) *Practicing Philosophy: Pragmatism and the Philosophical Life*. New York and London: Routledge.

Thrift, N. (1999) 'Steps to an ecology of place', in D. Massey, J. Allen and P. Sarre (eds), *Human Geography Today*. Cambridge: Polity.

Verene, D.P. (ed.) (1979) *Symbol, Myth and Culture: Essays and Lectures of Ernst Cassirer, 1935–45*. New Haven, CT, and London: Yale University Press.

Zukin, S. (1995) *The Culture of Cities*. Oxford: Blackwell.

Zukin, S. (1996) 'Space and symbolism in an age of decline', in A.D. King (ed.), *Representing the City: Ethnicity, Capital and Culture in the 21st-Century Metropolis*. Basingstoke and London: Macmillan.

Zukin, S. (1998) 'Urban lifestyles: diversity and standardization in spaces of consumption', *Urban Studies*, 35 (5/6): 825–39.

capturing markets from the economists

Don Slater

The division between economic and socio-cultural analysis constitutes a kind of deep structure of modern Western thought. While it has been a favourite pastime of critical thinking since early modernity to attack the formalism of economic theory, we have been less good at reflecting on how critical and cultural analysis has itself been structured by this opposition. Essentially, critical social thought has generally accepted the same terms of engagement as does economics, in which culture and economy are seen as macro structures operating on each other as externalities: each sees the other as a global force or potential impurity pressing on it from the outside. If economics has regarded any incursion of culture as something which renders its formal and normative models impure, the very notion of culture largely arose in the eighteenth century (as in Williams' 1985 analysis) as a defence against the incursion of economic rationality into more broadly conceived ways of life, or against the domination of economic 'value' over true social 'worth'. What we are always witnessing is a world-historical clash of titans, such as (in neo-liberalism) the purification of economy from all irrational cultural interventions, or the (traditionalist or Marxist) defence of culture from the virus of commodification.

There are two problems here, and a close relation between them: the macro level of analysis, and the way in which economy and culture are seen as externalities. I want to argue in this chapter that at the micro level of analysis we both can and indeed must grasp cultural and economic action as internally related to one another. Specifically, when we look at the preeminent sphere of conventional economics – markets and market relations – from the standpoint of specific social actors, we find that economic and cultural categories are logically and practically interdependent: neither can be reduced to or separated from the other. This is so for the very simple but strong reason that, in practice, social actors cannot actually define a market or a competitor, let alone act in relation to them, except through extensive forms of cultural knowledge. This, in turn, is because markets and competitors are defined by the perceived qualitative nature of the objects they transact, by whether an object is perceived as being the same as or different from other objects, a perception that requires complex cultural knowledges. At the same time, those cultural knowledges are strategically and instrumentally structured as part of competitive market actions. From this perspective, it is as wrong to reduce market features to cultural 'sign values' as it is to bracket qualitative features for the purpose of micro-economic analysis. This argument is initially presented in terms of an ethnography of one economic sector that has been crucial to the so-called 'cultural turn' in the sociology of economic life: the realm of culture industries and 'cultural intermediaries' such as advertising agents, designers and marketing people.

This is not simply a call to acknowledge the embeddedness of economy within the social. It is a stronger claim that economic and cultural categories are merged within the structures of market relations and micro-economic action. Yet this micro-economic level is precisely where most culturalist encounters with the economic fear to tread: where can we find a culturalist conceptualization of *markets*, or of fundamental market relations such as competition? Researchers may produce political economies of some cultural fields (for example of particular media), but these tend to employ economic categories unproblematically, perhaps reaching backwards to macro accounts of capitalism dimly remembered (and now only half-heartedly believed) from the days before Marx was *passé*. Or, worse, they reconceptualize economic categories *as* cultural categories, as in the case of Baudrillard's sign value or in the new grand narratives of a move from Fordist (materialistic) economies to dematerialized economies 'of signs and spaces' (Lash and Urry, 1994) or of information or culture. At the very least, such intellectual currents seem to be moves *within* rather than *against* the totalization of 'economy' and 'culture' as monolithic, defensive and hypostatized social moments. While there are very good grounds for investigating ostensibly new substantive developments such as the increasing centrality of 'cultural industries', or 'information commodities', or 'cultural intermediaries', this is quite a different thing from the methodological presumption that culture and economy have ever represented different logics or moments which are now empirically converging.

The line of thought pursued here would oppose the idea of culture as a separate social moment, and therefore complicates again the question of how to 'place' culture analytically, famously 'one of the two or three most complicated words in the English language' (Williams, 1976: 76). The issue for this chapter is to return to the most 'anthropological' senses of the term, those which equate it with the meaningful patterning of all social life (and therefore make it coterminous with social life as such) rather than with any specialized expressive spheres or forms, whether 'high' or 'low'. At the same time, apparently objectified structures, such as markets, clearly also need to be thought of in terms of 'meaningful patterning'; for example, in the present case, the very notion of a market requires qualitative understandings of the place and meaning of objects/commodities in ways of life. Against the deep structure of thought in which culture – in step with trajectories of modernity and postmodernity – retreats from or overwhelms various social locations (such as 'the economic'), one concern of this chapter is to bring market analysis into line with a perspective in which it is inconceivable that any social sphere could be 'without culture' and still persist as social order (similarly, John Law and Liz McFall, in this volume, start from the [Weberian] premise that 'culture is everywhere', and always has been). This stance also generates an advocacy of ethnography as a methodological approach: an analysis of 'cultural economy' has to be built up from engagement with lived social practices rather than deduced from macro characterizations of pre-given social moments.

What I would like to do in this chapter, then, is to interrogate various concepts of both economy and culture at the micro level of commercial practice and through this to question the macro and external forms through which we generally relate culture and economy.

two case studies: cultural and commercial calculation in an advertising agency   Advertising is a decisive test case in connecting economy and culture within everyday economic action. Briefly, although advertising is generally understood as paradigmatic of modern consumer capitalism, it is unthinkable within mainstream economic discourses, where it appears as a departure from perfect competition. It is a form of non-price competition by which firms attempt to exert control over the demand curves for their own products through psychological or cultural intervention, and hence represents a pressure away from formal rationality. Mirroring this position, within critical and culturalist discourse, advertising is almost never conceptualized as a form of business practice at all but rather as a cultural intervention in the domain of the economic. Although the literature recognizes that it is indisputably undertaken, and paid for, in order to accomplish clear commercial purposes – *selling things* – it is not itself theorized as a commercial practice. Over the course of the twentieth century, advertising was treated as a psychological technology, as semiotic process, as communications media, as modernist art, as ideology or as a production of sign values – as absolutely any cultural thing so as not to look at it as a common or garden business effort (for examples of each of these 'takes' on advertising, see, respectively, Galbraith, 1969; Barthes, 1986, or Dyer, 1982; Leiss et al., 1986; Schudson, 1984; Ewen, 1976; Baudrillard, 1998 [1970] or Goldman, 1992). Indeed, an entire hugely influential generation of advertising studies (e.g., Williamson, 1978) treated it exclusively as an ideological effort, without any reference to commerce at all, relating it to economy only at the most global level through the role of ideology in capitalist reproduction. Such formulations may reach deeply back into the 1970s and 1980s, but the same structure of thought is if anything more extreme today, at a time when thinking about economic reproduction has become increasingly reduced to thinking about cultural reproduction.

Let us start then with two routine examples of advertising thinking which, I would argue, are simply incomprehensible in these terms. The material comes from fieldwork done some time ago (1980) and may therefore be treated as historical. However, the onus is on current research to indicate exactly what *has* changed in the picture I am about to paint.

Johnson's Baby Oil　　Table 3.1 is a 'Strategy Selection Outline', a standard document within one of the agencies studied; most agencies have something similar. It formalized the central marketing categories in such a way as to connect them (vertically, looking down the rows) into coherent visions for the product, and then to compare them (horizontally across the columns) in order to reach a strategic decision. This example was from a training exercise carried out by younger agents, but the account had recently been taken through the same process for real. Johnson's Baby Oil (JBO) faced slow growth in its traditional infant care market due (they believed) to a declining birth rate rather than competitive forces. Having made a general decision to move towards the women's cosmetics and skin-care markets, the company could conjure up a seemingly infinite number of products that JBO could now become, each involving a myriad possible consumer groups, product uses and possible markets and competitors. The agency account director listed 20 different products which JBO could be defined as. Each definition started from a notion of 'use value', which was simultaneously the definition of a market. For example, given a general focus on women users, it was found that JBO was usable as an eye make-up remover. This was supported by clinical tests which identified relevant properties of the product ('gentle and non-sensitizing'). Taking this route implied a particular demographic ('Females 18–49 with emphasis against 18–34 year-olds, upscale'), but also intervention in a specific constellation of relations of consumption. Specific questions could be asked about this use value as a potential consumer market, such as frequency and volume of use in relation to eye make-up removal.

But this cultural calculation of consumption possibilities was inseparable from thinking about competitive relations. To be 'better than the leading cold cream' (in one example) means to characterize the use value in terms of its substitutability for other products in the same category: if one were to choose the Eye Make-up Remover route, then one would be simultaneously defining JBO as competing in a particular market ('All baby oils and eye make-up removers'). Indeed, the very heading 'Product class definition' simultaneously labels the product (eye make-up remover) and names its market ('All baby oils . . .'). The choice of this product/market definition involves more than who will use it and how. Rather, in choosing to be an eye make-up remover rather than a bath additive, one is entering different markets with different conditions of competition, such as different competitors, different levels of competing advertising expenditure, different valuations within financial markets, different legal and regulatory structures, and so on.

The Strategy Selection Outline copes with the fact that advertisers have to manage a complex simultaneous equation: a shift in use value, as one reads across the page, is at the very same moment a shift in markets, and vice versa. A shift in any element causes all the other elements – consumption and competition, cultural and market relations – to shift as well.

My claim is that the advertisers above are formalizing and seeking rationally to exploit potentialities for economic action which are inherent in the very idea of a market but which escape both the economic and culturalist view. For an advertiser the very idea of 'a market' is a malleable and fluid one. The supposedly 'economic' issues of 'what market are we in?' and 'who are our competitors?' are simply not economic in the conventional sense. Producers cannot know what market they are in without extensive cultural calculation; and they cannot understand the cultural form of their product and its use outside of a context of market competition. Moreover, the crucial question is not in fact 'what market are we in?' but rather 'what are the various interrelated definitions of product and competition that we can dream up, and how do we assess and choose between them as commercial strategies?' The answer to *that* question takes the form, eventually, of the identification of what we gloss as 'a market'. And even more slippery than this, advertisers distinguish this 'strategic market definition' (where they would like to end up) from 'the market' at the present moment (what they analyse through background market research). Hence, markets and market relations are not – for *practitioners* – an economic environment within which more cultural ('advertising') choices are made. To the contrary, markets and market relations are themselves defined within a broader calculation of possibilities. At the same time, supposedly cultural relations are not a backdrop or set of assumptions behind rational economic action. To the contrary, they are redefined and conceptualized *within* an instrumentally rational attempt to characterize optimal market positions.

Table 3.1
Strategy selection outline for Johnson's Baby Oil

	Strategy I (Preferred)	Strategy II	Strategy III	Strategy IV	Rationale/basis of preference
Product class definition	BROAD COSMETIC VERSATILITY All baby oils, hand/body moisturizers, make-up removers and bath additives.	MOISTURIZER All baby oils and hand/body moisturizers.	EYE MAKE-UP REMOVER All baby oils and eye make-up removers.	BATH ADDITIVE All baby oils and bath moisturizers.	Strategy I is preferred because it represents a potentially larger user base and appeals to the diverse cosmetic needs of the broad category of susceptible prospects. Although not stated, this positioning has an implicit economy appeal. Neither of the alternative strategies provides the broad user base nor resultant consumption afforded by the preferred positioning.
Target group selection	Females 18–49 with emphasis against 18–34, upscale, who are concerned with their appearance, may have a dry-skin problem, and are desirous of a skin-care product which is versatile, gentle and pure.	Females 18–49 with emphasis against 34–49 year-olds, upscale, who are concerned with their appearance, have a dry-skin problem, and are desirous of an effective overall skin moisturizer which is gentle and pure.	Females 18–49 with emphasis against 18–34 year-olds, upscale, who are concerned with their appearance and wish an effective make-up remover which is gentle, pure and non-sensitizing.	Females 18–49 who are concerned with their appearance, have a dry-skin problem, and want a gentle, pure bath product that will moisturize their skin.	

Message element selection	JBO is a versatile cosmetic product which is an effective moisturizer and make-up remover and is therefore a substitute for a wide variety of skin-care/cosmetic products.	JBO is an effective body moisturizer.	JBO is a superior eye make-up remover. ('Better than the leading cold cream.')	JBO is an effective body moisturizer when added to the bath.
Rationale based on information and/or judgement	(1) JBO is an effective body moisturizer and make-up remover fulfilling perceived consumer needs/desires. (2) JBO's versatility of usage makes it an ideal replacement for a wide variety of cosmetic products whose users are singular in nature, and in doing so provides an implied economic benefit to the consumer.	(1) JBO's properties make it an effective agent for the retardation of moisture loss from the skin, aiding in the alleviation of dry skin and making the body soft and smooth to touch. (2) JBO is an economical replacement for more expensive dry-skin products.	(1) JBO is a clinically proven superior make-up remover. (2) JBO is gentle and non-sensitizing.	(1) The properties of JBO make if an effective product for the retardation of moisture loss from the skin, aiding in the alleviation of dry skin. (2) Using JBO as part of the bathing regimen is an easy, convenient way to make the entire body soft and smooth. (3) JBO is an economical replacement for more expensive bath additives/moisturizers.

INFORMATION NEEDS

Detailed data relating to triers, non-users and non-triers of baby oil for cosmetic purposes, with particular attraction to frequency and volume by use occasion.

Energen crispbread   The JBO exercise focused largely on use value. In the second example, the concern was more evidently with how to pick a market. Energen, a division of Rank Hovis MacDougall, produced a range of low-calorie foods (crispbreads, rolls, jams, soft drink, breakfast cereal). It was introduced and marketed as a range of diet and slimming products. When the advertising agency won the account, this market was deeply troubled and declining, and Energen was looking for a way out. This defined the development of marketing and advertising strategy: what market should the products be in? How can we redefine the product so as to place it in a market which promises growth in sales? Energen had already come to believe that slimming products constituted a neurotic market based on neurotic consumption. The very notion of a specialist slimming food mainly for women implied that it was bought for periodic spasms of crash dieting, outside normal consumption patterns. Their most recent advertising focused on the fact that this disruption of eating habits separated women from their families: women felt they were excluding themselves from the central ritual of domestic integration (dinner-time) for the sake of disciplining their bodies. The tag-line of the previous advertisements had run: 'Did your last diet expect you to give up little things – like your family?' Energen was nowto be seen not as part of a special diet but as a range of low-carbohydrate substitutes for the elements of a normal meal; hence, you can diet without ostracizing yourself.

However, this did not shift the products far enough from the diet market, for the main use value was still seen as weight loss. This conflicted with a second consideration: by looking at a range of new consumption trends, marketers argued that the main movement was towards increasing consumer concern with a 'healthier way of life', characterized by regular exercise, natural foods and natural ingredients. Maintaining a certain weight was not seen as a special problem to be dealt with by special diets, but it was rather a part of a larger and more continuous concern with health and feeling good. In food markets, those products perceived to be both healthy and natural were increasing market share; there was 'increasing awareness of "good-for-you/bad-for-you" ingredients' (internal company report). So the products that were gaining share were of the wholemeal bread, real ale, cottage cheese variety. Significantly for Energen, slimming versions of normal foods, as opposed to specialist diet foods (e.g. diet soft drinks, diet salad creams), were taking increasing shares of their respective markets; again, they were seen not as part of a diet but as low-calorie versions of normal foods, the choice of healthier alternatives. Finally, the idea of healthy eating actually made redundant the idea of slimming as a special dietary regime.

In sum, Energen felt it was confronting a shift in the entire structure of markets and competition which could indeed be traced to shifting consumption patterns. However, these were simultaneously seen by the agents to require redefining the product in terms of new market relations (e.g. new distribution patterns emerged as the slimming market moved away from chemists to supermarkets, which were now including health food shelves). They felt that they were in the wrong market, competing with the wrong products; or, conversely, they felt that the market and competitive relations had shifted to such an extent that their strategies were no longer appropriate. So Energen was slowly to make the move from diet food to a notion of food and drink products 'each of which offers a more sensible and beneficial alternative to the usual product of the kind' (advertising strategy document).

This strategy was chosen from a longer list of formalized alternatives, much like the Strategy Selection Outline above. Among the out-takes we can find the following example: 'Energen is the producer of natural wholesome foods which are designed for people who are determined to have a healthy diet.' While this served to move the product out of dieting and tapped the new consumption trends, it was felt to target too small a consumer market – largely 'opinion formers', the vanguard of health food consumers, who were also largely up-market. Moreover, it placed the product in too constricted a competitive market: largely specialist health foods. The chosen strategy – Energen as alternative to normal generic foods – encompassed a wide audience (particularly a move from individual women consumers to the entire family's diet); competitively, it would feed off sales to generic products. (Once their crispbread, Brancrisp, was defined as substitutable for sliced bread, for example, there would be plenty of market slack to take up.) As in the previous example, this was assessed for both advertising potentiality and long-term market growth. In this case, it was argued that after competing first with, say, wholemeal bread for the health trade, the product could move on to compete with all breads generally. When I left the agency, they were discussing how, once Brancrisp was established as a staple – in competition with bread – it could ultimately take on the potato, competing with all carbohydrate staples in the family diet. This was accompanied by long, loving and sensuous discussions amongst the account executives as to whether you could ever use Brancrisp – as one would a great wedge of farmer's loaf or King Edward potatoes – to dip in a steamy soup or soak up every last drop of gravy: competitive and consumption relations were clearly well ensconced within a single frame.

what is a 'market'?   Let us summarize: first, marketing strategy appears in these examples as a simultaneous definition of both markets and products. Each possible choice of product definition – of what the product could be – is simultaneously a choice of consumption relations (different culturally defined product characteristics, uses and consumers) and a choice of competitors (goods which are perceived as similar or different). In short:

different product definitions delineate different markets. Conversely, a choice between different markets is a choice between different products, uses and consumers. These choices are not made independently of each other but rather, in these examples, are made in conscious connection with each other, in full cognizance of the fact that a shift along one dimension at the same time shifts all the others. Hence, economic and cultural decisions have immediate consequences for each other; indeed, each is merely the reverse side of the same coin.

Second, advertisers are not simply 'choosing' between an array of possible definitions of products and markets. They are creating and implementing them. That is to say, each market/product definition is in fact a strategy: by seeking to produce particular definitions of markets and products through advertising, distribution, public relations, redesign or repackaging of the product itself, the advertiser is seeking to establish in reality (in the social practices of economic and cultural actors) a particular constellation of both consumption relations and competitive relations. And the two cannot be separated. These are action plans for achieving socially and conceptually interrelated economic and cultural positions, different market structures and consumption relations.

Third, for that very reason, marketing strategy is not – in the first instance – a matter of competition *within* market structures; rather it is a matter of competition *over* the structure of markets. Markets cannot be defined – as in neo-classicism – as given structures within which we can analyse competitive behaviour. This would be to assume that actors treat product definitions as given. Yet, as we have seen, the entire aim of marketing strategy is to redefine products – and to treat these redefinitions as operational strategies – in order to alter the terms of competition.

In some respects this should all be perfectly obvious. On the one hand, in both everyday and economic language markets are defined as markets *for* product types or categories: we talk easily of markets for consumer electronics, financial instruments, soya beans, labour, and so on. A market – whatever else it is within normative economic definitions – is defined by certain boundaries that give it its structure: it contains goods that are homogeneous in the sense that they can be treated as substitutable, as *the same thing*, and therefore as competing; it excludes goods which can be treated as different (see Chamberlin (1948) for an early discussion of this issue). Hence, in order to be a particular kind of economic institution, a market must also be a certain kind of culturally defined domain: it depends on social categorizations of things as similar or not. However, on the other hand, in both everyday and economic language we bracket precisely those processes by which goods come to be treated as the same or different, and consequently are able to delineate and institutionalize markets as economic structures. The entire point of advertising practice, as we have seen, is that it constantly problematizes the entire notion of 'specific products', and constitutes a set of technologies for attempting both to destabilize markets and then to re-institutionalize them around new, strategically calculated product definitions.

In the case of conventional economics, this bracketing of product definitions and therefore of market structures (and therefore of the entire domain of advertising and marketing) is both necessary and perverse. It is simply a special case of economics' general bracketing of the cultural composition of demand, tastes, preferences and all other aspects of consumption: these are taken as given rather than treated as dynamic or needing explanation; they are frameworks within which rational choice can be carried out (see, e.g., Douglas and Isherwood, 1979; Fine and Leopold, 1993; Slater, 1997; Slater and Tonkiss, 2001). There can be no interference with the framework or else it would be impossible to disentangle the rationally allocative functions of price from changing qualitative states of demand itself (Slater and Tonkiss, 2001). A classic example is the so-called 'identification problem' (Robinson, 1983: 51): if the analyst is only looking at revealed preferences in the market, how can he or she distinguish movement up and down a demand function (which can be interpreted simply as the set of possible rational responses to different prices at a particular moment in time) from a shift of the demand function itself (which can only be interpreted as different or changing qualitative definitions of needs, goods and their relationship)? The typical economic answer to this conundrum is methodological: assume that market analysis focuses on a single moment in time, hence bracketing the entire issue of the nature of demand in order to get on with the more formal agenda of modelling rational calculation. The typical advertiser's response is entirely the opposite: assume that products, needs and their relationships can be altered over time in order to bring about quite different market structures and demand functions.

The conventional economic bracketing of all this can be summarized in terms of three issues. First, there is the assumption that product categories are self-evident. Kelvin Lancaster, who pioneered this kind of critique from within conventional economic theory, put it like this: 'The "goods" of traditional theory are typically such aggregates as "automobiles", "food", "clothing", rather than individual goods as strictly defined' (1971: 9; see also Ironmonger 1972). By using such gross categories, economics could treat markets as self-evident because the use values they contained appeared as obvious and unquestionable; this brackets the interpretation and definition of market boundaries and market relations.

Second, this self-evidence is made plausible because the economist simultaneously employs and hides the forms of cultural knowledge that are actually used to define markets as frameworks for economic analysis. Again following Lancaster, to identify market relations such as competition and complementarity requires a complex cultural knowledge which both advertisers and consumers use every day but which economists replace with abstract and simplified fictions:

> All economic textbooks use examples which draw upon common-sense knowledge of the relation between properties of goods – that butter and margarine will be closer substitutes than butter and sugar, that demand for gasoline will not depend much on the price of tea, and so on. But the actual demand theories set out in these books provides no warrant for statements of this kind and no necessary expectation that goods which are close substitutes in the eyes of one person will be close substitutes for others.
>
> (1971: 2)

The 'warrant' – which is the stock-in-trade of every marketing or advertising brief or discussion – necessarily invokes cultural expertise. That is to say, as our case studies demonstrated, defining such things as 'who is my competitor?' requires an advertiser (or economist) to make assumptions about relations of consumption, about the structures of use and perception in terms of which goods might be deemed substitutable, complementary, unrelated or whatever, and by whom. They are dealing with different consumers and competitors each of whom operates different categorizations of the world of goods. The notion of an internally homogeneous market requires us to be able to identify the produce of different firms as identical or perfectly substitutable. In order to make such a definition we must know the socially salient definitions of the product and of the need involved, and current definitions of sameness and difference. For example, whether small carrots are identical to large carrots or whether they constitute different markets depends on identifying their use value: it depends on social usages among particular consumer groups, on levels of discrimination, on whether the taste difference is appreciated, on the appropriateness of the size for various recipes and styles of cooking. One can easily imagine social classes to whom small carrots are in competition with *petit pois* rather than with other carrots, on the basis of a relation to cordon bleu cuisine. If 'my competition' means 'what alternative goods might various potential customers choose instead of mine?', then the answer is going to be heterogeneous, rapidly changing and based on background knowledge or research. This background knowledge, moreover, may be entirely wrong; but *some* cultural construction of how butter and margarine, or gasoline and tea, or big and litle carrots are culturally connected will nevertheless be essential in order simply to go about my business of market competition.

Third, in addition to treating product definitions as self-evident and obscuring the cultural knowledges on which they are based, economics also treats them as *fixed*, in two senses. On the one hand, like consumption in general, product definitions are treated effectively as natural, as facts of nature or environment. At the same time, they are treated as unchanging over time, as fixed frameworks: As Lancaster argues, when the economic analyst is faced with change over time,

> In traditional analysis, we can only do one of two things: (i) ignore the changes, and proceed as if the new variant is the same good as before or (ii) regard the variant as an entirely new good, throwing out any information concerning demand behavior with respect to the original variant, and start from scratch.
>
> (1971: 8)

That is to say, precisely because they naturalize product categories, economists also reify market structures. Yet, again, this is to bracket everything that an advertising agent does: advertising operates in an environment in which products and therefore markets are continuously and dynamically changing; moreover, advertising, as we have seen, *focuses* on exploiting these environmental conditions, creating variations between product concepts as a means to reconfigure both consumer demand and competitive market structures. They live off the very fact that competition occurs *over* market structures, not just *within* them; and that this is because – in the real world – the cultural constitution of market relations is very far from 'bracketed': advertisers do not take these things as self-evident, do not leave their cultural knowledges in the background and do not treat anything as fixed.

what is a 'product'?   Market structures and relations, then, follow the contours of culturally defined use values and the ways in which relations between use values can be conceptualized as the basis for market action. The conventional economic response to this issue oddly mirrors some of the more moralistic culturalist responses to it. For example, the possibility of goods within a market being perceived by consumers or advertisers as heterogeneous and non-substitutable is regarded as a (post?)modern issue of 'product differentiation', as a new problem that somehow distorts, rather than constitutes, competition. Hence, economists (rather like some critical theorists) might then seek criteria for distinguishing between 'false' advertising-produced product differences, which segment what is 'really' a single market, and 'real' product differences, which legitimately constitute different markets. In fact, what we are dealing with is neither a problem nor a new historical development but rather an artefact of an intellectual division of labour which has historically separated economy and culture and leaves analysts deeply perturbed when it finds them in close cahoots.

Following the line of argument presented here, at the heart of this division of intellectual labour is not so much the nature of markets as the nature of the 'goods' which are central to defining them in practice. If we (and practitioners) must necessarily remove the analytical brackets from around the products, then the central issue for social analysts, as much as for economic actors, is to unpack the very notion of an object or product as a categorizable entity, to see how it can be fixed or unfixed, taken for granted or problematized. We need a social theorization of the 'things' that are transacted and how they come to be defined and stabilized as things (Slater, in press, 2001). Both conventional economics and the cultural turn present fairly inadequate resources for doing this. On the one hand, economics persistently seeks to re-fix products methodologically as self-evident or natural. On the other hand, more culturalist accounts (discussed in the next section) take the opposite tack of reducing the product to 'sign'. It can thereby be treated as entirely malleable, and be understood largely in terms of encounters between readers and texts, hence entirely missing the relations, institutions and practices through which the meanings of things, and the things themselves, are destabilized or stabilized, negotiated or contested within complex power relations and resource inequalities.

Part of the problem is a persistent naturalism that stems from crude materialism. Neo-classical utility theory, on the one hand, reduces demand to subjective preferences within the domain of market behaviour, but constantly assumes, implicitly or explicitly, that these preferences are ultimately explicable in terms of such things as basic needs or 'cultural influences' that it is the duty of non-economic disciplines like psychology, anthropology or sociology to investigate. Within economic analysis itself, needs and goods appear as a natural and self-evident environment. In more critical theory, the use value/exchange value distinction within the commodity form has generally functioned as a proxy for the distinction between a 'natural metabolism' between man (*sic*) and nature, and the warped social form taken by needs and things within capitalist market relations. In fact, Lancaster (1971) himself focuses entirely on how – having discovered the non-homogeneous character of the products on which market definitions depend – an economist might go on to formalize the different objective characteristics of products so that analysis might relate more closely to the way in which product differences change market structures over time. Of course, by identifying products with their fixed material properties, he once again brackets the very different ways in which different consumers and different advertisers construe the 'objective' properties of goods in relation to their specific practices and purposes.

The converse danger is represented by various forms of culturalism which reduce the product to sign value and semiotic processes. The object becomes entirely dematerialized as a symbolic entity or sign, which is infinitely malleable (and hence never stabilized as a socio-historical object), and whose definition can be entirely accounted for in terms of the manipulation of codes by skilled cultural actors. In the process such approaches ignore both the materiality of the object and the material economic and social structures through which it is elaborated as a meaningful entity. It tends also to reduce market structures and relations to semiotic ones. It is rather difficult to imagine how markets could exist over time, as they patently do, if products have truly undergone the kind of semiotic reduction that culturalists assume. Markets are in fact routinely institutionalized, and are even stabilized, around enduring definitions of products, whereas the semiotic reduction would assume that – as sign value – goods can be redefined at will. In fact, visions of the complete destabilization of economy – for example, 'the new economy' – are precisely what is offered on the basis of such analysis.

If we turn back to advertising practice itself, we find a way of looking at goods which cuts across both cultural reductionism and naturalism. Moreover, the approach found there is not a million methodological miles away from the perspectives that have arisen out of material culture approaches to consumption (Miller, 1995; Slater, 1997). For advertising agents, a product definition is a simultaneous equation. It is not just the object and its properties construed as physical characteristics or functions; it is, rather, properties of the object (material and symbolic) as they are perceived by particular categories of people in the context of particular relations of consumption. At the same time, a product definition is not just a set of meanings attached to a thing in isolation (the object as text or sign); rather, it is an operation on the meaningfulness of a thing that exists in a real social context. We can define that context in terms of three aspects:

- the thing itself (material and symbolic) with properties that are designed, presented or perceived in particular cultural contexts;
- social relations of consumption in which things are understood to be needed, functional, desirable, etc. – to say that 'a good is needed or wanted' is to gloss all those social practices and contexts by which such a statement comes to have a meaning (Slater, 1997);
- culturally specific social actors: that is to, say, particular product characteristics and needs are constructed in relation to particular people or groups.

The definition of a thing cannot be solidly anchored in given material properties; but it also cannot drift off into a realm of floating signifiers. Rather, the definition of a thing extends across a broad social field, offering numerous different and related points of intervention to an equally broad range of competing social actors. Take the example of parent and child arguing over the dinner table as to whether the green, steaming pile on their plate counts as 'food'. This obviously invokes the perceived properties of spinach (health, edibility, Popeye's strength); it invokes broader relations of consumption around the meaning of meals (notions of nutritional needs, obedience and power, traditions); and it is perceived from the perspective of particular people (parental roles, class constructions of nutrition, gendered relations of power and responsibility). The construction of spinach as a use value extends across a social field in which parents, marketers, schools and health services, the media (cartoons in this case), and so on, can intervene, seeking to shift elements of the field towards establishing a definition of the good that fits in with their interests. This constellation of interventions may act to destabilize the object or re-fix it: one could at least imagine an advertiser, for example, moulding spinach into new shapes – say Popeye himself – in order to crack the youth market by repositioning the vegetable as a fun food, snack and media tie-in. Any of these processes would have implications for market structures, even if the motive was not originally commercial but, say, the initiative of health educationalists; conversely, any non-commercial, 'cultural' intervention in the definition of spinach would at least take place within, and take cognizance of, the market structure of competing goods.

The construction of a categorizable 'thing' as the basis of a market structure and competitive relationship is both conceptually and socially complex. It is also conflictual, perspectival and dynamic. As anthropological studies constantly foreground, relations of consumption are fields of power struggle and reproduction, are diverse and are sites through which people articulate and negotiate diverse 'cosmologies': for example, '[t]he choice between pounding and grinding [coffee] is . . . a choice between two different views of the human condition', as well as potentially representing competition between two market segments (Douglas and Isherwood, 1979: 74). In the context of contemporary consumer culture, such consumption sites are the objects of intervention by institutions with particular and highly rationalized interests in them as conditions of political power, market competitive behaviour, moral authority, and so on.

cultural studies in the market   If economics needs to be reconstructed to accommodate the practical social knowledges that economic actors necessarily employ in order to *be* economic actors, cultural theories in turn need to develop an appropriate micro-economics. Returning to the case study, advertisers definitely acted as cultural anthropologists and sociologists, conceptualizing goods and markets in terms of concepts of use value. However, they did so within an instrumentally rational framework, with the practical intent of increasing sales and beating competition. A relation between bath oil and make-up removal within everyday body maintenance is precisely not a matter of academic interest but simultaneously and indistinguishably also a relation of competition between their product and, say, Oil of Ulay (as it was then named). This is the logic of the advertiser's situation.

If one is trying to understand economic action – specifically business practice – it makes little sense to construe what is going on here in terms of a purely ideological or cultural intervention in, say, the structure of femininity or codes of representation. This is the problem with most culturalist accounts of advertising and marketing. Judith Williamson's influential *Decoding Advertisements* (1978) both picked up on a long line of cultural criticism and set the tone for most subsequent work. Williamson dismisses the micro-economic practice of 'selling things' as trivial or empirically undecidable in comparison to the ideological role of advertising in the reproduction of capitalist subjects, patriarchal power relations and historicist structures of thought. Compare Myers' more recent statement in an introduction to advertising for cultural studies courses that our primary concern should be with the 'broader' cultural or ideological impact of advertising (1999: 3–5). This position has become axiomatic. The point here is not that the micro-economic effects of advertising are any more important (or indeed empirically investigable) than the global ideological ones. It is simply that we cannot make any sense of economic action without attending to that micro level, and that if we do not make sense of how advertisers actually carry out their commercial actions, then the global ideological analysis degenerates into a kind of abstract, disembodied functionalism: it appears as if advertising (rather than advertisers) creates capitalist or patriarchal subjects' (Slater, 1997: 137–44).

The problem is that even where analysts are trying to understand forms of commercial representation as indeed commercial, they are either lacking the concepts of the market to do this adequately, or they perform a cultural reduction. The discovery of marketing by critical social sciences in the 1980s, when they realized that businesses treat markets as symbolically malleable entities, is treated as a new development in which the economy as a whole is 'dematerialized' and henceforth structured by a logic that can be entirely grasped through quasi-semiotic analysis. Baudrillard's analysis of sign value and the code is only the most extreme example. Contemporary analyses of globalization, the information society and 'new economies' suffer on the whole from the same problem: an analytic discovery, through which one could overcome the inadequacies of previous economic thought, is instead treated as the empirical discovery of a new economy which transcends all economic thought.

It is particularly crucial to debates within cultural studies and sociology of media and culture that the appropriate methodological response is not an 'additive' one, a matter of adding traditional questions of political economy to a fundamentally cultural analysis, or an argument about the increased centrality of cultural industries in contemporary economy. Simply producing 'political economies *of*' music or the Internet or other cultural industries is not the same as exposing the integral relationship between economic and cultural processes. First, if we simply resurrect political economy in relation to cultural sectors of the economy we must (and many do) make a host of so-far unconfirmed assumptions about the centrality of these industries to overall social reproduction in order to generalize outwards from a study of, say, music or fashion to the economy as a whole (e.g. Garnham, 2000). Second, importing old analytical categories (usually from an unreconstructed Marxism or an undigested encounter with 'new economics') and applying them to cultural activities simply reinforces the sense that 'the cultural' is a separate rather than integral moment. Finally, there is the constant danger of confusing new movements within thought (the new understanding that culture and economy cannot be theorized separately) from new empirical developments. Is it the case that culture is actually more central to economic process than it was before? We need to develop more adequate theories of the sociology of economic life rather than proclaim epochal social revolutions that are merely the artefact of the inadequate theories and theoretical division of labour we have inherited.

conclusion   The argument of this chapter is limited in its aims: it looks at the traditional domain of micro-economics from the perspective of some clearly 'cultural' intermediaries, advertising agents, and argues that the conventional division between economic and cultural analysis is inadequate, as are the reductive alternatives that arise from it. At the same time, the opening out of concepts of markets and products seems capable of leading to more productive use of what we have learned from studies of consumption and material culture and (as discussed in a further essay: Slater, in press, 2001) to an engagement with the institutional processes by which both markets and products are stabilized or destabilized. In addition to the substantive and theoretical claims there is also a methodological one: the ethnographic basis of this chapter is crucial not simply for the obvious reason of staying grounded in determinate social practice but also as a basis for elaborating theory. The claim in this case is that the space currently occupied by the culture–economy divisions and reductions can be reconstructed at least partially by treating concepts such as markets, products and competition as lived realities rather than formal categories. As noted by figures such as Callon (1998), this approach must include economic theory as an object of research, in that it plays a constructive role in the production of economic realities (through business training, policy and representations of the economy), but it enters the picture as a participant rather than an observer. However, by investigating the ways in which these economic categories are constructed and acted upon, we can disaggregate the monoliths of 'culture' and 'economy' and produce theorizations that start from their internal relation within forms of social practice.

references

Barthes, R. (1986) *Mythologies*. London: Paladin.

Baudrillard, J. (1998) [1970] *The Consumer Society: Myths and Structures*. London: Sage.

Callon, M. (ed.) (1998) *The Laws of the Markets*. Oxford and Keele: Blackwell and the Sociological Review.

Chamberlin, E. (1948) *The Theory of Monopolistic Competition*. Cambridge: Harvard University Press.

Douglas, M. and Isherwood, B. (1979) *The World of Goods: Towards an Anthropology of Consumption*. Harmondsworth: Penguin.

Dyer, G. (1982) *Advertising as Communication*. London: Methuen.

Ewen, S. (1976) *Captains of Consciousness: Advertising and the Social Roots of Consumer Culture*. New York: McGraw-Hill.

Fine, B. and Leopold, E. (1993) *The World of Consumption*. London: Routledge.

Galbraith, J.K. (1969) *The Affluent Society*. London: Hamish Hamilton.

Garnham, N. (2000) *Emancipation, the Media and Modernity: Arguments about the Media and Social Theory*. Oxford: Oxford University Press.

Goldman, R. (1992) *Reading Ads Socially*. London: Routledge.

Ironmonger, D.S. (1972) *New Commodities and Consumer Behaviour*. Cambridge: Cambridge University Press.

Lancaster, K. (1971) *Consumer Demand: A New Approach*. New York: Columbia University Press.

Lash, S. and Urry, J. (1994) *Economies of Signs and Space*. London: Sage.

Leiss, W., Kline, S. and Jhally, S. (1986) *Social Communication in Advertising: Persons, Products and Images of Well-Being*. London: Methuen.

Miller, D. (ed.) (1995) *Acknowledging Consumption: A Review of New Studies*. London: Routledge.

Myers, G. (1999) *Ad Worlds: Brands, Media, Audiences*. London: Arnold.

Robinson, J. (1983) *Economic Philosophy*. Harmondsworth: Penguin.

Schudson, M. (1984) *Advertising, the Uneasy Persuasion: Its Dubious Impact on American Society*. New York: Basic Books.

Slater, D. (1997) *Consumer Culture and Modernity*. Cambridge: Polity.

Slater, D. and Tonkiss, F. (2001) *Market Society*. Cambridge: Polity.

Slater, D. (2001), 'Markets, materiality and the 'new economy', in S. Metcalf and A. Warde (eds), *Market Relatins and the Competitive Process*. Manchester: Manchester University Press.

Williams, R. (1976) *Keywords: A Vocabulary of Culture and Society*. Glasgow: Fontana.

Williams, R. (1985) *Culture and Society: 1780–1950*. Harmondsworth: Penguin.

Williamson, J. (1978) *Decoding Advertisements: Ideology and Meaning in Advertising*. London: Marion Boyars

work ethics, soft capitalism and the 'turn to life'

Paul Heelas

A good way of arguing against those who hold that the economic realm is (largely) autonomous and (relatively) impervious with regard to cultural influences is to draw attention to the role played by work ethics. Having made the point that work ethics are at once cultural and economic, attention is paid to distinguishing between four (ideal-type) work ethics. This paves the way for the main purpose of what then follows, namely that of explaining the development of what has become an important work ethic, the 'self-work ethic' of 'soft' capitalism, in particular in its 'exploratory' mode. And a key argument in this regard is that the development of soft/exploratory capitalism is largely due to the failure of other work ethics, in particular their inability adequately to handle the widespread cultural 'turn to life'.

the cultural-cum-economic   Work ethics – of whatever variety – involve the ascription of value to work. Work is valued as the means to some end (including the possibilities that work itself serves as the end or that work is not valued *per se*). And, being bound up with the attainment of some state of affairs which is valued, people are motivated to work.

There is little doubting the fact that economic activities are associated with work ethics. People can readily give reasons as to why they are working; the values they associate with their work: as the means to the end of doing a professional job; as the means to the end of helping others; as the means to ends beyond work, such as the necessity of paying the mortgage. But does this mean that work ethics serve to provide a *necessary* link between the economic and the cultural? That is to say, is it possible to imagine economic activity being carried out in the absence of some kind of work ethic?

I think not. It is certainly possible to think of cases in which 'negative' work ethics are operative, as when people work for 'wrong reasons' (such as getting by with as little effort as possible whilst still obtaining an income). But it is difficult if not impossible to think of people working without ascribing *some* value to what they are doing. Which means that there is something approaching, if not demonstrating, a necessary connection between economic activity and cultural values.

varieties of work ethics   Given the importance of Weber's *The Protestant Ethic and the Spirit of Capitalism* (1985 [1904–5]), it is perhaps not surprising that the term 'work ethic' has tended to be associated with a particular work ethic, namely the Protestant variety which – Weber argued – was developed by many of the Reformist sects of earlier modernity and contributed decisively to the development of capitalistic modernity. However, there are other quite different work ethics.

With the primary purpose of this chapter in mind, namely exploring the growth of exploratory capitalism and its self-work ethic, I now develop a language which serves to distinguish between different kinds of work ethics. This language will then be used when it is argued that the growth of exploratory capitalism owes a great deal to its promise to be able to deal with problems associated with other work ethics.

Steven Tipton's (1984) analysis of four 'styles of ethical evaluation' provides a useful starting point for distinguishing between different work ethics. The four styles are as follows:

1   The authoritative style is 'oriented toward an authoritative moral source known by faith'. It asks, '"What does God command?" and answers with which act is "obedient" and "faithful".' Action in terms of this style 'is right because the authoritative source commands it' (1984: 282).

2   The regular style is 'oriented toward rules or principles known by reason'. It asks, '"What is the relevant rule or principle?" and answers with which act is "right" or "obligatory" according to the rules.' Action in terms of this style 'is right because it conforms to the relevant rules and principles' (1984: 282).

3   The consequential or utilitarian style is 'oriented towards consequences known by cost–benefit calculation'. It asks, ' "What do I want? What act will most satisfy it?" and answers with which act will be most "efficient" or "effective" in producing the consequences that satisfy a given want.' Action in terms of this style 'is right because it produces the most good consequences; that is, maximizes satisfaction of wants' (1984: 282–3).

4   Finally, the expressive style is 'oriented toward the quality of personal feelings and of situations known by intuitions'. It asks, ' "What's happening?" and answers with which act is most "fitting" in response.'

Action in terms of this style 'is right because it constitutes the most fitting response to the situation and the most appropriate or honest expression of one's self' (1984: 282–3).

Applying Tipton's analytical scheme to the task of distinguishing between different (ideal-typical) kinds of work ethics, what can be called the *tradition-informed work ethic* ascribes value to work by way of belief or faith. Thus the Protestant work ethic, as portrayed by Weber, valued work as a key means to the end of signifying that one is of the Elect. Or, to give a related example, a later version of the Protestant work ethic values work as a key means to the end of obtaining salvation.

The second of Tipton's styles of ethical evaluation translates into what is here called the *organizational work ethic*. Work is valued as a means to the end of professional or community status and career advancement, as defined by the organization. Work ethicality is 'in-corporated', as portrayed, for example, by William Whyte in *The Organization Man* (1963 [1956]) or Robert Jackell in *Moral Mazes* (1988). This is the work ethic of the organizational dimension of the Enlightenment project. Enlightenment values – such as efficiency and accountability – are brought into play; rules are constructed accordingly. Once constructed, the system might appear to function as a tradition, as 'the way we do things'. But the organizational work ethic differs from the tradition-informed variety in that it is derived from the explicit, 'formal' application of rationality, and is open to questioning and revision. The organizational work ethic, that is to say, involves 'the committee' or some other kind of decision-making process.

The third of Tipton's styles sees the locus of authority resting with what is taken to be the 'autonomous' self rather than with traditions of faith and belief or 'traditions' of established rules and regulations. The work ethic of the third style can be called the *instrumentalized work ethic*. The value of work is individualized. Work is valued as a key means to the end of self-gratification or satisfaction. It serves to satisfy those desires which belong to – are defined and constructed by – consumer culture. This is the work ethicality vividly portrayed (and criticized) by Christopher Lasch (1977, 1980, 1984, 1991).

As for the last of the four styles of ethical evaluation and their associated work ethics, the locus of authority-cum-value now rests with another kind of individualization. Not the self as constituted by consumer culture, but the self as a self which considers itself to be something more, something much 'deeper', more natural and authentic than the self of what is taken to be involved with the superficialities of the 'merely' materialistic-cum-consumeristic; the self as a self which has to work on itself to enrich and explore itself, in the process dealing with its problems. The *self-work ethic*, that is to say, treats work as something to be valued as the means to those ends espoused by expressive or therapeutic culture. This is the work ethic advocated by Abraham Maslow (1965) and E.F. Schumacher (1980), for example.

Finally, by way of introducing different work ethics, it must be emphasized that these are ideal-type differentiations. In real life, it goes without saying, analytical distinctions collapse; mutually transformative fusions take place; contradictions co-exist. But this is not to say that ideal-type differentiations are not useful. Far from it. They enable the researcher to identify what is going on; to make claims concerning what might be dominant (or not) in any particular setting; indeed, to trace the dynamics of fusion or tension.

soft capitalism   Having introduced a language for distinguishing between different work ethics, I now pave the way for the main argument of this chapter – that 'soft capitalism' has developed as a response to the (perceived) failure of three long-standing work ethics (the tradition-informed, organizational and instrumentalized) – by saying something about this form of culturalized economy.

Soft capitalism has come into its own during the last fifty or so years. The basic idea, as Larry Ray and Andrew Sayer put it, is that economic success is held to lie with ' "soft" characteristics rather than straightforward technological or cost advantages' (1999: 17). And as for the 'soft' characteristics themselves, 'emphasis' is attached to 'culture, knowledge and creativity' (1999: 17).

Given what has already been argued concerning the fact that work always involves work ethicality, there is nothing new about the 'soft' dimension with regard to economic activity. What is (relatively) new, however, is the *degree* to which culture is called upon; the *degree* to which experts (management consultants, training organizations, etc.) exercise their judgement; the *degree* to which creativity is called into play to construct more and more over and above the technological and rational activities of (supposedly 'pure') cost–benefit analysis and performance. *Elaboration* has taken place with regard to cultural inputs. Rather than thinking in terms of instilling a particular work culture (according to a particular tradition or corporate vision), experts exercise their freedom to draw on globalized culture to try out cultural items to see 'what works' best for their particular concerns.

Soft capitalism involves narratives, more specific discourses, and practices to do with enhancing commitment and motivation; identifying and unblocking 'barriers' to success; seeking identity (what it is to *become/be* a good manager or telephone call centre operative, for example); working as a team or as a company; exercising responsibility or initiative; engaging in emotion work (as in the classic portrayal by Arlie Horchschild [1983]); 'closing the sale'; believing in one's product; and so on. To give a vivid illustration, enter a Lexus car salesroom; encounter the smooth, carefully paced (one is inclined to say well-oiled) process whereby highly trained personnel engage in a carefully devised series of mini-discourses and actions which are of course aimed at 'the sale' but which also provides a distinctive, culturally laden, car-focused way of life. Or consider a recent fashion involving Shakespeare as a cultural input (see also Chapter 11, this volume). As Matthew Campbell writes,

> American business and government have found an unlikely guru in William Shakespeare, whose plays are being used as a tool for teaching modern management techniques. . . . In one session recently, executives from Northrop Grumman's electronic sensors and systems sector watched in bewilderment as their boss was invited to put on a cardboard, ruby-studded crown and utter the famous lines delivered by Henry V to rally his men on the eve of the battle of Agincourt: 'Follow your spirit; and, upon this charge/Cry "God for Harry! England and Saint George!" ' The message, Adelman tells clients, is that 'successful corporate leaders dig deep within themselves which makes that critical difference between victory and defeat'.
>
> (2000: 25)

Soft capitalism is indeed about 'culture, knowledge and creativity' (to recall Ray and Sayer); about identity; about values, beliefs and assumptions; and, as we shall see in greater detail as we proceed, about cultural expertise concerning the *psychological* realm of life – how to explore it in order to develop it.[1]

What, though, of the work ethics of soft capitalism? There is little doubting the fact that there is a strong utilitarian dimension to much of what has developed. Thus Ray and Sayer write of 'work culture, which some firms attempt to mould in order to improve company performance', continuing:

> Although this elevates the place of culture, it is clearly an attempt to instrumentalize culture for economic ends. . . . Motivating people in purely instrumental ways – 'do this and there will be a pay-off' – may sometimes be successful on its own, but arguably, external goals such as profit can be attained more effectively by harnessing cultural norms.
>
> (1999: 16–17)

Consider such claims in connection with those hundreds of thousands of people – in Britain alone – who work the phone. Cultural beliefs, values and assumptions are well in evidence, forms of training instilling what has to be done to sell or persuade. Although there is often talk of telephoning serving to provide the opportunity to develop as a person (thereby facilitating self-work ethicality), the meanings ascribed to the practice would appear to be primarily to do with obtaining economic ends. The telephonist, that is to say, basically engages with culture through the wire – including assumptions to do with what it is to develop as a person – because it serves as the means to the end of income and the bonus. The dominant work ethic is of an instrumentalized nature, at least for those on pay-by-selling services.

There is also little doubting the fact that other forms of work ethic are abroad within the domains of soft capitalism. Consider, for example, the Eddie Stobart haulage empire (easily the largest in Britain). Here, it would appear, skilful interplay of the organizational and the (Christianized) tradition-informed is at work on the road, in militaristic, crusading mode, cathecting employees to a strong cultural/corporate/encorporated frame of reference.

Broadly conceived, soft capitalism can involve instrumentalized, organizational and tradition-informed work ethicalities. Soft capitalism, in this regard, simply intensifies and elaborates work ethicalities which have been long been in the making. This said, however, what really justifies the term 'soft capitalism' – given that it is surely the most significant development since the 1960s – concerns the role which has come to be played by the self-work ethic.

We are in the land of what can be called the *exploratory* mode of soft capitalism. Work, that is to say, is taken to provide the opportunity to 'work' on oneself; to grow; to learn ('the learning organization'); to become more effective *as* a person (du Gay, 1996). The utilitarian aspect (in particular) is by no means absent, with discourses and practices teaching that by working on oneself through one's work (in particular associated trainings and supervisions) one learns how to become a more efficient producer. But motivation to work is also – and crucially – enhanced by virtue of the fact that *personal* development is involved. Work, in other words, is meaningful, serves as a 'source of significance', because (among other things) it provides opportunities for 'inner' or psychological identity exploration and cultivation. Telephone work might be strongly instrumentalized, but the training manuals are replete with psychological rules and assumptions to do with overcoming personal negativities. Lex salespeople are not simply working for the sale; they are also working to be/become *themselves at work*. Management trainings, of the exploratory kind, might have an instrumental dimension, but they typically attend in great detail to the psychological betterment of participants.

'the problem of work'   During the 1960s and 1970s, a number of commentators – within the worlds of business, the academy and public life – drew attention to what Peter Berger (1964) called 'the problem of work'. As I shall shortly be arguing, the development of soft capitalism owes a considerable amount to this (perceived) 'problem'. First, though, a few observations on the nature of the 'problem'.

According to Berger, the heart of the matter lies with the fact that by the 1960s work had lost its significance; its meaning. As he puts it, 'To deal with "the problem of work" is to deal with a peculiarly modern phenomenon. The focus of the "problem" is the question of "meaning". . . . [The meaning of work is no longer] taken for granted, organized in institutions, and fully legitimated in the symbolic systems of the society' (1964: 213). Also, according to Berger, work has lost its value as a source of significance because modernity has developed two spheres, the 'private' and the 'public', with the values and assumptions of the former eroding the significance of the latter:

> The two spheres are geographically and socially separate. And since it is in the [private domain] that people typically and normally locate their essential identities, one can say . . . that they do not live where they work. 'Real life' and one's 'authentic self' are supposed to be centred in the private sphere. Life at work thus tends to take on the character of pseudo-reality and pseudo-identity. . . . The private sphere, especially the family, becomes the expression of 'who one really is'. The sphere of work is conversely apprehended as the region in which one is 'not really oneself', or . . . one in which one 'plays only a role'.
>
> (1964: 217–18)

The claim, then, is that work 'culture' if indeed this sphere is meaningful enough to be called 'culture' – is unfulfilling. And the obvious entailment of this is that people who do not put their hearts into their work do not work as well as they could or should.

Another major theorist of modernity, Daniel Bell (1976), provides a related account of the problem of work. Discussing 'the cultural contradictions of capitalism', he writes:

> [These] have to do with the disjunction between the kind of organization and norms demanded in the economic realm, and the norms of self-realization that are now central in the culture. The two realms which had historically been joined to produce a single character structure – that of the Puritan and his calling – have now become unjoined. The principles of the economic realm and those of the culture now lead people in contrary directions.
>
> (1976: 15)

The principles of the economic realm require discipline, delayed gratification (in order to save and invest) and commitment to work. However, those norms of self-realization – which are central to the culture – serve to undermine the economic realm. For, as Bell puts it, '[t]he cultural, if not moral, justification of capitalism has become hedonism, the idea of pleasure as a way of life' (1976: 21–2). The value accorded to consumptive self-realization-cum-gratification, that is to say, renders work problematic in that work comes to be treated as a mere means to the end of private activities, in the process undermining those values associated with successful enterprise.

For Berger and Bell, the key to the problem of work lies with 'private' – self, personal or familial – concerns undermining commitment to the 'public' workplace. This basic account can now be enriched by considering matters from the point of view of how work ethics were faring by the time of the 1960s and 1970s.

Thinking, first, of the tradition-informed work ethic, there is no doubting the fact that this source of work significance has more or less disappeared in 'Western' settings. Consider, for example, what Hunter has found in his study of evangelical Christianity in the conservative heartlands of the 'Bible belt' of the USA, writing that '[t]he caricatures of Evangelicalism as the last bastion of the traditional norms of discipline and hard work for their own sake, self-sacrifice, and moral asceticism are largely inaccurate' (1987: 74). Such erosion of the tradition-informed has undoubtedly contributed to the problem of the meaning of work. Quite simply, when work is no longer valued in terms of those ultimate values provided by religious tradition its value becomes highly problematic; unless, of course, other values come into evidence.

Thinking, second, of the organizational work ethic, this product of modernity – with the importance attached to specifying and valuing work in terms of rationalization, bureaucratization or scientific evaluation (Taylorization) – has for some time been seen as self-defeating. After all, Weber wrote of the 'iron cage' some one hundred years ago. True, and given the uncertainties of the immediate postwar period, this work ethic came into prominence during the 1950s. But with the '1960s', the organizational work ethic became increasingly suspect. Quite simply, it failed to meet the expectations and values of those (predominantly younger) people who valued autonomy, creativity, equality; people who thus found little significance, indeed much of counter-significance, with the world of the hierarchical, regulated, bureaucratized.

Third, and turning now to another product of modernity, the instrumentalized work ethic – with the importance attached to the values and assumptions of consumer culture – has contributed to the problem of work by generating a 'raiding work' outlook. Utilitarian individualists, that is to say, treat work as merely the means to that end (income) required to satisfy their ultimate end, namely self-interest and gratification. Not being valued *per se*, work is problematized in that those concerned are not really engaged.

Overall, those writing of 'the problem of work' during the 1960s and 1970s pointed to evidence concerning disenchantment and 'iron cage' barrenness. The traditional, authoritative work ethic was no longer significantly at work; the organizational work ethic was taken to be in increasing crisis; and the instrumentalized work ethic was taken to involve loss of commitment to work, other than, that is, as a means to supporting the activities of the privatized consumer. Work, it appeared to many, might still have utility or self-interest/serving value, but had come to be little valued in any more 'serious' fashion – in terms of personal or professional/career identity, let alone salvational – fashion.

soft capitalism as a response to 'the problem of work'   Whatever the 'actual' truth of claims concerning the problem of work, it can hardly be disputed that during the 1960s and 1970s it was widely assumed that work had indeed become problematic. And academics and others could point to evidence apparently showing 'the problem': strikes, unrest, the criticism or forthright rejection of mainstream work by counterculturalists or those so inclined. Accordingly, it seemed to many – those directly involved in the workplace, commentators, as well as academics – that what was needed was an injection of 'culture'. What was needed was ways of responding to the problem of work by developing meaning, value and motivation. And the solution was to develop 'soft' capitalism, by no means least in its 'exploratory' mode.

The argument that the development of soft/exploratory capitalism can – at least in measure – be explained by reference to the (perceived) problem of work is supported by two considerations. First, and most simply, the timing is right. Soft/exploratory capitalism has indeed proliferated during the decades since many identified the (supposed) problem of work. And, second, it certainly appears to be the case that soft capitalism – in particular its 'exploratory' variant – addresses the loss of 'significance' within the workplace.

Towards the beginning of her study of Amerco, a Fortune 500 company located in the midwest of the USA, Arlie Hochschild writes,

In *Haven in a Heartless World*, the social historian Christopher Lasch drew a picture of family as a 'haven' where workers sought out refuge from the cruel world of work. Painted in broad strokes, we might imagine a picture like this: At the end of a long day, a weary worker opens his front door and calls out, 'Hi, Honey! I'm home!' He takes off his uniform, puts on a bathrobe, opens a beer, picks up the paper, and exhales. Whatever its strains, home is where he's relaxed, most himself. At home, he

> feels that people know him, understand him, and appreciate him for who is really is. At home, he is safe.
>
> (1997: 36)

Haven in a Heartless World was published in 1977 when – as we have seen – 'the problem of work' was very much on the agenda. Writing twenty years later, Hochschild provides much evidence to paint a very different picture. For, as the title of her book – *The Time Bind: When Work Becomes Home and Home Becomes Work* – serves to indicate, she charts a massive reversal, from living at home to living at work; from working at work to working at home.

With specific reference to Amerco, Hochschild writes that '[t]he emotional magnets beneath home and workplace are in the process of being reversed. . . . Overall, this "reversal" was a predominant pattern in about a fifth of Amerco families, and an important theme in over half of them' (1997: 44–5). And indeed she provides a great deal of evidence of 'home' being found at work. To illustrate, one can consider the following passage:

> In its engineered corporate cultures, capitalism has rediscovered communal ties and is using them to build its new version of capitalism. Many Amerco employees spoke warmly, happily, and seriously of 'belonging to the Amerco family', and everwhere there were visible symbols of this belonging. While some married people have dispensed with their wedding rings, people proudly wore their 'Total Quality' pins or 'High Performance Team' tee-shirts, symbols of their loyalty to the company and of its loyalty to them. In my interviews, I heard little about festive reunions of extended families, whilst throughout the year, employees flocked to the many company-sponsored ritual gatherings.
>
> (1997: 44)

And so to the crucial point. The 'meaning' of work, the value or significance found by way participating with the Amerco company, is surely bound up with the fact that soft capitalism is very much in evidence. Without going into too much detail with regard to Hochschild's rich ethnographic material, we can thus reflect on the following passage:

> At its white-collar offices, Amerco was even more involved [than with regard to the 'self-managed production teams'] in shaping the emotional culture of the workplace and fostering an environment of trust and cooperation in order to bring out everyone's best. At the middle and top levels of the company, employees were invited to

periodic 'career development seminars' on personal relations at work. The center-piece of Amerco's personal relations culture was a 'vision' speech that the CEO had given called 'Valuing the Individual', a message repeated in speeches, memorialized in company brochures, and discussed with great seriousness throughout the upper reaches of the company. In essence, the message was a parental reminder to respect others. Similarly, in a new-age recasting of an old business slogan ('The customer is always right'), Amerco proposed that its workers 'Value the internal customer'. This meant: Be polite and considerate to your coworkers as you would be to Amerco customers. 'Value the internal customer' extended to coworkers the slogan 'Delight the customer'. 'Don't just work with your co-workers, delight them'.

'Employee empowerment', 'valuing diversity' and 'work–family balance' – these catchphrases, too, spoke to a moral aspect of work life. Though ultimately tied to financial gain, such exhortations – and the policies that follow from them – made workers feel the company was concerned with people, not just money. In many ways, the workplace appeared to be a site of benign social engineering where workers came to feel appreciated, honored, and liked.

(1997: 43)

Work ethicality at Amerco, it would appear, is a sophisticated blend of what we are calling the organizational and the self-work ethic. The organizational is in evidence in that employees (typically) take great pride in living in terms of company visions and missions, seeking to become yet more professional by following corporate pathways. At the same time, the professional, organizational collectivity is brought alive by the operation of self-work ethicality. There is a strongly 'exploratory' aspect to much of what is going on, with the 'Valuing the Individual' message, the development seminars on personal relations at work, the 'Value the internal customer' programme.

And soft capitalism at Amerco, it can be said, 'works'. Whatever 'problems of work' the company might have experienced in the past, the 'meaning' now found at work surely goes a long way in explaining why the workforce is so committed; so enthusiastic; so much at home at work. Indeed, explains why it is by no means uncommon for people to arrive at work early and leave late – without extra pay.

Moving beyond the confines of Amerco, soft capitalism takes many shapes and forms. Christian, tradition-informed work ethicality, for example, has been 'brought alive' by direct selling organizations, such as Mary Kay Cosmetics, through particular integrations of work, family, community, religion and ritual (see Biggart, 1989). Or one might think of attempts to 'enrich' instrumentalized work ethicality, as when telephone sales and advice workers are provided with the opportunity to release themselves from their 'blocks' or barriers' and cultivate their 'intentionality'. However, it is highly likely that the most significant development since the 1960s concerns the self-work ethicality of exploratory capitalism.

Following in the footsteps of the 1960s pioneers – Douglas McGregor with his *The Human Side of Enterprise* (1960), Frederick Herzberg and his *Work and the Nature of Man* (1968) and Abraham Maslow with his *Eupsychian Management* (1965) – management consultants, advisers, trainers, personnel officers, and so on, have blazed the way 'forward' with their messages proclaiming 'the humanization of the workplace', the importance of 'self-development for productivity', the value of being 'yourself' at work, the 'unlocking of human potential' at work. To illustrate by reference to some publications, one can think of Roger Harrison's *Organization Culture and Quality of Service: a Strategy for Releasing Love in the Workplace* ('to balance the powers of intellect and human will in organizations with the powers of intuition and will' [1987: 3]); Mike Pedler et al.'s *Learning Company Project* ('how can we create organizations which are opportunity structures enabling people to grow and develop . . .? [1988: 9]); and Craig Hickman and Michael Silva's *Creating Excellence* ('By applying the art of meditation to organizational introspection, you gain a deeper understanding of a business and its environment' [1985: 32]). Or, to give an example from India, there is V.S. Mahesh's *Thresholds of Motivation*, the subtitle of which is 'The corporation as a nursery for human growth', with the 'Introduction' beginning with a section on 'Corporate excellence through human self-actualization' (1993: xv).

And then there are all those New Age management trainings and consultancies which have proliferated since the 1960s and which take the exploratory message of soft capitalism to what one can only assume is something approaching its limit. For the self-work ethic is here taken to have a spiritual dimension. One is not simply working on oneself, through work activities (including trainings), to develop as a human being, for one is now working on onself to experience that spirituality which is integral to one's very nature or essence. The workplace is valued, that is to say, as a vehicle to the end of self-sacralization. And inner spirituality can then be put to work to enhance productivity.[2]

'bringing life back to work'   Thus far I have been suggesting that the development of soft capitalism can – in measure – be explained as a way of handling what was taken to be 'the problem of work'. However, there is more to the story than this.

Experts and trainers interviewed by Hansfried Kellner and Frank Heuberger during their study of the 'hidden technocrats' of the 'new class' of the 'new capitalism' stressed that industry should take into account

> the importance of an individual's quest for an 'unfolded' personality; the justified demands for self-realization, autonomy, and authenticity; the prerogatives of the subjective life, emotional well-being, and intimacy against the demands of rationalized industry, with its controlling pressures, coldness, and abstractness; the rights of private over public life; the individual's search for 'meaning' in a world that is held to be devoid of meaningful symbols, plausibility, and credibility; the individual's need for 'spontaneity', 'immediacy', and expression of hedonistic impulses; the importance of creativity and fantasy.
>
> (1992: 57)

The problem of work is by no means absent in this formulation, those interviewed attaching importance to providing personal meaning, value and significance for those faced with 'the demands of rationalized industry'. But Kellner and Heuberger are also pointing to another factor: namely that the experts and trainers are attaching importance to ensuring that the workplace caters for cultural values to do with expectation concerning what it is to *live* a full *life*.

One of the great slogans of soft capitalism, in particular in its exploratory mode, is 'bringing life back to work'. Taking this as my cue, I now want to argue that the development and current popularity of soft capitalism owes a very great deal indeed to what shall be called 'the cultural turn to life'. The argument runs that (a) this cultural turn involves many of those at work, which means (b) that forms of soft capitalism promising 'life' at work are likely to be well received. The slogan 'bringing life back to work' is *just* what many want to hear.

The cultural turn to life   In 'Western' cultures it is widely assumed that cultural values like 'freedom', 'equality' and making progress with what the material world of commodities has to offer are of central importance. Mention is rarely made of what is here taken to be a – if not the – central value of our times, 'life'. Since this value is not often highlighted, I shall first provide some evidence regarding its centrality, thus lending plausibility to my argument.

'Life' plays itself out in various ways within 'Western' cultures. One might think of the massive investment in scientific research, attempting to 'create life' (as the media often put it) or to manipulate life at the genetic level. Or one might think of the massive investments in prolonging life, not simply with regard to scientific methods but also with regard to the very considerable percentages, in many countries, who turn to alternative/ complementary healings. Then there are the huge investments in improving the quality of personal life, whether by way of consumer activities or therapies, trainings, exploring nature and the like.

The importance of 'life' is also shown by the fact that the ethic of humanity – so important in international relations and law, all the specifics of human rights legislation, and also all the specifics of equal opportunities programmes, harassment procedures, and so on – is the dominant ethical complex of our times. And it is premised on the value ascribed to 'human life'. Furthermore, the vitality of this ethic is seen in the fact that the so-called 'culture wars' are battled out over the conflicting values of the ethic (e.g. 'life' [for the anti-abortionists] vs freedom [for the abortionists]). And the vitality of the ethic is also seen in how 'life' is, so to speak, extending into nature, in the sense that it comes to provide the basis of animal (and other) rights.

Or one might think of the importance of 'life' with regard to religion, the most successful religions – in Western contexts – being those which dwell on what it is to *be* alive in the here-and-now rather than those religions which concentrate on preparing for life in the hereafter. Consider, in this regard, the rather extraordinary growth of what Robert Wuthnow (1994) calls 'small groups' or 'support groups'. Little in evidence prior to the 1960s, some 80 million Americans were involved by the earlier 1990s. According to Wuthnow, the 'small group that meets regularly and provides caring and support for those who participate in it' (1994: 45) adds up to a phenomenon which 'is at least as important to understand as the political system or the economy' (1994: 26). And the small group movement, generally underpinned by religion, is very much oriented towards 'life': 'the life of the soul', as Wuthnow puts it (1994: 5). As Wuthnow also writes,

What happened [in the groups] took place so incrementally that it could seldom be seen at all. It was, like most profound reorientations *in life*, so gradual that those involved saw it less as a revolution than as a journey. The change was concerned with daily life, emotions, and understandings of one's identity. It was personal rather than public, moral rather than political.

(1994: 3, my emphasis)

Writing in 1918, Georg Simmel claimed that 'this emotional reality – which we can only call *life* – makes itself increasingly felt in its formless strength . . . claiming [such forms] their inalienable rights as the true meaning or value of our existence' (1997 [1918]: 24, my emphasis). This claim directs us to the sense of 'life' which is of most relevance to the argument which I am developing. It is 'life' in the sense of that 'inner' realm, which – ultimately – belongs to the individual alone, and which has to do with one's experiences, one's consciousness, one's sense of being alive in the here-and-now, drawing on memories and expectations to enhance the present whilst neither diminishing the quality of life – now – for the sake of obeying the past or investing too much in the future.

Furthermore, this 'life' is not 'life-as' – that is, as constituted and regulated by the roles, duties and obligations of the institutional order. Indeed, it has been argued that this is a 'life' that has come into prominence precisely because 'life-as' a traditionalist Christian, family member, businessperson or 'public man' has proved unsatisfactory. Thus, according to Simmel – and then Arnold Gehlen (1980 [1949]), Peter Berger et al. (1974) and Thomas Luckmann (1967) – 'life' in the sense we are discussing has come into prominence because modernity has resulted in significant numbers becoming disillusioned with what the 'primary' institutions of society have to offer with regard to 'the meaning of life'. From religious tradition, to political ideologies, the nuclear family, the workplace (Weber's 'iron cage'): the claim is that the institutional order no longer succeeds in providing sound sources of identity, purpose or value-in-life. Accordingly, so the argument goes, people have been 'thrown back' on *themselves* as the *key source of significance*. With little to have faith in what lies beyond themselves, what matters thus becomes a matter of what lies inside: one's psychology, one's personal ethicality; the quality of one's emotions; the health/vitality of one's nature; the importance of being authentic; the imperative of being true to oneself; experiencing and the value of finding out what one truly is and capable of experiencing and becoming.

'Life as . . .', that is, as constituted by the roles and promises of primary institutions, has come to be replaced – in sectors of the population – by 'subjective-life' as the key source of significance: the ultimacy of 'feeling alive'; of self-exploration and growth; of getting in touch with as much as possible of what life has to offer; of experiencing 'the quality of life'; indeed, of staying alive for as long as possible. Or, to amend a fashionable injunction, in 'getting oneself a life'.[3]

The account which I have just been summarizing, it has to be admitted, is flawed in that it is over-generalized. For surely great swathes of the population remain firmly locked into various forms of 'life-as . . .' which take life into roles, duties, obligations. Having said this, however, the fact remains that 'subjective-life' has become of very considerable significance. Fewer today than in the past are convinced by that great traditional promise, namely life in the hereafter; many more are convinced by the value of what the here-and-now, the immediacy of the experiential, the widths and depths of consciousness, have to offer. And there is little doubting the fact that the turn to life is well in evidence among better educated, more expressivistic members of the population; precisely those who, if they enter the world of business, are (the most) likely to seek out – and thus help develop – exploratory capitalism.[4]

The cultural turn to life and soft/exploratory capitalism   In passing, Wuthnow (1994: 40) mentions business trainings as a version of the small group. And this provides us with our cue. Work, today, has well and truly entered the realm of the small group by virtue of the fact that we live in the 'Age of the Training', with management trainings leading the way. And management trainings increasingly take a soft/exploratory form rather than dwelling on the Taylorized externals of life.

Remaining with managers, the cultural turn to life has certainly entered the workplace, thereby contributing to the development of exploratory capitalism. Many (MBAed etc.) managers want work to cater for the exercise, expression and development of personal life; the aliveness or rejuvenation of subject-ive life; the aim of being all that they can be. Many do not want to waste their time by 'just' working without also 'growing'; many feel that life is too short and working hours too long for them to be content with the 'raiding work' attitude; many feel that their own lives are too significant to be sacrificed or disciplined for the sake of 'the company' (unless, that is, their 'growth' is somehow still assured). What many are expecting, in other words, is work which includes all those practices (most especially 'the training' and the self-work ethic) which promise to 'bring life back to work'. In short, exploratory capitalism, especially at the managerial level, is fuelled by 'life-values'; a 'life ethic'. It might be life 'as-a' manager, but – being of a soft or exploratory nature – the 'role' of being a manager involves self-expression, the acting out of one's life.

In sum: at least for sectors of the workplace the argument is that work only *really* matters, or matters *most*, when it caters for what it is to *be* alive (as well as, of course, providing income or status). Without the training, without the opportunity to *be*, *explore* and *develop* oneself, work is deemed unsatisfactory. Cultural vehicles are sought, but not those authoritative work ethics which are life denying (as with the aesthetic disciplines of the traditional Protestant work ethic, aimed at preparation in the life to come, with which capitalistic modernity arguably began), or regulated work ethicality which requires sacrificing one's own life for 'life-as' the 'encorporated', or the instrumentalized work ethic where work is envisaged as simply 'life *as*' the means to other goals.

Work is necessary; but there is more to the meaning of life than 'mechanical' productivity. Soft capitalism, especially in its exploratory mode, with all its ways of ensuring that work is experienced as catering for the life of the subject, thrives with the cultural turn to life. Roger Lewin and Biute Regine's *The Soul At Work* (1999), as the title of a recent publication puts it: thereby exemplifying what has come to matter in certain sectors of the contemporary culturalized economy. Not life as disciplined for God, as in the early days of modernity, but life explored and expressed at work.

What is somewhat ironic is that that very loss of faith in what the working environment has had to offer, resulting in the problem of work, should have contributed to the turn to life – which has in turn contributed to the (supposed) 'enrichment' of the culture of the workplace by way of the development of soft/exploratory capitalism.

Certainly much less is heard these days about 'the problem of work' as it was formulated by Berger (and others) during the 1960s. Problems, of course, remain. One thinks of the perils of the short-term contract, for example. But Berger's claim – 'they do not live where they work' – has been severely undermined by the 'they really live at work' kind of development which we have been charting (with particular reference to Hochschild's research). And that culturalized form of economy known as soft/exploratory capitalism surely has consequences for the economy. Consequences which have yet to be adequately charted . . .

notes

1. So far as I know, Hansfried Kellner and Frank Heuberger (1992) were the first to use the term 'soft' in connection with capitalism. As they write of 'modern' management, as opposed to 'classical' (Taylorian) 'scientific management', it 'has very much to do with the cultural, behavioural, and psychic aspects of people and events of an organization. From this 'soft' side, it 'organizes the organization' just as systematically as classical consulting does from its more technical side' (1992: 51). Nigel Thrift (1996, 1997, 1999 and this volume) has developed usage of the term. Kellner and Heuberger, together with Thrift, provide good illustrative material of soft capitalism. See Art Kleiner (1996) for a historiography of some of the wilder reaches of this development.

2. I have discussed New Age management trainings and their contribution to 'life' in greater detail elsewhere (Heelas, 1996). See also Huczynski (1993).

3. Don Cupitt's *The New Religion of Life in Everyday Speech* (1999) provides evidence for this cultural turn by examining how life idioms (such as 'Get a Life') have entered everyday discourse.

4. Inglehart (1990, 1997) provides a massive amount of evidence to support the claim that a cultural turn to life has taken place. (Concerning this turn to life, he writes, for example, of 'the increasingly subjective nature of life experience in advanced industrial society' [1997: 76], and of the shift to 'the pursuit of individual subjective well-being' [1997: 75].) Evidence that the turn to life is to the fore among better educated, more expressivistic members of the population is also provided by Ingelehart (1997): such members of the population are the most likely to have ' "postmaterialist" priorities', namely those to do with 'self-expression and the quality of life' (p. 4). Evidence that those involved in exploratory capitalism are indeed 'turn to lifers' is also provided by Ronald Inglehart (1997): 'Postmaterialism', he writes, ' has penetrated deeply into the ranks of professionals, civil servants, managers . . .' (p. 142; see also Inglehart, 1990: Chapter 9).

references

Bell, D. (1976) *The Cultural Contradictions of Capitalism*. London: Heinemann.

Berger, P. (1964) 'Some general observations on the problem of work', in P. Berger (ed.), *The Human Shape of Work*. New York: Macmillan.

Berger, P., Berger, B. and Kellner, H. (1974) *The Homeless Mind*. Harmondsworth: Penguin.

Biggart, N. (1989) *Charismatic Capitalism: Direct Selling Organizations in America*. Chicago: University of Chicago Press.

Campbell, M. (2000) 'Cry God for sales as the Bard goes centre stage in US boardrooms', *The Sunday Times*, 9 January, p. 25.

Cupitt, D. (1999) *The New Religion of Life in Everday Speech*. London: SCM.

du Gay, P. (1996) *Consumption and Identity at Work*. London: Sage.

Gehlen, A. (1980) [1949] *Man in the Age of Technology*. New York: Columbia University Press.

Harrison, R. (1987) *Organization Culture and Quality of Service: a Strategy for Releasing Love in the Workplace*. London: The Association for Management Education and Development.

Heelas, P. (1996) *The New Age Movement: The Celebration of the Self and the Sacralization of Modernity*. Oxford: Blackwell.

Herzberg, F. (1968) *Work and the Nature of Man*. London: Staples Press.

Hickman, C. and Silva, M. (1985) *Creating Excellence: Managing Corporate Culture, Strategy and Change in the New Age*. London: George Allen & Unwin.

Hochschild, A. (1983) *The Managed Heart: Commercialization of Human Feeling*. Berkeley: University of California Press.

Hochschild, A. (1997) *The Time Bind: When Work Becomes Home and Home Becomes Work*. New York: Metropolitan Books.

Huczynski, A. (1993) *Management Gurus: What Makes Them and How to Become One*. London: Routledge.

Hunter, J.D. (1987) *Evangelicalism: The Coming Generation*. Chicago: The University of Chicago Press.

Inglehart, R. (1990) *Culture Shift in Advanced Industrial Society*. Princeton, NJ: Princeton University Press.

Inglehart, R. (1997) *Modernization and Postmodernization: Cultural, Economic, and Political Change in 43 Societies*. Princeton, NJ: Princeton University Press.

Jackell, R. (1988) *Moral Mazes: The World of Corporate Managers*. Oxford: Oxford University Press.

Kellner, H. and Heubeger, F. (1992) *Hidden Technocrats: The New Class and New Capitalism*. London: Transaction.

Kleiner, A. (1996) *The Age of Heretics: Heroes, Outlaws, and the Forerunners of Corporate Change*. London: Nicholas Brealey.

Lasch, C. (1977) *Haven in a Heartless World*. New York: Basic Books.

Lasch, C. (1980) *The Culture of Narcissism: American Life in an Age of Diminishing Expectations*. London: Abacus.

Lasch, C. (1984) *The Minimal Self: Psychic Survival in Troubled Times*. London: Picador.

Lasch, C. (1991) *The Only True Heaven: Progress and Its Critics*. New York and London: Norton.

Lewin, R. and Regine, B. (1999) *The Soul at Work*. London: Orion.

Luckmann, T. (1967) *The Invisible Religion: The Problem of Religion in Modern Society*. New York: Macmillan.

McGregor, D. (1960) *The Human Side of Enterprise*. London: McGraw-Hill.

Mahesh, V.S. (1993) *Thresholds of Motivation: The Corporation as a Nursery for Human Growth*. New Delhi: Tata McGraw-Hill.

Maslow, A. (1965) *Eupsychian Management*. Illinois: Richard D. Irwin.

Pedler, M., Boydell, T. and Bourgoyne, J. (1988) *Learning Company Project*. A report. Lancaster: Lancaster University.

Ray, L. and Sayer, A. (1999) 'Introduction', in L. Ray and A. Sayer (eds), *Culture and Economy after the Cultural Turn*. London: Sage.

Schumacher, E.F. (1980) *Good Work*. London: Abacus.

Simmel, G. (1997) [1918] 'The conflict of modern culture', in G. Simmel, *Essays on Religion*. New Haven, CT: Yale University Press.

Thrift, N. (1996) *Spatial Formations*. London: Sage.

Thrift, N. (1997) 'The rise of soft capitalism', *Cultural Values*, 1 (1): 29–57.

Thrift, N. (1999) 'Capitalism's cultural turn', in L. Ray and A. Sayer (eds), *Culture and Economy after the Cultural Turn*. London: Sage.

Tipton, S. (1984) *Getting Saved from the Sixties: Moral Meaning in Conversion and Cultural Change*. Los Angeles and London: University of California Press.

Weber, Max (1985) [1904–5] *The Protestant Ethic and the Spirit of Capitalism*. London: Unwin.

Whyte, W. (1963) [1956] *The Organization Man*. Harmondsworth: Pelican.

Wuthnow, R. (1994) *Sharing the Journey: Support Groups and America's New Quest for Community*. New York: Free Press.

from Holloway to Hollywood:
happiness at work in the new cultural economy?

Angela McRobbie

> We must look towards entrepreneurship as the form of working life that can renew the common values once supported by the institution of the career.
>
> (J. Gray and F. Flores, 'A Wing and a Prayer', *Guardian*, 16 May 2000, p. 17)

introduction: may a million novels now be written

This chapter considers the consequences of the recent growth of (self-) employment in the creative industries and the convergence of notions of culture with those of work.[1] The marriage of culture with work heralds a new and important relation. Culture in this specific context refers to the creative, expressive and symbolic activities in media, arts and communicative practices which demonstrate, in this instance, potential for gainful activity. As the UK Department of Culture, Media and Science (DCMS) Mapping Document (1998) indicated, this is a sector which has expanded dramatically over recent years, one which is also constantly renewing and re-inventing itself in response to changing technology and the development of new media. Indeed, in as short a period as two or three years, we can see seismic shifts in such unstable fields as these (McRobbie, 2001). So profoundly subject to changes are these growth areas of the cultural economy that they come to represent 'permanently transitional' work. Requiring risk-taking activity and high degrees of mobility of its workforce, cultural work also relies on disembedded and highly individualized personnel. Never before have generational differences and the factor of age played such decisive roles in shaping career trajectories, so much so that one strand of the argument here is that young people now find themselves on the side of a new divide between old work (and older workers) and new work with its more youthful workforce. This is most pronounced in the cultural and new media field, where there is an inversion of the bureaucratic model of work patterns associated with the professions, the public sector and also with organized labour and enshrined in employment law. (Ursell describes this shift away from professionally organized work in media fields as a 'discursive rupture' [2000: 816]. Where youth and talent – and, of course, endless resources of energy – are at a premium, and where culture is opened out to embrace the vast field of communications industries, including the entertainment sector, sharp new modalities of inequality appear. These do not replace older 'depth' variables of class, gender and racial disadvantage, but neither do they simply compound them. Instead social determinations are de-stabilized, disorganized and endlessly re-shuffled as though by a restless and nervous card player. Sociological vocabularies are strained to the limit to encompass such a fluid terrain. In cultural studies the turn to work and employment emerges from broader discussions of the 'cultural turn' as society and economy appear to be increasingly enculturalized, but a vocabulary for fully engaging with creative work is still at an early stage (see du Gay, 1997; Nixon, 1997). What I want to flag as integral to this current debate are three key features: youth; 'permanently transitional' work; and creativity, understood as a sovereign space for finding 'pleasure in work' (Donzelot, 1991).

In the UK, where culture is now so central to local and national economies, it is being removed by large companies from the hands of the small-scale cultural producers, who are reduced to 'dependent' subcontracted 'independents' and who become suppliers of services (Leadbeater and Oakley, 1999). These are not company employees but rather freelance, franchised or casualized labour. This pattern is repeated as larger organizations attempt to shed their costly permanent staff in favour of hiring their labour for projects and 'one-off' commissions. As Ursell (2000) has described, television production work now comprises a majority (60 per cent in 1996) of freelancers. The demand for cultural goods on an ever-increasing scale brings into being new kinds of labour markets, hence new kinds of work. Where, in Raymond Williams' sense, culture as a 'way of life' was deeply embedded in social institutions and practices, now, as a 'way of earning a living', it is increasingly disembedded, rapidly disconnected from any notion of vernacular as soon as its potential for commodification is spotted. (See Naomi Klein [2000] for the use by companies like Nike and Gap of 'youth stalkers' who are paid fees to spot trends by closely observing their friends and peers.) At the same time local colour continues to make highly commercial global culture. (From *Trainspotting* to *High Fidelity*, from Roni Size and Reprazent to Radiohead.) Increasingly cultural practices are seen primarily and immediately in terms of commercial opportunities; this eliminates the space, time and rationale for an independent or alternative sector. But this new prominence doesn't eliminate the irregular and insecure livings being made in these creative fields; instead it intensifies them.

The job opportunities opened up with the expansion of the cultural sector resonate with government as it looks to work, and the ideal of full employment, as a means of retaining its place in office and of endorsing (with penalties to those who default) a mode of citzenship through employment. Culture and work are critical to policy and thus to change. As Stuart Hall has said, 'not since the workhouse has labour been so fervently and single-mindedly valorised' (1998: 11). Since 1997 work has been a site of endless government activity. Let me itemize just some of these initiatives: these include 'welfare to work' programmes, designed to move lone parents from dependence on benefits into waged work; the New Deal, for young people with low-level qualifications; the introduction of a minimum wage; encouragement to young women to avoid low-paid careers in traditionally gendered work like hairdressing; renewed calls to employers to ensure that women get equal pay; new legislation to ease the pain of bankruptcy; encouragement to older unemployed people to get back into work; and finally the winding down of access to early retirement schemes. These schemes more than confirm the validity of the party's very name, New Labour. Work comes to mean much more than just earning a living; it incorporates and overtakes everyday life. In exacting new resources of self-reliance on the part of the working population, work appears to supplant, indeed hijack, the realm of the social, re-adjusting the division between work and leisure, creating new modes of self-disciplining, producing new forms of identity. (For the first time in recent history women as a whole are to be defined in wage-earning rather than child-bearing capacity.)

What do I mean by proposing that work replaces ' the social'? Diverse strands in contemporary life feed into this. These include the devaluing of the public sector and public and social services. This was a determining feature of the government of Mrs Thatcher, but has continued unabated since then. More generally there are changes in family life and new patterns of individual mobility which have detached individuals from more settled, and thus more socially rooted, ways of existence; there is also the replacement of older, again more sociable, working lives with impersonal connections and transactions; and there is the emergence of new hierarchies which celebrate wealthy individualized lifestyles and consumer culture at the expense of social obligation. Public service and with it social services are now relegated to the margins of contemporary life. These are increasingly replaced by competition, the seeking of self-advancement in work, and, in commercialized leisure spheres, self-improvement techniques. As self-reliance becomes a way of being, a means of conducting the self, ideas of the social become emptied of meaning. This, then, is the background for the encroachment of work into every corner of everyday life, including 'flexible' working at home, 'sociable' working in cafés with plug-in points for laptops, and mobile working from indeterminate 'non-places' (Augé, 1995). Work is promoted as the sole means of ensuring personal security, and the very idea of social security fades in significance.

In leisure there are also good reasons to find the meaning of life in the rhythms of work. Leisure, too, comes to be mined for added values which can enhance performance and reward in the workplace, hence the culture of 'pampering yourself' with beauty treatments, health farms and any number of body-toning therapies. This is particularly important in the new service sector, which, as recent studies have shown, now expects its workforce to look especially attractive and stylish for what they label 'aesthetic labour' (Warhurst et al., 2000). These features are particularly important for women, now entering the workforce and expecting to remain there over the course of a lifetime. The present British government is practising what Rose (1999, following Foucault) describes as 'etho-politics', that is, 'the aesthetic elements . . . in the crafting of the self', through its almost microscopic concern for personal conduct and body image. This is most evident in its support for the UK version of the US Dress for Success campaign. While the latter was initiated by a non-profit-making organization to help poor women improve their chances at job interviews by lending them suits donated by more affluent working women, in the UK it is the government's subcontracted agency, the privately owned Reed International, which has undertaken to provide women on the 'welfare to work' schemes (which it has been running) with cast-offs, including some from a celebrity guest list including Cherie Blair.[2]

From the perspective of New Labour in office, the commitment to work marks continuity with, as well as a shift away from, the free market values which characterized the previous Conservative government. These tolerated high levels of unemployment alongside the inflated salaries of the city yuppies. Key dynamics of 'the social' ironically remained in place as long as there were individuals in substantial numbers who were signing on for social security. But now the new work ethic functions as an ideological means of combating social exclusion. It extends to incorporate disenfranchised sectors of the population. Getting people into work as a strategy of government becomes also a definition of government. It requires that people become more entrepreneurial, irrespective of their education, skills or expertise. It is not a matter of creating employment by swelling the old public sector. It is about making people want to develop their own capacities to create their own jobs and, it is hoped, employ others. Despite the short life of the 'Cool Britannia' episode, the model of creative work (fashion, music, new media) epitomizes the talent-led economy which the Blair government favours and wants to see more widely extended.[3] The combination of youth, talent and culture is a heady mix providing Blair with an egalitarian gloss, especially when some of the successes (e.g. Damien Hirst and Tracey Emin) come from poor or disadvantaged backgrounds.

New Labour appears to be inventing a new youth-driven meritocracy by this means. But in practice the move from welfare to work is more punitive and the jobs on offer for low-skilled people far from rewarding or creative. It is not just that there is a downside to the talent-led economy, it is more that the concept of talent is aggressively deployed to dramatic effect. In the cultural sector, those up to the age of approximately 40 now normatively self-exploit themselves by working hours no employer could legally enforce; they also do without all the protection afforded by employee status, including sickness benefits; they are largely non-unionized; they are expected to take out private pension plans (which many cannot afford to do); they are unable to claim benefits for non-work time between jobs or 'projects'; and they also cover their own workspace and equipment costs. All of this in the hope of talent paying off. Labour is reorganized along wildly free market lines by promoting talent as that which lies within us all, waiting to be tapped into. Indeed there is even a danger it will be wasted if we are not attentive enough to its idiosyncratic, temperamental and certainly unpredictable ways. This encouragement to uncover personal talent is most directed towards youth. Success, wealth and even fame and celebrity are now routinely held out as possibilities for those prepared to take the risks and put in the long hours. If there is an increasing divide between old and new work, young people are firmly positioned in the latter. They do not lose the inequities of class, gender and ethnicity in this new 'milieu of innovation' (Castells, 1996), and pure talent (whatever that means) does not win out, but the emergent patterns of success and failure are volatile and as yet insufficiently documented to allow us to do anything more than speculate on outcomes (McRobbie, 2001).

The ideal of self-expressive work is now mediated by a new rhetoric of mobility and success. As social groups and communities seem to disperse and give way to more atomized biographies, so also do individualized pathways become more culturally resonant. While in the past the idea of rags to riches was never anything more than a delicious popular fantasy, the very stuff of Hollywood dreams, now in what has been described as a lottery economy characterized by the 'chaos of reward' (Young, 1999), the systemic features of class, gender and ethnicity, as they have become less stable, are pushed further into the political background as populist and 'feelgood' ideas of chance, good or bad fortune, the contingency of occasion and the value of individual effort are taken to be more reliable indicators of achievement. These ideas pulsate through the entire cultural fabric, but they are so dispersed, without any apparent attachment to a central node, that their power and impact are easily overlooked.

May a million novels now be written. Media mogul Chris Evans started life as a cheery milkman; single mother J.K. Rowling wrote her first Harry Potter book in cafés in Edinburgh while her baby slept in a pushchair.

The emphasis by government and media alike on 'talent' not only infects popular culture ('Posh and Becks'), but it also becomes a way of securing common values. Although some government ministers have expressed misgivings about the huge popularity of TV quiz shows like *Who Wants To Be a Millionaire?* for promoting materialism and thus contributing to the erosion of community values, these are mere murmurings. New Labour makes it a mark of its own modernity to recognize the new opportunities of the talent-led economy for individuals who demonstrate capacities for inexhaustible resourcefulness, resilience and entrepreneurialism.

Before considering the handful of empirical studies which track some of these careers in the new cultural sector, it is useful to reflect briefly on how the changing world of work has been analysed by a number of leading commentators. Though lacking in an explicitly cultural focus, four recent and highly influential books – Sennett's *The Corrosion of Character* (1998), Beck's *Risk Society* (1992) and, more recently, *The Brave New World of Work* (2000), and Leadbeater's *Living on Thin Air* (1999) – provide different, indeed opposing, perspectives. These could be characterized as narratives of loss (Sennett), narratives of risk and transition (Beck) and narratives of self-invention, stardom and success (Leadbeater). Sennett's style is elegaic, American and literary; Beck's is German and 'documentary-realist'; Leadbeater's is slick Anglo-American postmodernism.

Sennett in America   Sennett depicts a band of American workers who have each experienced the full force of the transition to the flexible economy. His argument, that they have suffered a loss – a loss of self, a loss of character – is constructed through their accounts of the impact of new working conditions. The book focuses on the relation between character and work in the new capitalism, with what the latter does to the former as the basis for critique.

The men and women Sennett writes about are not young. Even in early middle age they feel already used up and depleted. They have been buffeted by a range of forces beyond their control: from the need to re-locate again and again, with the lack of rootedness which avails of such mobility, to being excluded from youthful socializing and networking by dint of age and appearance (an older woman who tries her hand, mid-life, in advertising); from the loss of skill and craft of baking bread to the usurpation of even newly acquired computer skills to cheaper programmers living thousands of miles away. Sennett reveals the underside of flexibility, the way in which the more relaxed or informal codes of association, for example the network or teamworking, in fact do not just weaken the social bonds between people in contrast with more traditional forms of work, they are also much more easy to dismantle. Thus the new work marks the end of loyalty to others in a shared workplace, the end of dependence, which is replaced with a more detached, self-reliant outlook. Here social interaction is more fleeting and the person protects him- or herself by acting the part of cooperation and involvement, while in fact retaining a primary commitment to self-interest. He or she must also be able to anticipate trends and move before being pushed. Routinized time and dedicated space were more able to produce a set of social bonds based on need and mutual dependence, the very fabric of a decent society. Neo-liberal capitalism, in contrast, flourishes by stigmatizing dependence and by casting people so adrift that they have no sense whatsoever of being needed. It succeeds in making its own operations so opaque as to be 'illegible'. Where old-fashioned Marxism used to typecast workers' confusion regarding their own condition as 'false consciousness', confusion now stands as an 'accurate reflection of reality'. How many times can people re-invent themselves? In a winner-takes-all market, risk taking takes its toll.

More stable contours of time and place allow life narratives to be told which are meaningful and social. Better to have conflict and discussion between full and rounded characters than superficial game playing and failure to communicate. Arguing against what he describes as Salman Rushdie's postmodern notion of the fragmented self, elaborated through literary montage, Sennett says there is 'little room for understanding the breakdown of a career if you believe that all life history is just an assemblage of fragments' (1998: 133). Sennett envisages individual life histories as might be told and retold in the pub or round the kitchen table, as comparable to fuller literary narratives. The implication is that traditional realist literature (the great American novels of John Updike, Philip Roth and Saul Bellow spring to mind, and are echoed in Sennett's prose) is more capable of invoking self-understanding than is contemporary culture. Sennett's own fine literary style, as well as the persuasive force of his argument for an enlarged sense of community where people are valued for more than their short shelf life in the new labour market, are intertwined in his own distinctive narrative sociology.

Sennett's book raises a number of critical questions. What, for example, might be the consequences not just of the kind of individualization he describes, but of hyper-individualization brought about by being in perpetual motion from place to place, from 'hub' to 'hub', from job to job? How can there be workplace community when there is no workplace? If the new capitalism makes working patterns seem illegible, if it creates fragmented selves no longer capable of telling a whole story, and if in the process individuals are deprived of social bonds, do not the 'non-careers' of the 'others' of industrial and now post-industrial capitalism (of women, black people, immigrants, youth) become more normative? Disorganized labour reconvened along the lines of the talent-led economy brings more and more people closer to the working conditions of those who were never part of the American and European postwar settlement between capital and labour. Increasingly substantial numbers of men and women are expected to participate in 'risk work' where there is no long-term security, no guarantees they will be 'looked after'. But this is not a matter of turning the clock back; rather the clock is re-set to fit with the accelerated requirements of high-tech global capitalism. What the talent-led economy means in reality is a deeply individualized dream of affluence based on sheer effort and without the resources of welfare. For 'talent' read 'looking out for and after the self'.

Sennett is writing very much against the grain of the post-structuralists as well as the postmodernists, for whom the idea of character is itself a kind of fiction, a mythical wholeness held up as the ideal and hence a kind of benchmark, a means of judging 'humanity' and also loss of humanity. The problem with a perspective like this is that, while it can be demonstrated for those to whom the author speaks or who are interviewed by him (and hence represented by him), it is impossible to imagine how it might apply to a whole strata of much younger people for whom working in the new (cultural) economy has been in a sense mapped out for them by the entrepreneurializing discourses of government and who have no other experience of work. Are they therefore 'corroded' in advance? Perhaps the questions have to be re-posed. If young people know no other way of working than frenetic networking, self-exploitation and the maximization of talent and creativity as inner resources, expressions of self (i.e. self-expression), then maybe it is the job of the sociologist to examine the discursive means by which these 'inner qualities' are new forms of disciplining, new regimes of power all the more effective since they are connected with freedom and self-realization (du Gay, 1996; Rose, 1999). What is it to 'be' creative? How is talent perceived and mobilized as a strategy for individual success?[4]

Beck in Brazil   Like Sennett, Beck (2000) recognises the role of temporality and spatiality as critical to the experience of work, and he argues that the new work is characterized by 'spatial de-concentration'. Likewise the temporal security of lifelong full-time work is rapidly being replaced by interrupted short-term and part-time work. Beck argues that the key issue is the decline of the employment society and the consequent redistributive attempts undertaken by government and employers to spread what there is of work around, hence the rise of part-time work. The boundaries between work and non-work become more fluid, there is a spread of work over a different organization of 'hours' and a proliferation of 'sites', and work broadly is 'de-standardized'. Beck indicates how this new thin spread of work will impact on lowering income and creating new forms of social insecurity.

In addition, while the flexible forms of under-employment might be convenient for young people with families, these changes also herald the privatization of work with the burdens of health and safety shifted away from the big employers to the self-employed and semi-employed themselves. The new work marks an attempt to move from an unemployed society to one which is under-employed. And increasingly under-employment becomes normative, a replacement for traditional work, achieved through shortening the working week, introducing early retirement and extending the time of higher education. What Beck portrays is a patchwork and pluralized economy of diverse 'informal' jobs. With boldness (and complete inattentiveness to the complexities of the Latin American labour market) he talks of the Brazilianization of work (Beck, 2000). More and more people are rushing into this world of semi-employment, risk work where social responsibility for working lives is offloaded onto the individual him- or herself. Thus Beck argues that the 'reflexive modernization of the employment society' is such that not only can it defuse the explosive political potential of unemployment through redistributing work in a new time and space dimension, but it can also extract even more from this widely dispersed and highly individualized workforce who pick up the costs which in the past were covered by the employer. Thus capital (and government) gets more from the new workforce through the productive forces unleashed by flexible working while also avoiding the political consequences of widespread unemployment. The workforce itself is dismembered and the gains of flexibility, what Beck describes as 'partial freedom and sovereignty', are set against the risk of irregular work and the real prospect of poverty.

Just as Sennett describes the emergent work as illegible, Beck registers that as firms outsource their work and employ freelancers working at home, the daily working practices of the workforce fade from view. But the question is: does Beck offer insights on work that are useful for the analysis of new forms of creative work in the UK economy? Beck of course is not restricting himself to Germany, but implicitly it looms large in his analysis. However, there are elements to warrant useful comparison: first, the accumulation of jobs (or projects) held by persons, but each operating according to its own contract, its own timespan and spatial location; second, the illegible and invisible characteristics of many of these jobs; third, the acceptability of under-employment in the form of 'time between jobs', that is, irregular work (or, in Hollywood terms, the actor's time off work as 'resting periods'); fourth, the apparent sovereignty over work in the form of being freed from a desk and rigid schedule; fifth, the toll of responsibility for personal social insurance consequent upon the risk of self-employment; and, finally, the restructuring of family life and domestic commitments. Beck recognizes the urgent need for new forms of social insurance, including the guarantee of a minimum income to all. But in *Brave New World of Work*

(2000), his defence of social welfare allows him to reveal his own Euro-centricity by brandishing the spectre of Brazilianization (as in street vendor-ing) – otherwise uninvestigated and thus possessing only rhetorical power in this context – to alert and alarm European employment policy makers as to the consequences of neo-liberalism in the workplace. Ultimately he is warn-ing them of the Third Worldization of emergent labour markets in the hope that they will take action to avoid this 'catastrophe' scenario. Beck provides a rich account of work as it is in the process of being reorganized. In relation to this current discussion of youth, 'permanently transitional' work and creative activity as self-realization, what is most pertinent is the process of that reorganization as indeed transitional; work is being redistributed along new lines. What in the past might have been understood as a *rite de passage*, a transitional job leading to something more secure, is now a more permanent state of being.

Leadbeater in Silicon Valley   Leadbeater's (1999) book is a provocatively upbeat account of working in the new economy, or as he puts it, 'living on thin air'. Closely associated with New Labour, he is also a staunch advocate of neo-liberal values being more aggressively pursued in the context of the UK economy. He could not be described as a social theorist or indeed a sociologist; instead he is a journalist and an 'ideas person' who brings an iconoclastic American vocabulary to advocate entre-preneurialism in the cultural field and in the new media. The great institu-tions of the Victorian age, including those of work, are, he claims, now outdated as the knowledge economy makes new requirements of us all. Leadbeater's perspective is Anglo-American and his mission is to bring to the UK's and the current government's attention the lessons learned from Silicon Valley. His book is popular in tone and it is full of breezy announcements, as in 'everyone seems to have the chance to make it' when discussing the meritocratic nature of the new knowledge economy. His method is journal-istic, anecdotal and the evidence he presents is pulled from a wide variety of sources, including his own visits to new working environments. Leadbeater is also attempting to make a decisive break with old ways of thinking about work. In place of all the old terms which have applied in work, including 'democracy', 'solidarity', even 'bureaucracy', he introduces terms like 'trust', 'self-reliance', 'innovation', 'creativity', and 'risk taking'. These, in fact, he borrows from US management gurus, including the infamous Tom Peters and several others.[5]

Leadbeater wants to make entrepreneurs of us all. This opportunity is afforded by the growth of the knowledge economy and the decline of manu-facture. You can sell what you have inside your head. The examples he offers include the well-known TV cook Delia Smith, whose television programmes, books and other spin-offs, including branded kitchen utensils, have made her a multi-millionaire. Her success, he suggests, rests on the combination of her 'recipes' and her 'know-how'. Without analysing in depth Smith's business career, Leadbeater none the less argues that she fills a gap in people's knowledge opened up by the decline of learning 'from mother'. Now that most mothers go out to work, the basic skills of cooking have become highly marketable commodities. She is a 'knowledge entrepreneur'. Leadbeater provides other examples. He (mistakenly) implies that Alexander McQueen is a 'boy with no formal education' who has none the less 'become one of Europe's most precocious fashion designers' (1999: 33). (In fact McQueen completed an MA at Central St Martin's College of Art and Design.) This kind of work is 'more exciting' and the opportunities are enormous: 'the new economy will reward celebrities and stars, gamblers and entrepreneurs' (1999: 64). The old institutions which stifle this kind of attitude must be swept away, particularly the great public sector institutions like the universities. There should be greater diversity in educational provision, including that made available by successful entrepreneurs like Rupert Murdoch; knowledge should be more accesssible, like that on offer at the Phoenix University in the US (otherwise dubbed the 'drive-by university'), where courses can be taken through various different means. The Hollywood model is the most desirable for its 'dense social networks' and for its endless capacity to turn failure (only a few films get made from the thousands of scripts written) into success.

Leadbeater embraces the talent-led economy and envisages it as representing the best possible future for UK labour markets. With full support from Tony Blair (in the form of a blurb of recommendation on the book cover), Leadbeater's vision also represents most forcefully the presence and import of New Right thinking in New Labour's governmental vision.[6] The new talent-led meritocracy appears to be egalitarian by virtue of its seeming openness, and its commitment to social inclusion through work. In practice it is an unambivalently neo-liberal strategy, already being adopted by US Republicans (Walker, 2000). Leadbeater's account of new work relies on the elevated status of working in the media (the TV cook or gardener) as providing the model for success and achievement. It is a wholly individualized image of work, with little or no place for loyalty, association, never mind trade unionization. Instead it is about personal brilliance and the values of perseverance. 'You can make it if you really want' is the by-line. This human capital account of the new world of work has no time for anything other than resilience, self-help and motivation. Leadbeater's vision is one where we are almost all self-employed and able to buy into customized forms of private insurance. The conditions which he outlines with such enthusiasm are indeed close to the reality of (some) young cultural entrepreneurs. They are plugged into the knowledge economy and they do work from cafés with laptops and mobile phones, but he overlooks the much harsher realities of their working lives and the high levels of self-exploitation they must maintain to achieve a pretty threadbare existence. Nor does Leadbeater have any sense of the continuing existence of gender and ethnic constraints on labour market participation. He is uncritical of the limitations of the new meritocracy and unconcerned by those hard workers in the new cultural economy who, despite great effort and some degree of success, have still only got midway up the ladder of mobility by the age of 40.

the Hollywood sign, the Holloway Road *High Fidelity*, the best-selling novel by Nick Hornby (1995), chronicles the daily activities (and neurotic masculinity) of an 'indie' music fan turned storekeeper whose record shop is located on the busy, dirty Holloway Road, one of the main artery routes into central London. The shop is run less along sound business lines, more as a passion. In this sense it exemplifies the spirit of 'subcultural entrepreneurialism' (McRobbie, 1994), acting as an intermediary between producers and consumers of popular music ignored or as yet undiscovered by the mainstream. The novel itself also represents the small-scale creative successes of which the UK government has recently come to be so proud. However, for the book to translate into film, it was necessary to relocate the narrative to Chicago and production to Hollywood. 'UK talent', in this instance, was embodied in the persona of author (Hornby) and director (Stephen Frears). The export value lies in the creative abilities of two key individuals, and this example is representative of a cultural flow which includes fashion designers (Stella McCartney, John Galliano and Alexander McQueen to Paris), film directors, pop stars, actors, stylists, journalists, photographers and writers, whose route is most often in the direction of New York or Los Angeles.

The more general point is that the culture industries in economic and commercial terms actually comprise a small (but growing) band of atomized individuals who we can assume connect with relevant others through a network, but whose career pathways are quite distinct from the more normative 'work biographies' which have been documented in the social sciences. Indeed they are spectacularly different. So far we have only the beginnings of a critical vocabulary to deal with this shift. This would require the transition from the familiar 'sociology of work and employment' to a full account of the appeal of glamour and 'stardom'. In fact this transition is also incorporated into the narrative of *The Full Monty* (again written in the UK but produced in the US). While there is a substantial literature on employment in the steelworking industry, the entertainment careers dependent on the aestheticization of bodily attributes to which the unemployed ex-steelworkers in the film aspire as male strippers have attracted little sustained attention.[7] In this final section it will be argued that the couplet 'creativity/talent' has recently come to represent the most desired of human qualities, expressive of, indeed synonymous with, an 'inner self', and hence a mark of uniqueness, and particularly resonant for young people poised to enter the labour market. Creativity is not unlike what 'soul' used to be, a mark of the inner, meaningful self. But these resources are not simply there, on tap. They have to be worked at. The various incitements to uncover these abilities can be understood as 'technologies of the self'. These are also strategies of self-governance and thus demonstrative of recent modalities of power.

As various authors drawing on the work of Foucault have pointed out, it is through practices of freedom that the most positive and effective disciplining of individuals is achieved (e.g. Rose, 1999). By handing over responsibility for the self to the individual, power is both devolved and accentuated. So it is with creativity/talent. Where the individual is most free to be chasing his or her dreams of self-expression, so also is postmodern power at its most effective. Donzelot (1991) has argued that for capital to hand over the management of labour to a population for whom this self-management is increasingly understood as constituting 'pleasure in work' is to achieve unprecedented and sophisticated levels of regulation. As Ursell points out in relation to work in television production, this process of casualization and extended freelancing shows 'how late capitalism associates with a very particular technology of the self' (2000: 806).

Drawing from my own recent work on the careers of young fashion designers (McRobbie, 1998) as well as Ursell's (2000) analysis of working practices in television and other recent studies, including the British Film Institute's *Television Tracking Study* (1999, also on television workers), the Society of Authors' study of writers (Pool, 2000) and finally on Leadbeater and Oakley's (1999) account of 'cultural entrepreneurs', a number of themes appear with increasing regularity. Perhaps the most critical and intransigent of these is the pleasure with which individuals enter into this kind of work, notwithstanding low pay (sometimes no pay), extraordinarily long working hours (many of my respondents mentioned regularly working through the night) and volatile and unpredictable patterns of work. Both Ursell and I acknowledge the disciplinary impact of the many incitements across the media and in popular culture to participate in this kind of activity. We might call this the 'Hollywoodization' of the UK cultural labour markets. Even failures and knock-backs are, according to Leadbeater, helpful in encouraging resilience and determination. In *British Fashion Design* (McRobbie, 1998) there are any number of quotes from young designers about the passion they have for their 'own work'. It is this which allows them to keep going despite the seeming inevitability of bankruptcy.[8] Ursell, again drawing on Foucault, describes how television workers are also governed by these 'passions' for their work. As she says, 'in television production you can pursue your sensual pleasures' (Ursell, 2000: 821).The encouragement, indeed the exhortation, to the individual to find the meaning of life in work, and to identify with work, is a new normative way of ensuring 'civilisation through identification' (Rose quoted in Ursell, 2000: 810). Like Ursell, I also described this kind of working as a 'labour of love'. Ursell asks 'Why do they do it?' and argues that 'The willingness of individuals to work in television production is partly to be explained by the tantalising possibilities thereby for securing social recognition and acclaim . . . and partly [by] the possibilities for self actualisation and creativity' (2000: 819).

Those possibilities are, however, consequent on early days in the sector. Youthfulness is more or less a requirement for participation in the 'new work', not because a bodily essentialism kicks in later in life disallowing the 'long hours' culture, but rather because the expectation and indeed legitimacy of some degree of struggle and even failure to 'make it' reduces with age as other requirements for status and authority replace youthful resilience. That is, the technologies of self themselves undergo substantial modification to ensure middle-aged economic well-being. In my own study (McRobbie, 1998), among designers who were in their late thirties I found strategies of diversification: many had moved into teaching fashion design in art colleges; others had abandoned their 'own label' work and had taken jobs in large fashion companies. The BFI tracking study (1999) has found increasing numbers of television workers developing other sources of income, once again many from teaching. The same is true for the authors surveyed by the Society of Authors (Pool, 2000), whose very low annual earnings were supplemented by other forms of work. Independent creative work is thus transitional in terms of lifecycle, with high levels of investment in the early years following the completion of education or training. Youth itself is not a stable category, and a determining feature of new work in cultural fields is to extend the age range of 'youth' so that creative workers well into their late thirties and even early forties are still thought of as young and can be called upon at short notice to work in any geographical location for an indefinite period of time. Thus the traditional conditions of youthfulness are normatively expected of this workforce independent of family life. As a result many young women I interviewed had postponed motherhood indefinitely. The BFI study also shows that of a sample of approximately 500, one half of the women surveyed had no children, but only one quarter of the men. Another feature of enforced youthfulness is the expectation of working for nothing. In my study I found that even journalists on staff contracts regularly did unpaid work in other ' more creative' outlets to keep their names in circulation and thus 'for exposure'. There is a certain indignity about middle-aged persons indicating their willingness (or desperation) to work unpaid.

But the redirection of creative careers in mid-life does not, it seems, mean stability: the 'permanently transitional' stage gives way instead to multi-skilling and the generation of revenue from more than one source. Increasingly, 'portfolio careers' means working for more than one 'employer' over a prolonged period, perhaps even a lifetime. The talent-led economy is clearly capricious in its rewards. As Ursell (2000) points out, across the sector and across age ranges the discrepancy between very high wage earners (a small minority) and relatively low-paid workers is increasing with a diminishing of middle-range salaries. Likewise only a handful of writers earn the huge advances which take up so many column inches in the press. Indeed, in writing, five per cent earn on average over £75,000 and 'three-quarters of members earned less than the national average wage; and two-thirds less than half the average wage and one half less than the minimum wage' (Pool, 2000). In fashion design the majority of interviewees were living on take-home pay of less than £20,000, although of course for the few figures at the top (McQueen, Galliano, McCartney) the rewards were enormous.

Beck is therefore right, I would argue, when he characterizes new work (although he is inattentive to creative work) as work spread more thinly across a wider cross-section of individuals. In the UK context the rise of creative work especially for young people can indeed be seen as a strategy for reducing unemployment. What Beck described as capital without jobs I suggested in relation to fashion designers were actually jobs without capital. These are mostly 'made-up jobs', sustained by the euphoria and enthusiasm of a large cast of energetic actors who by necessity must believe in their own talent. Thus the encouragement to become 'entrepreneurs of the self' (du Gay, 1996) is almost wholly accomplished within that sector of young people increasingly drawn to the cultural and creative fields. According to Andrew Ross (1998), this terrain has recently expanded to include workers in the new media, which, in the US context, are similarly subject to the effects of the lottery economy, that is the winners take all and the others work in a 'labour-intensive workplace' which, like many other, less prestigious environments, is prey to the 'low wage revolution'.

Even just a few years ago creative types could normatively have access to unemployment benefit when a job ran out and before another one started. But this cushion is now removed and the only alternative is to stack up other jobs (cab driving, bar work, data input, temping) until more fulfilling opportunities arrive. But this intensification of work weakens almost all social bonds beyond those of the creative network (often the agency) and personal and familial relationships. In low-status temporary jobs taken to tide the worker over until something better appears, there is neither the prospect of 'narrative sociality' preferred by Sennett (1998), nor the so-called 'network sociality' described by Lash (2000). De-spatialized as well as de-socialized, the entire range of work activities is inevitably de-politicized. An increasing gap divides young and older, where the latter have (only) just managed to be incorporated into the old work settlement of pensions and employment rights. For the under forties, the 'regimes of subjectification' with which they have grown up have inculcated individualization and entrepreneurialism as alternatives to traditional careers (as Gray and Flores describe in the opening epigraph). It is almost impossible to imagine how the inequities which arise from this wholly neo-liberalized cultural labour market might be redressed. Murmurs of trade unionization among 'dot.com' workers in the US are yet to translate into any degree of self-organization among this band of dissociated workers in the UK. Workplace politics is virtually unknown in the fashion industry, and, according to Ursell (2000), union membership by young television workers is negligible. Being freelance or self-employed appears to negate the idea of the politics of work. But in this context, where ideas of equal opportunities belong to a bygone era, black and Asian people are wholly under-represented as 'talented' cultural entrepreneurs, as even Leadbeater and Oakley (1999) note, and the BFI study (1999) also shows that new young entrants into television in 1999 were 94 per cent white. Women, too, find themselves faced with having to make a decision between having children and having work. Against this backdrop, and for the moment, New Labour can sit back. They have succeeded in reducing unemployment and they can rejoice in a generation who in the meantime at least appear to love their labour.

notes

1. Leadbeater and Oakley suggest that there will soon by 1.5 million working in the cultural sector, the majority of whom are self-employed. Handy (2000), writing in the *Guardian*, claims that '60% of British businesses have only one employee, which is why the statistics of self-employment understate the real degree of independence in work. We call ourselves businesses, not "the self-employed".'

2. Boughton (2000), in the *Guardian*, reports that what started in the US as a self-help initiative was re-invented in the UK by Reed in Partnership as a means of encouraging 'corporate goodwill' with companies organizing 'suit drives' where employees donate their cast-offs at collection sites in offices.

3. The 'Cool Britannia' episode was an ill-fated attempt in the early days of the New Labour government to involve young artists, pop musicians, fashion designers and other celebrities in a campaign to export UK talent abroad and promote the creative sector as integral to New Labour's modernizing process.

4. In *British Fashion Design* I made some attempt to begin such work of investigating the social construction of talent, creativity and imagination in the context of the working lives of fashion designers (McRobbie, 1998).

5. Franks (2000) has written a scathing critique of the publications of the think-tank Demos, and the recent writing of Leadbeater, as vapid management speak

borrowed from US business gurus. He also connects Leadbeater's celebratory rhetoric with the pernicious effect of cultural studies writing, including my own.

6. I argued this influence on Tony Blair was evidence of the 'new right by stealth' (McRobbie, 1999).
7. One of two TV programmes screened in the week starting 8 January 2000 on young women and body image include a feature on 15-year-old girls seeking breast implants on the basis that 'you can't be famous if you don't have boobs'.
8. In the week starting 1 January 2000, it was reported that one of the stars of UK fashion design, Hussein Chalayan, had filed for bankruptcy. In the same week one of my own respondents, Ally Capellino, was reported as having 'gone under' in 1999 but was about to re-launch a small accessory range having repurchased her own name.

references

Augé, M. (1995) *Non-Places: Introduction to an Anthropology of Supermodernity.* London: Verso.

Beck, U. (1992) *Risk Society.* London: Sage.

Beck, U. (2000) *The Brave New World of Work.* Cambridge: Polity.

Boughton, I. (2000) 'Suits you at interview', *Guardian*, 20 November ('Office Hours' section), p. 2.

British Film Institute (1999) *Television Industry Tracking Study.* Third Report. May. London.

Castells, M. (1996) *The Information Age.* Oxford: Blackwell.

Department of Culture, Media and Sport (1998) *Creative Industries Mapping Document.*

Donzelot, J. (1991) 'Pleasure in work', in G. Burchell, C. Gordon and P. Miller (eds), *The Foucault Effect: Studies in Governmentality.* Hemel Hempstead: Harvester Wheatsheaf.

du Gay, P. (1996) *Consumption and Identity at Work.* London: Sage.

du Gay, P.(1997) 'Organizing identity: making up people at work', in P. du Gay (ed.), *Production of Culture/Cultures of Production.* London: Sage.

Franks, T. (2000) *One Market Under God: Extreme Capitalism, Market Populism and the End of Economic Democracy.* London: Secker and Warburg.

Hall, S. (1998) 'The great moving nowhere show', *Marxism Today*, November pp. 9–15.

Handy, C. (2000) 'On why work sharing works', *Guardian*, 20 December, p. 11.

Hornby, N. (1995) *High Fidelity.* Harmondsworth: Penguin.

Klein, N. (2000) *No Logo: Taking Aim at the Brand Bullies.* London: Flamingo.

Lash, S. (2000) *Network Sociality*, unpublished paper. London Goldsmiths College.

Leadbeater, C. (1999) *Living on Thin Air: The New Economy.* Harmondsworth: Viking.

Leadbeater, C. and Oakley, K. (1999) *The Independents.* London: Demos.

McRobbie, A. (1994) *Postmodernism and Popular Culture.* London: Routledge.

McRobbie, A. (1998) *British Fashion Design: Rag Trade or Image Industry?* London: Routledge.

McRobbie, A. (1999) 'On Trust' *The Guardian*, 22nd July, p. 21.

McRobbie, A. (2001) 'Club to company: the decline of political culture in the speeded-up world of the cultural economy', *Cultural Studies*, Special Issue (P. du Gay and S. Nixon, eds).

Nixon, S. (1997) 'Circulating culture', in P. du Gay (ed.), *Production of Culture/Cultures of Production*. London: Sage.

Pool, K. (2000) 'Love, not money', *The Author*, Summer, pp. 58–66.

Rose, N. (1999) 'Inventiveness in politics', *Economy and Society*, 28 (3): 467–93.

Ross, A. (1998) 'Jobs in cyberspace', in A. Ross, *Real Love: In Pursuit of Cultural Justice*. New York: New York University Press.

Sennett, R. (1998) *The Corrosion of Character*. New York: W.W. Norton.

Ursell, G. (2000) 'Television production: issues of exploitation, commodification and subjectivity in UK television labour markets', *Media, Culture and Society*, 22 (6): 805–27.

Walker, D. (2000) 'In the know', *Guardian*, 24 July, p. 21.

Warhurst, C., Watt, A. and Nickson, D. (2000) 'Looking good, sounding right: style counselling for the unemployed', *Industrial Society*. London: Industrial Society Report.

Young, J. (1999) *The Exclusive Society: Social Exclusion, Crime and Difference in Late Modernity*. London: Sage.

identities and industries:
the cultural formation of aesthetic economies

Keith Negus

Accounts of cultural production and the workings of media and communication corporations have, on the whole, tended to draw exclusively from mainstream systems-oriented organization studies, occupational sociology and political economy. An emphasis has been placed on the determining influence of institutional constraints and corporate structures, which have been viewed monolithically and unambiguously as detrimental to the work of creative artists and the choices available to consumers. When explaining processes of cultural production, such approaches have privileged the determining influence of an economic 'logic' of commerce, the corrupting motive of corporate greed, and confined their focus to the formal institutions of commercial exploitation and legal regulation. It is a recurring and familiar story: commerce (the economic imperative) has been corrupting creativity (the cultural impulse).

In this chapter I seek to provide an alternative view of cultural production by highlighting the broader dynamics which shape the formation of aesthetic economies. I want to argue that we need an approach which is sensitive to, and prepared to understand critically, the social relationships within market-oriented institutions, and which is also open to consider the broader dynamics within which these organizations are constituted. It is not that exploitation or incompetence and greed are not present, as they are in numerous areas of life, influencing the most trivial everyday activities as much as the most revered creative practices. But this is only part of the story. Drawing on research into the music industry in Britain and the United States (Negus, 1992, 1999), I want to argue that the practices of industries, audiences and artists are shaped within a broader cultural context. My argument here is against the assertion that we can understand any aesthetic forms that we might encounter in the marketplace in terms of simple stimulus–response models of marketing and publicity, or the effects of the impact of the industry on the public and on creative artists (or, in reverse, the ability of audiences to 'resist' such pressures, effects, systems and manipulations).

I wish to highlight how cultural processes shape (what are assumed to be) economic practices, beliefs and criteria, and how this informs the contexts within which creativity can be realized, judged and valued (and also the conditions within which any transformative politics might become possible). I will argue that what often appear to be fundamentally economic or commercial decisions (which artists to sign; how much to invest in them; how to market them) are based on a series of historically specific cultural values, beliefs and prejudices. Social relationships that are often perceived to be 'outside' of corporate organization and the economic relations of production are always an integral part of production (hence the cultural dynamics shaping the extra-economic practices of 'consumption' should not be separated from the way these intersect with the formal organizational worlds of production). This chapter is an exploration of these ideas and a consideration of the conditions within which creativity can be realized, recognized, refuted and rewarded.

Within the context of this collection it is perhaps obvious that in aligning myself here with a particular take on 'cultural economy' I do not mean the distinct research tradition which emerged during the late 1970s known as 'cultural economics'. Concerned with the 'economics of the arts' and with attempts to apply formal economic models and theories to various artistic activities (Throsby, 1994; Towse and Khakee, 1992), this type of thinking has operated with a clear distinction between the economic and cultural (with the cultural routinely approached in terms of a series of apparently 'objective' economic indicators and 'variables'). In contrast, I adopt the term 'cultural economy' as a way of raising critical questions about the fusing, blurring and interaction of practices understood with reference to the analytic distinctions between economy and culture.

In adopting this approach I have drawn from a number of theoretical tendencies, one being the type of 'cultural economy' that was adopted as part of the vocabulary of writers such as John Fiske and Arjun Appadurai during the 1980s as a way of initiating a culturalist critique of economics and political economy. Fiske and Appadurai made significant interventions into the study of culture, and when engaging with debates about commodification, used the term 'cultural economy' to point towards the 'social life of things' (Appadurai, 1986) beyond straightforward market exchange values. Fiske (1992) employed a notion of cultural economy when writing about the significance of fans as producers of popular meaning, and Appadurai (1990) wrote of the various 'scapes' that make up what he termed the 'global cultural economy', highlighting how the movements of people and things can be approached as simultaneously cultural, economic and political (although his account tended to privilege the cultural 'flows' over the economic movements and political circumstances). The emphasis was placed on how commodities are used and appropriated and are imbued with or accrue additional meanings, uses, sign values, and how, in turn, this dynamic contributes to the social value of things and is therefore significant for their continuing circulation and exchange. This argument was an important challenge to a crude version of the distinction between use value (social needs) and exchange value (economic market), and was part of a more general concern with the extra-cultural value which can be accumulated by commodities. In a broader context, these arguments – about the cultural character of economic relationships – intersected with the writings of Pierre Bourdieu (particularly notions of 'cultural capital'), Nestor García Canclini (cultural capitalism of artisans, cultural economy of citizenship) and Jean Baudrillard (the stress on the sign value of commodities). Whilst this type of thinking has clearly been important, and contributed to an understanding of the interrelations between the categories of economy and culture, it has sometimes been used to imply that the economic is ultimately cultural, with a concomitant tendency to reduce or recast social divisions and political processes as 'cultural'.

Whilst Fiske and Appadurai were more concerned with the cultures of consumption, my focus is on the 'cultures of production'. However, in pursuing this line of thinking I do not intend to imply a neglect of political and economic circumstances, and the quite clear way that corporate intervention and government regulation can impact upon occupational practices and artistic activity (whether pressure from shareholders results in companies being closed, sold and artists and workers losing their contracts; or whether immigration legislation or employment codes impact upon who is able to participate in the corporate world of cultural production in a given time and place). Political economists have provided many insights into the various ways that corporate ownership impinges upon cultural practices (the writings of Graham Murdock and Vincent Mosco being some of the most significant here). These have highlighted how production occurs within a series of unequal power relations, how commercial pressures can limit the circulation of unorthodox or oppositional ideas, and how the control of production by a few corporations can contribute to broader social divisions and inequalities of information not only within nations but across the world. That the major entertainment arts corporations are continually seeking to control and thus maximize their profits from cultural production is a point that has been repeatedly emphasized, and not only by political economists.

Despite its insights, however, the conclusions reached by many who adopt the perspective of political economy have tended to become rather predictable, portraying corporate ownership leading to rigid forms of social control and having a detrimental impact upon the activities of creative artists and the public. Writers who have followed this line of reasoning have, in recent years, been rather reluctant to embrace the tenets of classical Marxist political economy. Hence, the optimistic belief that such circumstances can be overcome through some form of revolutionary socialist transformation has been superseded by rather vague musings about the possibilities for 'democratizing' or regulating media corporations via various policy interventions.

To wish to intervene in and regulate 'the industry' is to neglect the conditions within which the industry has been formed. 'Cultural policies' cannot depend solely upon finding ways of dealing with an industry, occupational tasks or administrative concerns, nor with the issues arising as a consequence of 'ownership' (corporate control, monopolies and oligopolies) in any simple sense. These will be ineffective without an understanding of how industries are formed within a broader context or, to return to my earlier phrase, how culture produces industry.

The possibility of gaining access to, participating in and becoming formally recognized within cultural production (whether in the domains of literature, painting, music, clothing, design, theatre, film or investigative journalism) is clearly dependent upon presenting a 'marketable' product. But it is also informed by patterns of power and prejudice arising from the ways in which the formation of particular industries has been shaped by such factors as class, gender relations, sexual codes, ethnicity, racial labels, age, political allegiances, regional conflicts, family genealogy, religious affiliation and language. Depending where you are located in the world, some of these may appear to be more significant than others. In making this point, I do not wish to reduce the production of culture and creative work to a series of social variables or bodily distinguishing marks, but to emphasize how broader social divisions are inscribed *into* and become an integral part of business practices.

In adopting this approach I therefore also seek to move some distance away or outwards from the orientations of those writers who have adopted a 'production of culture perspective' (Peterson, 1976, 1978, 1997), 'organization set analysis of industry systems' (Hirsch, 1972), 'institutional economics' (Breen, 1995), a 'culture/cultural industries' approach (Garnham, 1990; Miége, 1989) or an orientation to a 'cultural industries production system' (Pratt, 2000). Although, again, these approaches have provided numerous insights, they have tended to focus solely on the dynamics of production within culture, media and entertainment organizations or systems and have had little to say about the broader social contexts within which cultural forms are received and appreciated and how this shapes occupational activities. They have also had little to say about the influential practices that, and people who, link producers to audiences. Hence, my concern is less with how *industry produces culture* and more with how *culture produces industry*. I argue that production takes place not simply 'within' a corporate environment or the systems of production structured according to the requirements of capitalist production, organizational formulas, occupational groupings and state regulation, but in relation to broader culture formations and practices that may be outside the direct control or understanding of the producing institutions. Hence, I am acknowledging the critique of production put by those who argue that the industry and media cannot simply determine the meaning of cultural forms and that these may be used and appropriated in various ways by artists and the public (the point made by Fiske and Appadurai). More specifically, in adopting this perspective I am drawing insights from the trajectory of thinking initiated by Raymond Williams' conception of culture as a 'way of life' and the writings of Stuart Hall in which he has placed an emphasis on culture as the discursive practices through which people create meaningful worlds in which to live. Hence, I am concerned with culture as practice, way of life and representation – all collide in the aesthetic economy.

There are a number of implications of adopting this type of approach. First, the activities of those within culture-producing organizations should be thought of as part of a 'way of life'; one that is not confined to the formal occupational tasks within a corporate world, but stretched across a range of activities that blur such conventional distinctions as public/private, professional judgement/personal preference and work/leisure time. Second, it is misleading to view practices within entertainment and arts institutions as primarily economic or governed by an organizational logic or structure. Instead, work and the activities involved in cultural production should be thought of as meaningful practices which are interpreted and understood in different ways (often within the same office) and given various meanings in various social situations.

In pursuing these themes I have, like a number of contributors to this book (see the chapters by Nixon and McFall), drawn from Bourdieu's suggestive although sketchy observations about the work of 'cultural intermediaries', those occupational groupings providing 'symbolic goods and services', occupying a position *between* the producer and consumer (or artist and audience) and operating across and exerting influence within a nexus of social relationships which the term 'habitus' seeks vaguely to signpost. However, whilst Bourdieu has perceptively analysed the impact of class divisions on cultural production and consumption, he has had relatively little of much substance to say about the influence of other social divisions of race, ethnicity, age, gender, sexuality and religious affiliation – all can become an integral part of cultural production. Not all of these dynamics will be featuring in this chapter, but they are clearly significant when considering the cultural constitution of aesthetic economies. The following sections are intended as an exploration of these issues through brief sketches of the music business in Britain and the United States.

repertoires and rewards: aesthetic hierarchies and the cultural valuing of commercial criteria In thinking about the cultural formation of aesthetic economies and the conditions within which any creative practice can be realized, I want to start by focusing on the criteria that guide the judgements which record company staff make about repertoire acquisition and the level of financial investment accorded to different types of music, performers and departments. These criteria are usually taken for granted and thought to be either 'obvious' or 'intuitive' by the staff mobilizing them. The criteria are most apparent when staff are making judgements about whom to select from the talent available, and imagining what the public would most like to hear. Yet such habitual and routine everyday beliefs about musical qualities and commercial potentials are not based on business decisions and objective economic judgements in any straightforward sense. Instead they are informed by beliefs arising within a series of gendered and radicalized class divisions, and these have decisively contributed to the formation of the working practices of record company departments.

Most of the key decision makers within the British music industry share many features in common, and constitute a coherent class grouping. Those executives who have been in the business for 25 to 30 years and who find themselves in senior management or running labels have been drawn from a very particular class background and habitus. Recruited into the music industry during the 1960s and early 1970s, most senior executives are middle-class white males who have received a privately funded education at 'public schools', or attended state grammar schools, and completed studies at university. Their formative experience was shaped during the era when rock was gaining cultural value, becoming self-consciously intellectual and respectable, and when a simultaneous expansion of the universities and institutions of cultural production provided an impetus which facilitated the recruitment into the music industry of a group of mildly bohemian young people associated with the 'counter-culture'. Many of these young executives in jeans had initially been involved in booking bands, often as university entertainment officers, and a considerable number had played in rock bands. The 'genre culture' of British rock music had provided a particular series of orientations, assumptions, dispositions and values, and these were carried into the organizations of music production and came to dominate agendas within the expanding recording industry during the late 1960s and 1970s. Despite often being presented as a fairly 'liberal' business, populated by personnel who are 'in touch with the street', these agendas were in no way a 'reflection' of the diversity of music being played and listened to in Britain. Instead they represented, in condensed form, the aesthetic preferences and value judgements of a small, relatively elite, educated, middle-class white male cohort.

At a decisive phase in its expansion and growth, the British music industry was reorganized around a series of dichotomies in which rock artists were favoured over pop or soul performers; albums were favoured over singles; and self-contained bands or 'solo artists' who are judged (from a position derived from Romanticism) to 'express' themselves through writing their own songs were favoured over the more collaborative ways in which singers or groups of performers may work with arrangers, session musicians and songwriters in putting together a composition or project. Most obviously, conventional 'live' male guitar bands were treated as long-term propositions, whilst soul and rhythm and blues music came to be treated in a more *ad hoc* and casual manner. These distinctions were hier-archically inscribed into contracts, investment and financial decision making. As many feminist writers have observed, rock also instituted a particularly sexist approach to gender relations and a male-dominated mode of heterosexual expression (McRobbie, 1991; Meade, 1972; Whitely, 1992). This not only limited the range of expressive possibilities available to female performers and placed women in a particular position in the narratives of rock songs, it also tended to marginalize women into specific sectors of the music industry. Apart from administrative and secretarial positions, the most notable area where women have managed to establish a presence over time has been in public relations work, where working practices have involved female publicists 'servicing' male journalists.[1]

In addition, as rock was being institutionalized, most companies tended to employ very few black staff, and then only the occasional accoun-tant, post room assistant or messenger (a notable exception here, during the 1970s, was Island Records). Not only have there been conspicuously few black people in key decision-making positions, there have been few staff with an in-depth knowledge of and expertise in managing rhythm and blues and soul music. This has directly contributed to the de-prioritizing of the recordings produced by Britain's black musicians and R & B performers. These practices were integral aspects of the 'culture of production' that con-stituted the context within which recordings were being made and mediated by the music industry.

In acquiring new artists, staff in the British music industry have not been responding, in any neutral or obvious way, to the 'talent available' or 'public demand'. Equally, the working practices that have been institutional-ized and which result in these aesthetic hierarchies are not explicable in terms of formal occupational titles, systems models nor arguments about the type of pressures exerted by corporate capitalist control of production and distribution. These working practices have emerged and been shaped histor-ically as a result of broader social divisions within Britain and as a conse-quence of how the beliefs, practices and aesthetic dispositions of those cultural intermediaries who constituted a rock genre culture have contributed to the formation of a particular type of music industry.

This has established an agenda which has endured and proved resilient, despite the fact that a number of individual executives and music business organizations have subsequently sought to give greater representation to woman and black workers within the industry, and also attempted to invest equally in genres of music other than rock. The 1990s saw the British music business prominently promoting and gaining widespread coverage for very conventional all-male guitar rock bands, most notably Oasis and Blur. These bands were promoted with comparisons made to the Beatles and the Rolling Stones, establishing them as part of a very particular rock tradition. Although the local popularity in Britain of 'rave' and 'dance' music has prompted claims that repertoire agendas and aesthetic experiences have profoundly changed, this has not necessarily been reflected in patterns of - strategic long-term economic investment. Neither does it seem very relevant when listening outside the isles and considering the type of British artists prioritized for international marketing.[2] In addition, much new dance music has come from a constituency of technology-fixated white boys with computers, not that different to the young men with electric guitars who continue to form into bands and stand in line waiting for recording contracts. Meanwhile, soul, rhythm and blues and the music of Britain's black and Asian populations continues to be treated in a more *ad hoc* and less strategic manner, finding outlets through affiliations and alliances with some of the more innovative and less easily labelled sounds that have circulated since the mid-1990s (such as the various collectivities associated with Bristol and the West Country, including artists such as Portishead, Massive Attack, Roni Size and Reprazent and Tricky).

In 1995 Ray Hayden, Chairman of the British Rhythm and Blues Association, explained that he was gaining most of his investment for British black music from overseas sources because British companies were reluctant to commit themselves to it. He commented, 'it's taken British companies to witness the overseas reception of British soul music [Des'ree, Omar] before they'll even grumble positively about it' (Springer, 1995: 17). A year after Hayden made these comments, a new award was introduced with the aim of drawing attention to, and remedying, this neglect. This was the UK Music of Black Origin (MOBO) Awards. Speaking after the fourth event, singer Beverley Knight gave voice to the enduring frustrations of Britain's rhythm and blues community:

America only sees one colour. And that's green. They don't give a shit that Jay-Z is a black guy from the hood, they don't care that Mary J. Blige came from Yonkers.

> Mary J. Blige sells. Over here, at a time when R & B-influenced singles are hitting the Top Ten regularly, real roots-level R & B is being totally cut back at radio. . . . It's the grassroots R & B that they find a bit scary. 'It's not accessible enough, it's not commercially viable.' But I remember when they were saying hip hop couldn't sell. Then the Stone Roses used a hip hop influence and had a massive smash with 'Fool's Gold', and the whole Madchester thing exploded. All the break-beat stuff that's happening now is from hip hop. We're always at the root of what goes on. But when it comes to exploiting the innovation and getting the sales, everybody shrinks away – they think it's too dark, it's too black. . . .
>
> (Quoted in Mullen, 1999: 28)

These comments are just one illustration of how an agenda that was established during the late 1960s and early 1970s has continued to influence how executives are recruited, artists acquired and rewarded, and money is invested across genres. Yet Beverley Knight's assumption that green is the only colour that matters in the US music business is itself rather optimistic, and can be countered by moving across the Atlantic and briefly considering the connections between social divisions, cultural identities and commercial decisions.

identities, genres and commerce: culture within and without the corporation

Many executives in record companies consider the issue of culture to be important, not only in terms of representation (the sounds, words and images of their artists), but as a way of understanding the day-to-day working world or 'culture' within the organization. Whilst numerous senior personnel have been influenced by the prescriptive literature which suggests that a company's distinctiveness and economic competitiveness is dependent upon its 'corporate culture', there is an additional aspect to notions of company culture here that is particular to record companies (and which manifests itself in discussions and working beliefs which draw on a historical knowledge of the 'great labels' of the past): when seeking to attract artists and senior executives, most companies can match each other's financial offers, so an additional appeal is made based on claims about how a company can provide the most sympathetic conditions for creative work and the most supportive environment for the idiosyncratic temperaments of musicians.

These aspects are often alluded to when executives are recounting anecdotes about how they did or did not manage to sign a particular artist. For example, Don Ienner, when reflecting on his inability to attract Green Day to Sony, remarked;

> We were the first major label that was out to sign Green Day. They walked into the Warner Bros. building in Burbank, which is a beautiful, wooden building, three floors, very homey. They're California kids. And after spending a couple of days in our marble and stone building here in New York, they decided to go with Warner Brothers.
>
> (Quoted in Zimmerman, 1995: 19)

Whether or not the 'homey' building was the sole factor in such a decision, it was considered to have an important influence on the company's ability to attract artists. Another non-economic factor that is judged to be crucial for attracting performers is the roster of artists signed to a label. Artists are not simply and straightforwardly construed as 'economic assets' but recognized as unstable human commodities and hence located within a continually monitored portfolio of rising talent, established stars and declining has-beens. Companies not only face a problem when deciding which new assets to acquire and how much to invest in them, they also have to judge when they are about to move beyond their sell-by date. The decision-making process and criteria of judgement are by no means straightforward. Whilst, anecdotes abound about how, at certain moments, stars such as Neil Young, the Beatles, David Bowie and Aretha Franklin have attracted artists to their respective labels, there are just as many less known but significant artists who have attracted people due to their critical acclaim, even though they would be considered a poor investment in terms of simple economic indicators. Such personas can contribute to a company's ability to attract performers and staff to a 'creative' environment. As Bob Merlis, Director of Media Relations at Warner Brothers, explained when speaking to me in the same building that Green Day had apparently found so attractive:

> There is something to be said for the profile of the company. We've had artists here who have not really sold a lot of albums but who have been kind of touchstones for other artists. I know that REM have always been impressed with the fact that this was the company that for ever maintained Van Dyke Parks, Ry Cooder and Randy Newman, despite the fact that they basically didn't sell a whole lot of records.[3]

It is these types of beliefs and this narrow understanding of the inter-relationship of 'culture' with music business economics that has prompted so many companies to introduce 'cultural changes' assuming that this will influence the talent (executives and artists) who will wish to join a record label. A typical example of this occurred at the EMI record label in New York City during 1996, where Davitt Sigerson, having been appointed as President and CEO in September 1994, was requested to 'change the culture', a directive initiated by EMI Group North American Chairman Charles Koppelman. When I interviewed Davitt and asked about these changes he gave an explanation which indicated the quite instrumental way that cultural change was understood and implemented. As he recalled:

It needed a culture. I needed to do it very dramatically and the way to do it was by bringing in a lot of different people. . . . I mean EMI was the last place that someone would have thought of to bring a quality artist. We were known for the fast buck and the quick fix and the pop sensation and the one-hit wonder. . . . It was very important to me to eradicate what had been the very unhealthy old culture, which was a place that was obsessed with success and making money and having a certain style and profile and turn it into a place which was really passionate about music. . . . I fired 18 senior executive in my first afternoon here on the job. . . . and it was a tremendously liberating thing for the artists who had been signed here, almost all of whom were miserable, and for the junior people here, who felt that they were working in a place that didn't have a soul and that didn't care about the music. It created a tremendous initial burst of high spirits for everybody.[4]

Sigerson estimated that by March 1996 (when I spoke to him), 70 per cent of the people who had been working at the company when he took over (September 1994) were no longer employed. Other members of staff I spoke with acknowledged the impact of these changes, and also spoke of how Sigerson not only changed the staff working for the company, but cut the artist roster. In his first year the label released 24 recordings as opposed to a quantity of 63 that had been issued in the previous year. He also brought in staff who he judged were committed to the philosophy of developing artists for the 'long term' rather than simply having short-term successes. When I spoke to Davitt in March 1996 he was building on these initial changes and putting in place a label which he believed would be able to attract talented artists who would wish to stay with the company for a long term. He was seeking artists who would 'build catalogue' and grow as 'career acts' by creating 'a body of work' over a long period. His assumption was that this would attract other artists and committed staff who wished to work in this way. Somewhat ironically, Sigerson's 'culture' changes, his 're-tooling' and reconfiguration of the company and his belief in a long-term and committed approach requiring some degree of patience was ultimately to be thwarted by movements at a higher corporate level. Just over one year after my interview, in May 1997, in yet another exhibition of the cost-cutting and restructuring that had been such a feature of the company, EMI corporate headquarters sacked Sigerson, along with 34 other senior executives, and closed down the EMI New York office.

The 'culture' that Sigerson was attempting to 'put in place' relied heavily on his experience of working with rock artists and his formation as a music business executive during the epoch when rock and soul were the dominant commercial forms in the United States. He was attempting to create a unified, 'organic', coherent shared 'culture'. Although, at the time, soul singer and songwriter D'Angelo was being treated as integral to this new culture, Sigerson was not particularly interested in working within the post-soul networks that had most notably been carved out by hip hop artists and their possees, labels and affiliations. Indeed, the EMI Music group had made a conscious decision to distance itself from hip hop and contemporary R & B in February 1996 when the company closed its Capitol Records 'urban division', cancelling the contracts of most artists and sacking 18 members of staff (most of them black). For J.R. Reynolds (1996), a columnist working for trade paper *Billboard*, this event represented 'the systematic extermination of black music at Capitol Records' and 'cut the company's ties' to the 'r'n'b community'. As such, this was far from simply an 'economic' decision. Although EMI publicly stated that it had been taken in order to streamline the corporate portfolio and to concentrate resources on 'stars' and 'modern rock' artists, Reynolds pointed out that it could not be justified in market terms: in 1995 R & B and rap had sold 132 million albums and accounted for over 21 per cent of the music market in the US. To many people, inside and outside the company, this looked suspiciously like racism and a distinct lack of commitment (in terms of staff and investment) to sustain an involvement in black music and what Nelson George (1989) has called the 'rhythm and blues world'. George has used this phrase to refer to the 'extramusical' significance of rhythm and blues as an 'integral part' of and 'powerful symbol' for 'a black community forged by common political, economic and geographic conditions' (1989: xii).

For Sigerson, who was given the immediate task of dealing with the few artists who were retained and passed on to the EMI label, the issue was perceived in a more instrumental manner. Yet his comments highlight how R & B acts were not considered integral to the 'culture' he was seeking to create within EMI. This he acknowledged explicitly when I asked how he was managing the acquisition and production of R & B and hip hop artists:

I don't have anyone doing r'n'b A & R [artist and repertoire]. What I've adopted as a model is to have a bunch of different production deals or first-look arrangements with entrepreneurs who bring me stuff . . . it's a very affiliative sort of creative community and process and I don't need to be in a camp.[5]

The action of the record company and Sigerson's explanation suggest far more than changes to internal company 'culture' and 'business decisions' and point to how the recording industry in the US intersects with cultural identities and enduring social divisions: how the music business confronts performers and public alike as a fragmented, multi-divisional polyarchy of genre-specific operating units, charts, retail spaces, radio stations, television channels, clubs and magazines. The fragmentation of socio-cultural identities is a characteristic feature of life in the United States, with the commercial segmentation of markets for apparently neutral business reasons connecting uncomfortably with the social segregation of the country and breaking up of cities into ghettos defined by class and ethnicity. The cultures of music production have been shaped by the way in which the US music business has been constituted within this broader context, with the recording industry dealing with different genres according to discrete organizational units, promotional media and marketing routes. Contemporary record companies may use the jargon of 'portfolio management' which has developed since the 1970s, but the basic way of dealing with different genres in discrete units has a long history. This can be traced back, at least, to the 1920s, when performers and songs were allocated into three distinct categories: 'race' (African-American popular music), 'hillbilly' (white, working-class rural styles) and 'popular' (the type of music then produced by Tin Pan Alley).[6] Such practices have led to the division of black and white music, artists and audiences and contribute to the separation of different groups of people. They are far more than organizational arrangements that simply facilitate efficient marketing to a 'targeted' public. Such divisions are compounded by segregation according to class, language and geography.

Whilst most major companies' black music divisions are located in New York City (with offices in Los Angeles), country music has been instituted as a company sub-division or label (a business unit within the 'corporate portfolio') located in Nashville and geographically separated from the day-to-day setting of agendas at corporate headquarters. For much of the genre's history, staff based at the head offices of the major companies had little interest in what went on in Nashville: the music was 'an exotic, regional music that outsiders – those record executives in New York and LA – could never really understand' (Gubernick, 1993: 20). Such corporate neglect halted slightly during the 1960s and in the 1970s, and again during the country boom of the early to mid-1990s.

Yet, despite providing significant profits for the corporations, there are enduring divisions between those working with country artists and other parts of the record companies. The relationship between management in Nashville and corporate head office is not only informed by commercial concerns (is the country division meeting financial goals?), but influenced by the fact that Nashville is firmly part of 'the South' – with all the burden of accumulated meanings that small geographical signifier carries. As David Sanjek (1995) has observed, those involved in producing country music have had to deal with ignorance, antipathy and uncritically received stereotypes about their music and the place of the South within the United States: country production and intra-organizational working relationships are mediated by sentiments formed as a result of how practices within culture and media organizations bifurcate along urban/rural and North/South divides, and residues of antagonisms and prejudices which can be traced back to the Civil War in the nineteenth century.

In a similar way, staff working with US Latin music are located in regional offices in Miami, and embroiled in a set of organizational relations which are not only symptomatic of institutional tensions between the English language and Spanish language cultures of the United States, but indicative of the relationships which uneasily connect the USA to Cuba, Puerto Rico and the Caribbean regions of Latin America in the East, and to the Latin populations of Texas, California and Mexico in the West. Such tensions endure as part of the cultural dynamics within the same corporations, influencing how staff interact and how artists are prioritized, produced and circulated.

There are complex working relationships involved here, not easily explained according to systems models of cultural industries or straightforward political economic processes, and certainly not fully elaborated in this brief sketch. The working practices of staff are shaped by an unstable collision of commercial organizational structures; the activities of fan cultures; musician communities and historical legacies within broader social formations – all come together and inform the aesthetic economy of cultural production.

This fragmented system does have one clear benefit. These separate units have provided a space for people who might not otherwise have gained employment in the industry: African-American staff, Latino/a personnel and the 'hillbillies' from the South. In addition, such divisions have ensured that musicians are managed by personnel with knowledge, skills and understanding of their music. This offers a clear advantage over the situation that has developed in Britain, where soul bands have been dropped from rosters in the past simply because the rock-oriented A & R manager had neither the understanding nor the will to work with them.

However, these divisions lead to the separation of musical knowledge and result in a number of highly distinct, identifiable and institutionalized boundaries erected between listeners, musicians and workers within the same record companies. This is, in turn, reinforced by the equally divisive segmentation of listeners by radio broadcasters, with the result that 'the audiences for hard rock, salsa and rhythm and blues are often mutually exclusive and divided neatly (and at times antagonistically) along racial and cultural lines' (Garofalo, 1986: 81). A further consequence of these divisions is that creative practices and aesthetic discourses have come to be fragmented into genre-specific codes and conventions, boxed into social containers which either do not meet or meet under conditions of mutual incomprehension or contempt – 'I don't understand your music' or 'I don't like your music it is boring/repetitive.' These types of statements are far more than musical judgements. As Simon Frith (1996) has argued, in his work on popular discrimination, our aesthetic judgements imply ethical agreements and disagreements, moral evaluations and assessments: the feelings that accompany aesthetic pleasure and displeasure are simultaneously emotional, sensual and social. Staying within or moving across popular genres is about more than the aesthetic or the market. Crossing genre boundaries is not only a musical act, it is also a social act, a way of making connections, of creating solidarities.

Many of the most critically acclaimed cultural forms (whether painting, music, novels, film) have been created when different cultural practices, peoples and aesthetic traditions have met and got mixed up; when different genre cultures have interacted and combined. Artists and cultural producers may be notoriously individualistic, continually questing for 'autonomy' and 'independence' and desiring the 'freedom' to pursue their own whims. Yet, at the same time, creative artists are continually contributing to solidarities in a way that dissolves any simple individual/collective dichotomy or pattern of us/them prejudice and discrimination. The practices of cultural producers continually bring about such possibilities.

It is ironic that the media arts and entertainment industries have sought to capitalize on such mixtures, yet, in producing organizations to profit from this, the industries have set up units within which such cultural dialogues can be contained. As a consequence, the creation and crossing of bridges to other genre worlds is a process which has occurred and continues to happen despite, rather than because of, the ways in which the major entertainment arts corporations have sought to organize the production of contemporary cultural forms.

notes

1. For a more extended discussion of this point see Chapter 7 in Negus (1992).
2. For elaboration of this point see Chapter 7 in Negus (1999).
3. Personal interview, Warner Brothers Records, Burbank, 25 April 1996.
4. Personal interview, New York City, 19 March 1996.
5. Sigerson's 'culture' changes, his belief in a long-term and committed approach requiring some degree of patience, his attempt to avoid artistic and social rivalries, was ultimately to be thwarted by movements at a higher corporate level; movements similar to those that had resulted in the closing of the 'urban'

division. Just over one year later, in May 1997, EMI corporate headquarters sacked Sigerson, along with 34 other senior executives and closed down the EMI New York office. This had little to do with Sigerson's initial changes and internal dynamics within the label in New York. Instead, it was informed by more profound corporate problems and sense of crisis within the British-based parent corporation. For further discussion of these issues see Negus (1999).

6. For further discussion of this see Garofalo (1997).

references

Appadurai, A. (ed.) (1986) *The Social Life of Things: Commodities in Cultural Perspective*. Cambridge: Cambridge University Press.

Appadurai, A. (1990) 'Disjuncture and difference in the global cultural economy', *Public Culture*, 2 (2): 1–24.

Breen, M. (1995) 'The end of the world as we know it: popular music's cultural mobility' *Cultural Studies*, 9 (3): 486–504.

Fiske, J. (1992) 'The cultural economy of fandom', in L. Lewis (ed.), *The Adoring Audience*. London: Routledge.

Frith, S. (1996) *Performing Rites: On the Value of Popular Music*. Oxford: Oxford University Press.

Garnham, N. (1990) *Capitalism and Communication: Global Culture and the Economics of Information*. London: Sage.

Garofalo, R. (1986) 'How autonomous is relative: popular music, the social formation and cultural struggle', *Popular Music*, 6 (1): 77–92.

Garofalo, R. (1997) *Rockin' Out: Popular Music in the USA*. Needham Heights, MA: Allyn and Bacon.

George, N. (1989) *The Death of Rhythm and Blues*. London: Omnibus.

Gubernick, L. (1993) *Get Hot or Go Home. Trisha Yearwood: The Making of a Nashville Star*. New York: St Martin's Press.

Hirsch, P. (1972) 'Processing fads and fashions: an organizational set analysis of cultural industry systems', *American Journal of Sociology*, 77 (4): 639–59.

McRobbie, A. (1991) *Feminism and Youth Culture*. Basingstoke: Macmillan.

Meade, M. (1972) 'The degradation of women', in V. Denisoff and R. Peterson (eds), *The Sounds of Social Change*. Rand McNally.

Miège, B. (1989) *The Capitalization of Cultural Production*. New York: International General.

Mullen, L. (1999) 'No-go MOBO?', *Time Out*, 10–17 November, p. 28.

Negus, K. (1992) *Producing Pop: Culture and Conflict in the Popular Music Industry*. London: Arnold.

Negus, K. (1999) *Music Genres and Corporate Cultures*. London: Routledge.

Peterson, R. (1976) 'The production of culture: a prolegomenon', in R. Peterson (ed.), *The Production of Culture*. London: Sage.

Peterson, R. (1978) 'The production of cultural change: the case of contemporary country music', *Social Research*, 45 (2): 293–314.

Peterson, R. (1997) *Creating Country Music: Fabricating Authenticity*. Chicago: University of Chicago Press.

Pratt, A. (2000) 'The cultural industries: the case of new media in world cities', in K. Kawasaki (comp.), *Cultural Globalization and Cultural Industries:*

Experiences in UK and Japan. Report for Ministry of Education, Science and Culture in Japan, Komazawa University.

Reynolds, J.R. (1996) 'Capitol Records setting a bad example', *Billboard*, 9 March, p. 18.

Sanjek, D. (1995) 'Blue Moon of Kentucky rising over the Mystery Train: the complex construction of country music', in C. Tichi (ed.), *Readin' Country Music: Steel Guitars, Opry Stars and Honky Tonk Bars, The South Atlantic Quarterly*, 94 (1), Winter: 29–55.

Springer, J. (1995) 'Hayden on the edge', *Blues and Soul*, 1–14 August, pp. 16–17.

Throsby, D. (1994) 'The production and consumption of the arts: a view of cultural economics', *Journal of Economic Literature*, 32, March: 1–29.

Towse, R. and Khakee, A. (eds) (1992) *Cultural Economics*. Heidelberg: Springer-Verlag.

Whitely, S. (1992) *The Space Between the Notes: Rock and the Counter-Culture*. London: Routledge.

Zimmerman, K. (1995) 'Year of turmoil', *Music Business International*, October: 18–22.

re-imagining the ad agency:
the cultural connotations of economic forms

Sean Nixon

Looking afresh at the once relatively settled relations between culture and economy is proving to be an important area of conceptual innovation within the human and social sciences. Germane to this work has been a prising open of the much vaunted autonomy of economic life and an emphasis on the constitutive role played by culture in the formation and operation of this domain. As Paul du Gay has succinctly put it, this has meant drawing attention to the way 'economic processes and practices . . . in all their plurality . . . depend upon and have cultural "conditions of existence"' (1997: 4). This conceptual insistence has been taken in a number of different directions. These have included, notably, the suggestive neo-Foucauldian work on the government of economic life, as well as the more recent studies derived from actor network theory on markets and market exchange (Callon, 1998; du Gay, 1996; Miller and Rose, 1990). It is the way in which this attention to the cultural conditions of economic practices and identities has surfaced in relation to cultural analysis, however, which has been most important for my own work. Looming large here has been the questioning of neo-Marxist (specifically, Althusserian) models of determination. It was this model which informed, often in a largely unacknowledged way, a good deal of cultural analysis, particularly of commercially produced popular culture. Within this model, an autonomous, primary domain of practice (the economic) acted on and ultimately determined another 'relatively autonomous' domain (the ideological or the cultural). Although in concrete studies cultural critics took full advantage of the licence given by the premise of relative autonomy to privilege the study of language and representation, this work remained anchored to the conceptual ranking of social practices furnished by the notion of determination by the economic in the last instance.

It was against this particular conceptual fudge and its shortcomings for cultural analysis that a number of cultural critics attempted to emphasize the interdependence of economic and cultural practices and their relations of reciprocal effect within the sphere of cultural production (Hall, 1986; Mort,

1996; Nixon, 1996). In my own work, a major impetus for rethinking these relations has stemmed from Ernesto Laclau's thoroughgoing critique of earlier forms of anti-economism. In particular, it was his emphasis on the contingency of all identities (including the economic) which opened up a different way of thinking about the relations between the incompletely formed fields of culture and economy. This precisely emphasized notions of imbrication and mutual constitution rather than direct determination by or interaction between fully constituted domains (Laclau, 1990: 24). This reconceptualization has significant pay-offs for cultural analysis. Once an *a priori* model of determination is dropped and the conceptual fudge of 'relative autonomy' discarded, it becomes possible to chart the contingent relations of effectivity and determination operating within and between specific domains. In the case of analysing cultural forms, this move is enormously generative. Rather than displacing the economic to the margins of analysis, it becomes possible – amongst other things – to pay attention to the role of cultural representations in the establishment of economic practices and relations. Thus, in earlier work on commercial representations of masculinity and the men's markets in clothing and lifestyle products with which they were associated, I explored the way attempts to know or represent the male consumer within market research were an integral part of the establishment of the commercial relations between advertisers, cultural intermediaries and consumers within this domain of gendered commerce (Nixon, 1996). Specifically, it was the representations of a new male consumer – the style-conscious young man – which formed a necessary part of the articulation of these commercial relations. In other words, representations of the consumer were an important determinant upon the formation and operation of this area of commercial or economic activity. They formed a necessary part of the conditions of existence of these markets.

In this chapter, I want to return to the imbrication of cultural and economic practices within the commercial domain. In doing so, however, I want to turn more directly and exclusively to a set of economic relations in order to push further at the value to cultural analysis of engaging with economic forms. In this case, it is the relations between clients and advertising agencies that I foreground. I want to suggest that the establishment of these economic or commercial relations – embodied in the contract of agreement agencies sign with clients – depends upon a set of cultural practices for their articulation. These are cultural practices bound up with the conceptualization and delimiting of the service relationship and the broader understanding of the identity of advertising agencies as particular kinds of service providers. In reflecting on the work of representation involved in articulating these economic relations, I want to place centre-stage the financial arrangements established within the contract of agreement. These financial arrangements – specifically forms of remuneration – are interesting because they have come to be seen by advertising industry insiders as carrying powerful meanings in themselves; meanings to do with the identity of advertising agencies as service providers. Thus, these financial forms have symbolic as much as direct economic significance. They are stakes in the game of re-imagining the ad agency. As such they play a strategic role in the broader cultural process through which the commercial relations between clients and agencies are articulated.

Exploring the constitution of these commercial relations has been made easier by the destabilizing of agency/client relationships brought about by developments within the British advertising industry. Figuring prominently within these have been a set of both local, conjunctural factors and more deep-rooted and long-term changes in the nature of the advertising business. In the first section of this chapter, I want to outline these factors, briefly, before turning in the second section to the specific debates about agency remuneration in Britain. In the final section, I explore the way one British agency – Bartle Bogle Hegarty – rewrote the contracts of agreement it entered into with clients in order to help it bring about a redefinition of itself as a different kind of advertising agency.

contemporary challenges   In early May 1996, *Campaign*, the British advertising trade newspaper, offered an upbeat commentary in its weekly leader column on the rather vexed question of advertisers' relationships with their advertising agencies under the headline 'Accountability benefits both agency and client' (*Campaign*, 3 May 1996, p. 27). The leader had been prompted by the moves by the body representing UK advertisers, the Incorporated Society of British Advertisers (ISBA), to make available to its members a common standard for assessing the performance of their advertising agencies. The standard had been devised following research carried out by the ISBA into its members' views on the service they received from agencies – and, in particular, their views on whether agencies delivered (in that most contemporary phrase) value for money. The researcher, Dr Ian Cheston, summarizing his findings in the press coverage which accompanied the publication of the proposal, noted that 'the high expenditure days of advertising are gone. Clients are looking for people to make their marketing programmes more successful. It's the agencies that are most professional that will survive' (*Campaign*, 26 April 1996, p. 7).

Campaign's response in its leader to Cheston's findings and the ISBA's proposal was to take both firmly on the chin. Whilst it wryly acknowledged that 'it's almost inevitable that when advertisers start to talk about greater accountability, mutinous mutterings emerge from agency boardrooms and creative departments', it went on,

> There is no need [to grumble]. The growing pre-occupation with accountability goes hand in hand with the recognition of the importance of agencies to commercial success. . . . If accountability is well managed, each side benefits. Agencies can get to grips with clients' needs and any renewed attack on margins can be nipped in the bud.
>
> (*Campaign*, 3 May 1996, p. 27).

There was more than a good dose of positive thinking, however, in *Campaign*'s response; of reading for the best interpretation amongst the more uncomfortable meanings of the ISBA's proposal. As the leader writer knew only too well, the demands for greater accountability articulated in the ISBA proposal were the product of a more widespread questioning of agencies by clients. This questioning had gathered pace since the early 1990s and was undoubtedly prompted by the sharp recession which affected key sectors of the UK economy during the early part of that decade. The recession not only put a significant squeeze on the marketing budgets of client companies, but also provoked some serious questioning amongst them of the commercial value of advertising. Big spending advertisers such as the processed food manufacturer Heinz and the confectionery giant Nestlé, for example, both took the decision in 1994 to promote individual brands through direct marketing – that is, media such as direct or 'junk' mail – rather than through television advertising. Other client companies also began to look much more closely at the effectiveness of above-the-line (principally, press and television) advertising and, in addition, turned a more questioning eye on the overall service which they received from advertising agencies. Under such scrutiny a worrying perception emerged amongst clients and their representatives. This was that advertising agencies were generally badly managed organizations which took a frivolous view of both their business strategies and their costs and routinely engaged in some rather sharp commercial practices. A welter of evidence appeared to confirm this: that agencies added anything up to a 40 per cent mark-up to the production costs of adverts when charging clients; that discounts gained from media companies were not declared to clients; that agencies made money by delaying payment to media owners and investing it on the overnight money markets; and that agencies were formerly run by meaninglessly large boards of directors, in which it appeared that board membership was routinely confirmed as a way of giving recognition to staff rather than helping to shape effective management practices (*Campaign*, 25 March 1994, pp. 12, 23; 10 May 1996, p. 12). Management consultant David Maister, picking up on this latter problem, went so far as to suggest that 'agencies are not so much badly managed as un-managed. They work like Fenian democracies, where everyone wears their sword to the gathering, but nothing gets decided' (*Campaign*, 25 March 1994, p. 12 and, *inter alia*, 14 November 1997, pp. 38–9).

This intensive scrutiny of agencies by clients and the demands for greater agency accountability which it generated where focused upon an industry itself suffering a major recession. Following a decade of constant expansion, advertising expenditure fell back sharply during the early to mid-1990s. This period also saw the industry contract, with employment levels dropping drastically.[1] These sectoral problems were closely related to the wider recession within the UK manufacturing and service industries, but were also sharpened by the highly leveraged nature of most agencies, which made them particularly vulnerable to even quite small reductions in their levels of income (Rawsthorn, 1989).

The local difficulties generated by the economic recession – including clients' demands for greater accountability – were unfolding at a time when agencies were also having to grapple with other, more deep-seated external pressures on their business. One set of challenges came from the increasing importance of global marketing to the big international client companies and their associated ambition to centralize their advertising into a smaller roster of typically larger agencies. The profound segmentation of the agency sector which the demands of these clients had already helped to form – with the sector split between a smallish number of genuinely global agency networks and other, smaller, privately owned agencies – continues to provide a major structural dynamic which individual agencies have to negotiate. For many – particularly medium-sized agencies – the intensification of the process of globalization in advertising and marketing services has meant taking decisions about entering into merger or acquisition deals with other agencies and communications businesses in order to avoid being squeezed out of an increasingly bifurcated sector (Daniels, 1995; Mattelart, 1991; Nixon, 1996).[2]

Agencies are also facing competition from other groups of symbolic intermediaries in the areas of expertise which they have traditionally monopolized. One set of challenges has come from management consultants, who are increasingly offering their services to clients as the providers of rigorous strategic advice about brands. The consultancy firm McKinsey & Co., most notably, garnered a good deal of disapprobation from agencies for its aggressive moves into the communications field in the early 1990s (*Campaign*, 15 July 1994, p. 29; 2 December 1994, pp. 36–7). Advertising agencies are also experiencing intensive competition from companies known as 'media independents' in the researching, planning and buying of media space as clients became more prepared to separate the media-buying services which they require from the other core services which they buy from agencies. This move by clients had profound consequences. Whereas in 1973 only the US giant Unilever and a handful of other clients used media independents and did not, as a consequence, integrate their planning, buying and creative work under one roof, by the early 1990s over half of all media buying was carried out at a different location from where the creative work was developed (*Campaign*, 4 June 1993, pp. 32–3). Many of the blue-chip clients were centrally involved in this process. In the year to May 1994, for example, £200 million worth of media business was centralized into media independents by Boots, British Gas, RHM and Cadbury's (*Campaign*, 13 May 1994, pp. 30–1).

Both these forms of competition – but most clearly that coming from media independents – were related to a further significant set of external developments bearing upon agency practice. These derived from changes in advertising media. The last decade has seen an acceleration of the process of media pluralization which had begun in the 1980s. At the root of this has been the policy-driven opening up of media markets – especially televisual markets – and the emergence of new media technologies and delivery systems. The scale of these developments has been phenomenal. For example, in 1980 there was just one commercial TV channel in Britain providing 88 minutes of ad time a day. By 1993, this had risen to 15 channels offering in excess of 1,500 minutes each day. Similarly, in 1980, there were just 16 national newspapers and 1,400 consumer magazines. By 1992, this had become 23 newspapers, each typically heavily sectionalized, and 2,300 consumer magazines. Commercial radio stations have also risen from 26 in 1980 to 125 in 1992 (*Campaign*, 4 June 1993, pp. 32–3). And the changes carry on apace.

These developments both in the established advertising media and in new media have raised practical questions for clients and agencies about the best way to reach consumers through the marketing process. One consequence of this has been that with more potential routes to the consumer, choices concerning the selection of media have moved up the list of priorities shaping the development of advertising and marketing campaigns. In many instances, then, the medium selected – whether it be TV, sponsorship, website, press advertorial or promotional event – has increasingly come to determine the overall marketing solution pursued by clients and agencies. One notable consequence of this has been that some of the established assumptions which have guided agency practice in most of the postwar period have been challenged. In particular, the assured centrality of the 30- or 60-second television commercial has come under intense scrutiny.

Amidst these heterogeneous developments, protecting their status and addressing the wider challenges facing them has become a pressing concern for the major players in the British advertising industry. This has prompted many to engage in a concerted effort to rethink the nature of their service relationship with clients and, in the process, to redefine what kind of businesses they are. It is these initiatives which are germane to my argument in this chapter. They precisely afford us a glimpse of the constitutive role played by cultural representations in the establishment and playing out of the commercial relations between clients and agencies. There are two dimensions to this. On the one hand, the current moves to redefine the identity of agencies reveals the contigent nature of the commercial relations which prevailed for much of the postwar period. Thus what looked like an autonomous economic relationship forged between agencies and clients is revealed to have depended upon an historically specific model of the ad agency and the service relationship. On the other hand, the current moves by agencies to protect their status also exposes the cultural work necessary to maintain and develop favourable commercial relations with clients. What this latter cultural work has thrown up has been a concern to extend and deepen the position of agencies as business partners offering extensive strategic advice to their clients and an equally strong ambition to resist the very different constitution of their identities as the mere suppliers of one-off ads. Pursuing this cultural vision has had significant consequences for agencies, forcing them into major programmes of organizational change. Rather late in the day compared with many of the client companies they deal with, agencies have been attempting to restructure themselves along more entrepreneurial lines. Whilst a number of different models of organizational change have been developed, common themes have emerged. Perhaps the most significant have been the moves away from a departmentalized organizational structure and the linear organization of the creative development process towards multi-disciplinary project team working.

Significantly, the cultural work associated with the process of re-imagining the identity of agencies which has generated these programmes of organizational change has become centred upon the question of how agencies should charge for their services and the nature of the contract of agreement they sign with clients. Three models of remuneration have dominated these discussions: payment by media commission, by project fees and by royalties. The debate about the relative merits of each of these models has become highly charged within the industry, in large part because they have become bound up with the moves by agencies to re-imagine their organizational identities. In fact, the remuneration question has become a synedoche for the broader cultural process of re-inventing the organizational identity of the advertising agency being undertaken by the sector's key players. It is to these exchanges about remuneration that I now want to turn.

the state of pay   At the heart of the contemporary debates about agency remuneration is the status and viability of commission-based forms of agency payment. This form of payment has its roots in the establishment of modern advertising agency practice at the end of the nineteenth century in which agencies acted as agents of the press. Commission-based payments were formalized into a legally regulated system – the fixed commission system – in 1932 and under this system agencies recognized by the Newspaper Proprietors' Association (NPA) could receive a 10 per cent commission on the costs of the media space which they bought for advertisers. Commission levels rose to 15 per cent by the late 1950s following the introduction of commercial television and remained at around that level into the 1990s, despite the ending of the fixed commission system in 1978.

The contemporary exchanges over commission-based payment were framed by evidence of its decline as a percentage of gross agency income. Whereas anecdotal evidence suggested that, in the late 1980s, commission payments still accounted for 86 per cent of most agencies' gross income, this had fallen to approximately 45 per cent by 1996. Although media commission has continued to remain the most important source of income for many agencies, income derived from fees and retainers paid by clients comes close to matching it (see, *inter alia, Campaign*, 13 August 1993, pp. 22–3; 20 January 1995, p. 25; 23 June 1995, p. 12).

For critics of commission-based forms of payment, its decline and the increasing importance of fees represented a positive development. Andy Tilley, managing partner of the media consultants Unity, argued, 'Nowadays there are so many bits to the media mix [such as new opportunities for sponsorship and the use of websites]. How does that fit with the commission system? The system is anachronistic and change is inevitable' (*Campaign*, 13 February 1998, p. 12). Mike Davis, of the agency LSDA, on the other hand, drew attention to the fact that media commission undervalued the full range of thinking contributed by agencies to clients' marketing problems. As he put it, 'commission only reflects media advertising usage. It puts no value on ideas and properties created by the agency that spread far beyond just ads' (*Campaign*, letter, 14 July 1995, p. 24). He went on, outlining the appropriateness and viability of fees as an alternative to commission-based payments: 'For those ideas, some form of usage payment is the answer. Fees can vary to reflect the value provided. . . . There's no Holy Grail, but having produced several ideas that give the client value way beyond media campaigns alone, we are working on various individual fee solutions.'

Fees were not the only alternative form of remuneration promoted by critics of media commission. Other industry insiders – from both the client and agency side – advocated royalty payments. Drawing the analogy between the creative ideas generated by agencies and musical or literary productions, Carol Reay of the agency Mellors Reay & Partners argued, 'We work in a creative industry, so there is a strong case for rewarding creative thinking. . . . With the royalty system, if the creative work is good, it has a longer life and you get bonuses on that' (*Campaign*, 21 November 1995, p. 14; see also 24 November 1995, p. 14 and 17 November 1995, p. 9).

It was the advertising newspaper *Campaign*, in its editorials, however, which – ventriloquizing the views of some influential agencies – offered the most elaborated and sustained critique of the commission-based form of remuneration. It argued that media commission was a significant block to agencies rethinking their role in a rapidly changing commercial environment. Specifically, it suggested, commission payment prevented agencies from moving beyond their established positions as producers of, pre-eminently, press and TV adverts and towards what it called the role of all-round marketing advisers to clients (*Campaign*, 16 January 1995, p. 13; 23 June 1995, p. 27). In an editorial from January 1995, the paper thus argued:

> [T]op of the agenda for every agency chief executive and marketing director should be the remuneration issue. For it is the method of remuneration that keeps agencies locked into a way of working that is less and less relevant. If you are paid by commission both your organizational structure, your product and, more importantly, your culture is skewed in certain directions. That may have been fine in the old days, when marketing and advertising were, relatively speaking, two-dimensional processes. But it is not relevant now. If you are paid in a conventional way, you act like a conventional ad agency. And that, sadly, is not what is needed.
>
> (*Campaign*, 6 January 1995, p. 13)

The critics of commission, however, did not have the arguments all their own way and their cultural vision did not go uncontested. For its supporters – amongst both clients and agencies – commission was nothing short of the financial glue which held the modern advertising agency together. As Arnold Brown, Vice-President for Europe of WCRS Healthcare, argued:

> [T]he commission system is based on a client's total marketing spend. It allows clients the freedom and flexibility to allocate to agencies and other fees based on equivalent commission. Without this umbrella costing procedure we would not have agencies. They would be creative, planning and media consultancies and controlling them would be clients co-ordinating all the activity and, probably, with advertising departments of their own.
>
> (*Campaign*, 30 June 1995, p. 25)

Hugh Burkitt, Chairman of Burkitt Weinreich Bryant, on the other hand, positively contrasted media commission with fees, suggesting:

> The key benefit to both sides of payment by commission is that it places the empha-
> sis on the value of the idea to the client, not the cost of producing it. The more an
> idea is used, the more an agency gets paid for it. The Andrex dog has, I hope, earned
> J. Walter Thompson millions because it has made even more millions for [the client].
>
> (*Campaign*, 20 January 1995, p. 25)

More prosaicly, John Sharkey, Chief Executive of BST BDDP, argued, '[It's] still the least time consuming and most effective way of rewarding agencies' (*Campaign*, 23 June 1995, p. 12).

Pragmatic considerations like Sharkey's notwithstanding, it is clear that for both sides of the argument, the debate over commission was about more than the survival of a particular system of remuneration. For supporters and detractors alike, the persistence of commission as a key element of remuneration raised questions about the nature of agencies' relationship with advertisers and about the kind of service providers they were. For its defenders, commission-based payments were integral to the identity of full-service agencies as the pre-eminent suppliers of well-researched and -planned advertising which added to the value of clients' brands.[4] For its critics, there was a need to move beyond commission payments and the model of the full-service agency which they had historically supported. What were needed were forms of remuneration which better fitted agencies' roles as more fully developed business partners and all-round marketing advisers to clients.

Amongst the advocates of this restructured vision of the advertising agency was Bartle Bogle Hegarty (BBH). I want to look in a little more detail at the way it set about attempting to redefine its identity as a service provider. In doing so I want to draw attention to the role played by the model of remuneration within this process of re-imagining the agency's identity.

Bartle Bogle Hegarty   BBH, one of the most successful and strongly branded advertising agencies in Britain over the last two decades, embarked upon a significant process of organizational change from 1995. The motivation behind this undoubtedly came from a concern to institutionalize the model of what it called 'integrated thinking' within the agency. Put simply what this meant was the ambition to link together in a more dynamic way both above- and below-the-line advertising[5] and to develop what were often called 'media neutral' solutions to a client's marketing problems. These were forms of promotion which did not, in advance, privilege any one form of media (such as the 30-second television advert) over another. At its root the pursuit of integration was central to the agency's desire to resist the drift amongst some clients to view agencies as merely the suppliers of one-off adverts or pieces of communication rather than as business partners. BBH hired the industrial psychologists Nicholson McBride in 1993 to help it bring about this programme of change. At the root of it lay the introduction of project team working in which teams consisting of each of the key agency disciplines would work on a set number of client accounts. As Martin Smith, the agency's Chairman, explained:

> That's very different from how it used to be where you'd have an account director who works on three pieces of business, an account manager who works to him on one piece of business but not necessarily on the other two. But now we have teams who have a set number of pieces of business. There's a symbolic oval table in the middle with more chairs than there are people because we want there to be, if it's relevant, somewhere for Motive [BBH's free-standing media department] to sit, Limbo [BBH's direct marketing subsidiary] to sit . . . somewhere for the client to sit, somewhere for the creative department to sit. It's about developing. . . . Flexibility is what it's all about. What we're trying to do increasingly is to get people to think more broadly, think more interestingly, more creatively. We're supposed to be a very creative business, and yet most of our practices stultify creativity.[6]

The reconfiguring of the organizational structure of the agency – a decision which Martin Smith also saw as about trying to 'build change into the culture' – was accompanied by the relocation of the agency from its offices in Great Poultney Street, Soho, London, to new, larger premises in Kingly Street, just off Regent Street at the heart of London's West End. Looming large in the move was, precisely, the requirement for a new open-plan office layout – difficult to achieve at Great Poultney Street – which could facilitate the desired ways of working. There was an important modification to the ideal-typical project team structure, however, when the teams were established in May 1996. In setting them up, BBH explicitly excluded art directors and copywriters – the advertising creatives – from them. Martin Smith again explained the logic behind this decision:

> [It] is important to strike a balance between a kind of openness, where. . .everybody works in a tight group and the fact that there is no doubt about it that creativity works best when there is a controlled tension. There has to be some kind of tension between the business needs that are being articulated by account management and planning and the creative solution which is being offered by the creative department. If it is all too nice and straight-line, you end up with Switzerland. You know, some-

thing wonderfully efficient and neutral and extremely dull. What you have to maintain is that tension, you have to get a creative tension going. And you still have to have the fevered argument, the temperaments and . . . that's important to get good work, because you have to get people feeling emotionally something is right, and some-one fighting them and changing it and bettering it. And that's important within a creative organization. So we've got to maintain the tension where it's relevant, and I think it is relevant between the people who are the primary connection with the client and the people who must be the ones who sprinkle pixie dust on the idea and create something which is a leap from where I and others like me would have got logically.

This defence of the separateness of creative teams and the concern to provide the working conditions under which they could generate the necessary imaginative leaps to bring a client's brief to life was undoubtedly underscored by BBH's view of itself as a purveyor of 'creative excellence'. It emphasized this distinction at every opportunity, drawing attention, for example, in a case study prepared for the Department of Trade and Industry, to its success at being voted International Agency of the Year for three consecutive years at the International Advertising Festival at Cannes. In doing so, it positioned itself as close to the heart of the UK's reputation as a centre of creative excellence. The emphasis on 'creativity' and 'creative excellence' often sat uneasily, however, for the agency with the traditional position of agencies as service providers. The agency captured this tension in its 1996 business practice publication produced for clients – and, in doing so, set out a statement of intent concerning how effective relations with clients ought to be ordered. In this extract we can see it beginning to elaborate upon a new identity for the agency:

Agencies work for clients and, traditionally, advertising has seen itself as a service industry. But all the available data show that the thing clients seek most is creativity. There is a potentially difficult balancing act here. It is not easy to play a responsible role as the specialist source of creative excellence and, at the same time, to be positioned as a service provider. . . . So, our mission is to strive for the complete confidence of our clients . . . in order that we may be given the responsibility that forces excellence.

(Bartle Bogle Hegarty, 1996: 3)

This statement had been provoked in large part by wider arguments within the industry concerning agency accountability and clients' perceived lack of trust in the agencies they contracted. BBH was keen to tackle head-on these difficulties affecting agency/client relations and to put itself ahead of the pack by developing clear and principled responses to them. One initiative which it developed – and which it promoted with a certain amount of flair[7] – was the guarantee of complete transparency in the financial arrangements associated with clients' accounts. Central to this was the declaration to clients of any discounts or commission which the agency negotiated with media suppliers.

These moves to put in place business practices which could encourage trust between the agency and its clients were clearly integral to BBH's ambitions to be more than a mere service provider of adverts. Significantly, it developed this further in its statement of good business practice by placing great weight on getting the remuneration deals right which it struck with clients. Looming large in this was a critique of not only commission payments, but also fee-based payments, and the advocacy of a novel model of financial compensation. The document suggested:

> Advertising can frequently be the difference between two products. . . . We think of ourselves as part of the manufacturing process, building advertising properties that fortify brands and that in themselves become company assets and deliver to the bottom line. How long does it take a creative team to think of an idea that may fundamentally change the fortunes of a brand. Five hours? Five weeks? Sadly, ideas do not materialize on command. Is that idea, which may endure for decades, worth only the hours it took to develop? Strange that we have perpetuated a payment system – commission – that encouraged the view that all agencies are the same. Equally strange that we should now be moving towards fee-based remuneration that encourages the perception of what we do as being a commodity, to be purchased by the hour, frequently to the lowest bidder.
>
> (Bartle Bogle Hegarty, 1996: 9)

It was against both these models of remuneration that BBH proposed a new alternative. It called this the 'salary concept'. This is how BBH described it:

> Our approach is simple. View the agency as a person. The clients who appoint BBH want the agency to become part of the team and to work in a spirit of real partnership. . . . Salary is not just a semantic re-expression of fees. It represents a different attitude to the issue. If an agency is to become part of the team and operate as a strategic partner, it cannot do so simply via the production and placement of the advertising. It must be able to contribute on a broader front, to take initiatives outside the specific sphere of advertising development. . . . We are not seeking to pad out our income. We simply seek a method of remuneration that reflects the scale of our input, the quality of our output and allows us to deliver in breadth to the best of

our ability. The fact that one agency may cost more or less than another does not, of itself, make a statement about which offers better value.

(Bartle Bogle Hegarty, 1996: 10)

At work in these pronouncements is the delineation of a distinctive cultural vision of the modern advertising agency and of its relationship with its clients, one in which the financial agreements struck with clients carried considerable symbolic importance. Getting them right represented a way of institutionalizing a particular kind of service relationship and of securing a higher status identity for the agency. This is one which the agency described as being the co-custodian of brands and which led – as in the case of its long-term client Levi-Strauss – to a place on the board of the client company as a trusted business partner.

conclusion   BBH's pursuit of new forms of remuneration and its associated moves to re-invent its identity as an advertising agency in changing times was not unique. Nor was its initiative the only one embarked upon by agencies in response to the challenges facing them. The example of BBH, however, dramatizes particularly clearly the way that the economic relations which structured agency/client relationships have conditions of existence which are not purely or narrowly economic. These economic relations are articulated through cultural practices associated with the delimiting and conceptualization of the service relationship and the identity of the agency as a particular kind of service provider. As we have seen with BBH, this has centrally involved agencies seeking to redefine their identities in order to defend their status as the pre-eminent suppliers of advertising and marketing services. Embroiled in this process of re-imagining the agency have been the forms of financial compensation which agencies receive from clients. Competing models of remuneration were seen to carry powerful meanings about the nature of the client/agency relationship and so rethinking remuneration has itself been integral to the broader process of defining the ad agency.

Driving this whole process were the dislocatory effects of various (largely) external pressures upon the established business practices of advertising. The routinized relationship with clients and the more or less fixed identity of each partner in the relationship which flowed from these stable commercial relations was what was precisely unsettled by the challenges to the business of advertising. And what had looked like an autonomous set of economic relations constituting the market for advertising services and the commercial relations entered into by agencies and their clients were revealed to contain sedimented assumptions about the service relationship and the identity of agencies. Defending their status in these changed circumstances then required, as we have seen, further cultural work to establish new favourable commercial relations with clients.

Significantly, the contemporary debates about remuneration and the status of agencies as service providers which I have charted has a noticeable historical parallel. During the 1950s and early 1960s, the Institute of Practitioners in Advertising (IPA), the corporate body of advertising agencies in Britain, also initiated a debate about commission-based forms of payments (Nixon, 2000). This was very much subordinated at the time, however, to a concern with the nomenclature of those individuals who practised advertising and what this said about their status and relationship with clients. Central to these earlier debates was a concern to eradicate the notion of the advertising agent – with its nineteenth-century association with Grub Street – and to replace it with the idea of practitioner. This formed part of a professionalizing project led by the IPA which it saw as the key way of securing the authority of advertising agencies as trusted experts and the exclusive suppliers of advertising services. Significantly, this project had only limited success and it is precisely the instability around the status of agencies which it left unresolved which was opened up again in the contemporary developments and debates. What this historical parallel also suggests, however, when read alongside the contemporary developments, is that the economic relations between clients and agencies are necessarily 'hydrid', always already 'cultural' and 'economic' in their composition. The implications for cultural analysis of this insight are important, however. They draw attention to the key role played by cultural representation within the domain of business and economic endeavour and alert us to processes – the imagining of business forms and identities – every bit as creative as the processes of cultural production which have typically caught the attention of cultural critics. The challenge for future work in cultural studies is to be involved in concrete studies of the relationship between the incompletely formed fields of culture and economics. As Don Slater argues in Chapter 3 of this book, it is time to take economic practices back from the economists.

notes

I am grateful to Martin Smith, Nick Kendall, John Bartle and John Hegarty at BBH for their generosity in putting time aside to see me, and to Kay Scorah for her invaluable help.

1. Advertising employment fell to a 30-year low of 11,600 in 1993. This was down from a peak of 15,400 in 1989 at the height of the sector's boom in the late 1980s (*Campaign*, 29 January 1993, p. 1; 13 January 1995, p. 1; 19 January 1996, p. 7). The sector begin to recover in 1995, reaching a level of 12,300 people.

2. The Institute of Practitioners in Advertising defines a large agency as one with a gross income of £12 million or more; a medium sized agency as one with a gross income between £2.25 and £12 million; and a small agency as one with gross income of less than £2.25m. In the *IPA Agency Census 1998*, there were 20 large, 44 medium and 142 small member agencies in the UK (IPA, 1999).

3. The 'Andrex' dog was a Labrador puppy which featured in the 'Andrex' television commercials and was the distinctive face of the brand. It was used to signify the softness of Andrex's toilet tissue.

4. The full-service advertising agency was a development and refinement of the service advertising agency which typically emerged in Britain during the interwar years. 'Full-service' referred to an agency which produced the adverts, researched them and bought the media space in which they were placed. During the 1990s, many full-service agencies separated off their media-buying functions into affiliated companies known as media dependants. These businesses retained financial ties with the parent company, but were free to compete for media business from other agencies.

5. Below-the-line advertising was a term used to describe promotional materials like direct mail and point-of-sale materials. Above-the-line referred to established advertising media like television and print.

6. Personal interview, August 1996, London.

7. BBH promoted this move by paying for a transparent polythene cover to be attached to that week's issue of *Campaign*, 16 April 1996, p. 1.

references

Bartle Bogle Hegarty (1996) *Business Practice.*

Callon, M. (ed.) (1998) *The Laws of the Markets.* Oxford: Blackwell.

Daniels, P. (1995) 'The internationalization of advertising services in a changing regulatory environment', *The Service Industries Journal*, 15 (3): 276–94.

du Gay, P. (1996) *Consumption and Identity at Work.* London: Sage.

du Gay, P. (1997) 'Introduction', in P. du Gay (ed.), *Production of Culture/Cultures of Production.* London: Sage.

Hall, S. (1986) 'On postmodernism and articulation: an interview with Stuart Hall', *Journal of Communication Enquiry*, 10 (2): 45–60.

Institute of Practitioners in Advertising (1999) *IPA Agency Census 1998*, April.

Laclau, E. (1990) *New Reflections on the Revolution of Our Time.* London: Verso.

Mattelart, A. (1991) *Advertising International: The Privatisation of Public Space.* London: Routledge.

Miller, P. and Rose, N. (1990) 'Governing economic life', *Economy and Society*, 19 (1): 1–31.

Mort, F. (1996) *Cultures of Consumption: Masculinities and Social Space in Late Twentieth Century Britain.* London: Routledge.

Nixon, S. (1996) *Hard Looks: Masculinities, Spectatorship and Contemporary Consumption.* London: UCL Press.

Nixon, S. (2000) 'In pursuit of the professional ideal: advertising and the construction of commercial expertise in Britain 1953–64', in P. Jackson, M. Lowe, D. Miller and F. Mort (eds), *Commercial Cultures.* London: Berg.

Rawsthorn, A. (1989) 'Falling behind in advertising', *Financial Times*, 17 October 1989, p. 15.

advertising, persuasion and the culture/economy dualism

Liz McFall

The real business of the historian of advertising is more difficult: to trace the development from processes of specific attention and information to an institutionalized system of commercial information and persuasion; to relate this to changes in society and in the economy: and to trace changes in method in the context of changing organizations and intentions.

(Williams, 1980: 170)

Raymond Williams' account of the advertising historian's remit was originally written around 1960. In one neat sentence it almost perfectly describes critical academia's approach to advertising in the interim. The structuring assumption that advertising was once, generally, informative and became, generally, persuasive can be found just about everywhere. From elaborate empirical expositions like Leiss et al.'s (1990) to detailed theoretical explorations like Wernick's (1991) to cursory references in Williamson (1978), Goldman (1992), Fowles (1996) and Falk (1994), the evolution of persuasiveness is axiomatic. Moreover, this evolution, as Williams explains, has, properly, to be related to changes in society and the economy. This is a job which critical theory has done extremely well. Baudrillard (1988), Leiss et al. (1990), Wernick (1991) and Goldman (1992) are amongst those whose accounts of advertising convincingly situate its current form in the needs and priorities of contemporary, epochally designated, consumption-driven economies.

I want to suggest here, however, that all this work has tended to be at the expense of Williams' last point: the need to trace changes in method in the context of changing organizations and intentions. These more modest and lower-level influences on advertising form and method have been much neglected in recent critical work. The many detailed ways in which, for example, mid-nineteenth-century press advertising differs from contemporary television advertising seem to have sprung magically from global economic transitions. This is a genuinely unfortunate consequence. In the banal arrangements which have historically constituted the advertising industry lies an insight into the motivations behind its forms and methods. That is to say, the institutional, technological and organizational forces which comprise the production context at any given moment shape the form advertising takes, and such contextual information is therefore crucial to even a rudimentary assessment of what advertising is about.

For this reason a production-centred focus is useful when considering the persuasiveness of pre-twentieth century advertising. The suggestion I am making is that persuasiveness is a contingent experience. In a context where the field of possibilities in advertising design was entirely different, even apparently mundane typographic effects might have a powerful persuasive intent and impact. Reviewing the field, moreover, gives a sense of the locally exigent nature of advertising product. Far from reflecting or producing global, societal changes in relations between culture and economy, advertising product emerges as the necessary, sometimes accidental, result of the constraints under which it was made.

In this chapter, I aim to do two things. First, I want to highlight a tendency, shared by advertising writers, to situate evidence and assumptions about the increasingly persuasive nature of advertising amongst broader concerns about changing relations between people and objects and between culture and economy. This tendency is rooted in the more general critical preoccupation with designating the epoch through delineating shifts in the culture/economy dynamic. But critical theorists writing in this vein define key entities like 'meaning', 'culture' and 'economy' in very particular ways. These definitions are essential to the epochalist account of advertising but other ways of thinking about these entities exist in the social and human sciences, particularly in anthropology, which can make this account seem far less convincing.

In the second section I will move on from the epistemological basis of critique to consider how an historical, empirical approach might shed light on the business of advertising. In this section I want to begin to explore the ways in which a lower-level analysis of the institutional, technological and organizational context provides a different sort of explanation of the appearance of advertising. By looking more closely at the production context of some pre-twentieth-century advertisements I mean to try to reconstruct a sense of how the use of typography in advertising was calculated, and experienced, as a powerful persuasive strategy.

In both sections the object is to show that epochalist explanations of advertising, despite their elegance and cogency, risk occluding the precise range of technical, organizational and institutional forces which led to the production of advertisements along particular lines at given historical moments.

persuasive advertising and the cultural economy

Critical theory has attributed to advertising a very particular historical role in the transformation of society. Advertising as an institution is understood to be structurally positioned between the domains of cultural and economic life. This mediative position grants it a unique capacity to intervene in both spheres of activity. In this vein, the most influential, even canonical, works in the sociological and cultural study of advertising locate its particular contemporary significance in this strategic situation between the fields of economic and cultural activity.

This is true despite the various directions taken by critique since Raymond Williams wrote his essay. From the semiotics of Barthes (1977), Leymore (1975), Williamson (1978) and Goldman (1992), the commodity fetishism of Haug (1986) and Jhally (1987), to the treatments by authors like Leiss et al. (1990), Wernick (1991) and Fowles (1996), one area of common interest has persisted: that is, a preoccupation with advertising's unique potential to transform society through its disruption and transgression of relations between the economic and the cultural spheres. Moreover, this potential has to be understood as of special consequence at the current historical moment. This special consequence arises from a conviction that contemporary advertising not only looks different from its historical predecessors but in addition it plays a fundamentally different economic and cultural role. At the most rudimentary level this conviction surfaces in the widespread belief that where contemporary advertising is persuasive, subtle, symbolic and emotional, pre-twentieth-century versions were informative, overt, literal and pragmatic. This change in form is widely understood to be symptomatic of a shift in advertising's role. Where previously it had acted as a system of commercial information, by the twentieth century it became an essential cultural strategy for the economic management of demand in Western societies.

In this respect, a diverse range of treatises on advertising share an 'epochalist' emphasis. This epochalism emerges in the desire to capture what is distinctive about advertising 'now' and how this articulates with other features understood as characteristic of specific 'epochs'. These loosely periodized epochs act to classify particular historical phases in terms of what Osborne has called 'overarching societal designations' (1998: 17). In this sense the spirit of the age, and advertising's constitutive role in it, is to be encapsulated in terms like post-industrial society, postmodern society, commodity capitalism or consumer culture.

Critical representations of advertising's transformative role are generally articulated around the effects that advertising is supposed to have upon meaning and the resultant impact on the domains of culture and economy. In Baudrillard's (1988) influential account, for example, the basis of society has shifted from the social to the cultural. Stable social norms and practices have disintegrated, leaving space for advertising to capture pre-existing meaning for commercial promotion. This is the society of the commodity sign, where the capacity of advertising to strip objects of their original meanings and install new ones has far-reaching consequences. This notion is also developed by Lash and Urry, for whom the mobility and velocity of objects in contemporary society have 'emptied' them of content, so that objects are better understood as sign values than as material items (1994: 4). Here, the long process of modernization has progressively depleted the meaning of objects, subjects and social relationships. Featherstone encapsulates this theoeretical position in the following:

> [C]onsumer culture through advertising, the media and techniques of display of goods, is able to destabilize the original notion of use or meaning of goods and attach to them new images and signs which can summon up a whole range of associated feelings and desires. The overproduction of signs and loss of referents . . . is therefore an immanent tendency within consumer culture. Hence within consumer culture the tendency is to push culture towards the centre of social life. . . .
>
> (1991: 114)

In Wernick's 1991 analysis the new system of advertising, or, in his terms, 'promotion', enables it to transform both objects and human subjectivity. This function logically extends beyond the level of objects and subjects to the level of culture and economy, such that the relation between the two is fundamentally altered. In this vein Wernick concludes that

> the expanded role of promotion, indeed of the circulation process as a whole, has led to a mutation in the relation between economic 'base' and cultural 'superstructure' such that the latter has become absorbed into the former – as the zone of circulation and exchange – while the former – as the zone of production – has itself become a major cultural apparatus.
>
> (1991: 19)

This is not a modest claim. What Wernick is arguing is that contemporary society is unique in producing a structural mutation in the relationship between culture and economy. In specific relation to advertising, he exemplifies the more general critical mood of the late eighties and early nineties in its preoccupation with delineating periodized shifts in the culture/economy dynamic.

There are two issues worth exploring further here: one refers to the notion of meaning inferred by this type of analysis; and the other to the apparent uniqueness of contemporary society in producing these types of effects on culture and economy.

Anxiety over loss of meaning has a pronounced hold on critical thought. Verbs like 'abducted', 'dissolved', 'captured', 'corrupted', 'emptied' and 'depleted' are summoned up to describe the effect that contemporary society, especially through advertising, has upon meaning. For meaning to be this vulnerable to the processes of consumer culture, however, it has to be understood as an otherwise relatively stable, existential category. It is as if meaning inheres in some kind of tidy cultural taxonomy where the proper relationships between meanings and objects are classified. This taxonomic or semantic approach to meaning, however, is very limiting. Systems of classification which group, record and describe the functions of objects may be a traceable, inherent feature of most cultures but such systems are inscribed in patterns of use which are intrinsically subject to change. As anthropologists like Appadurai (1986) and Sahlins (1976) have demonstrated, the meaning of objects derives from their uses, their forms and their patterns of circulation. Meaning, then, might be more accurately conceptualized as at once a semantic and pragmatic category. In Laclau and Mouffe's Wittgensteinian-inspired formulation (1990: 101–2), use cannot be easily separated from meaning precisely because use is itself a major factor in the determination of meaning.

When meaning is understood as based both in semantics *and* pragmatics, a sense of its fluidity and contingency begins to emerge. If meaning is bound up with the context of use it must, of necessity, be subject to change. This contingent dimension of meaning sits uneasily with the anxiety over its commercial devaluation. This anxiety involves an uncomfortable investment in a conception of meaning as at once a stable, existential category located *outside* of promotional culture and simultaneously a changing, fluid and vulnerable category manipulated *within* promotional discourse.

What becomes clear, however, is that it is not really change in meanings *per se* which is objected to; rather it is the origin of such change in a particular mode of economic organization. At base here is a concern that in contemporary industrialized economies, formerly autonomous cultural systems have given way to advertising and other forms of promotion, as the instruments of the economic system, to determine meaning and ultimately culture.

The problem with this argument is that it involves a normative understanding of culture and economy as separate and delineated spheres. And in this conception, moreover, we encounter further problems. The separation of culture from economy, it can be argued, is a convenient, but artificial, analytical abstraction. For example, for Sahlins (1976), material or economic forces cannot be understood to determine culture because the two are structurally interdependent. As he notes:

> The very form of social existence of material force is determined by its integration in the cultural system. The force may then be significant – but significance, precisely, is a symbolic quality. . . . Culture is organized in the final analysis by the material nature of things and cannot in its own conceptual or sociological differentiations transcend the reality structure manifested in production.
>
> (1976: 206–7)

What Sahlins highlights here are the conceptual difficulties inherent in the theoretical opposition of culture to the economy. This opposition for authors like Morris (1988) works only at the most reductive and vestigial level of conceptualizing 'the mode of production'. Anthropologists like Sahlins (1976), Appadurai (1986) and Miller (1997) have long insisted that in practice the relations between culture and economy are much more deeply intermeshed. Economic practices are culturally defined whilst cultural meanings are shared and disseminated through economic activities in any recorded society. If this inextricability at the level of practice is accepted as characteristic of cultures and economies across time and space, the theoretical account of advertising's mediative and transformative role seems increasingly problematic. How can the particular form of contemporary society be understood to blur or mutate a relation between spheres of activity which can only ever be separated as an analytical convenience?

The characterization of culture and economy as separate and opposed spheres, Turner suggests, artificially reduces and flattens our understanding of culture: 'As long as we talk of the relationship between culture "and" politics, culture "and" economics, between a realm of culture which pertains to human inwardness and a social realm which does not, we will miss the point completely. "Culture" *is not a sphere at all*' (1992: 43). What Turner is drawing attention to is Weber's much less restrictive definition of culture, which, rather than opposing culture to other 'spheres' of existence, whether 'economic', 'natural' or 'political', sees it as inherent in *all* areas of human endeavour. This encompassing view defines culture as referring to all the meaningful activities and practices which constitute a given society.[1] Where this usage is adopted, the analytical separation of culture and economy becomes increasingly problematic. In deploying a broader definition of culture, advertising, rather than acting as the instrument of capital to 'devalue' authentic culture, emerges as a practice which is neither cultural nor economic in essence. Rather, advertising is a constituent practice, consisting inescapably of both cultural and economic elements.

These issues all revolve around the theoretical constructs upon which the social and cultural critique of advertising has relied. I have argued that the epochalist tendency in critical accounts of advertising is underpinned by a very specific understanding of the nature of key entities like meaning, culture and economy. Meaning has to be understood as essentially stable, and culture and economy have to be understood as essentially separate, for these critical accounts to be wholly persuasive. My argument here is that an informed grasp of advertising cannot be derived from an overarching description of the epoch. It is not that large-scale processes of industrial and social change are unimportant or insignificant to the story of advertising. Rather, they provide a necessary explanation of the factors underlying changes in the form and content of advertising. But this explanation in itself is not sufficient to capture the contributions played by a range of institutional, technological and organizational arrangements in the final appearance of advertising. A closer look at the specific historical context of production of a small sample of advertisements may begin to make this clearer, and this will be the focus of the final section.

pre-twentieth-century advertising: typographical effects and persuasive strategies In this section I want to focus explicitly on the effects of the production context on the final appearance of advertising. There are pressing reasons for doing this. As I suggested above, the substantial differences in appearance between modern ads and their historical predecessors are often accepted as immediate evidence of the simpler and more restricted functions of early advertising. Early advertising is almost universally depicted as quaint and simple announcement distinct from the sophisticated persuasion of more recent versions. This increasing sophistication is often related to a broader concern with contemporary patterns of consumption as a corruption of earlier more pragmatic, utility-based patterns. Such concerns are usually based on some form of analyses[2] of the changing nature and content of advertising images over a given period. The question is whether advertisements, *by themselves*, can really support these types of argument. With sufficient effort, historical advertisements could be selected to lend support to a wide range of theses concerning their changing nature. The argument being put forward here is that such decontextualized interpretations tell us little about how specific advertisements operated or were understood at the time of their production. The *precise* significance, meaning and persuasive or other intent of early advertisements is probably lost to posterity, but a glimpse at these features may still be gained through considering the specific relations which existed with their fields of production. In the remainder of the chapter I will try to show how the final appearance owes a great deal more to the production system and operational contingencies than to the characteristics of the epoch.

One of the more curious things which emerges from a history of advertising is the extent to which the differences between the advertisements of the past and those of the present have preoccupied writers over the years. Regardless of the historical period being described, writers tend to understand the advertising of their own period as a 'zenith' (Presbrey, 1929: 259), far removed from any earlier attempts. It is this sentiment which underlies Johnson's often repeated claim that the advertising of his day was so near perfection that it was difficult to see how it could be improved. Figure 8.1 shows one of the many advertisements produced by the proprietors of the 'Anodyne Necklace', which Johnson cites as particularly impressive.]

Considering this advertisement in isolation may do little to challenge the immediate implausibility of Johnson's claim. It might seem to do the opposite. But it is very easy to make sweeping historical comparisons on the basis of evidence that we lack the contextual information to assess fully. The apparent simplicity and naivety of early advertising may be more

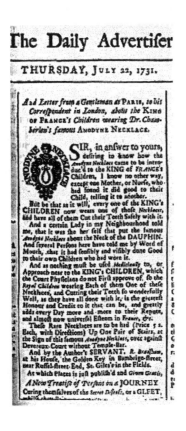

Figure 8.1

Anodyne

Necklace

advertisement,

1731

a function of our profound disengagement from the contexts in which they were produced and received than evidence of the different nature and role of advertising in earlier societies.

To make this point clearer I want to look at the context and uses of typography as a persuasive strategy in some pre-twentieth-century advertisements. There are particular reasons for considering this aspect. Display, layout and type are the most basic and fundamental elements of printed advertisements. As such their role as a particular method of appeal is often overlooked, especially by critics speaking from a platform where the manipulation of sound- and image-based media provides for a much more spectacular range of effects. Nevertheless the existence of a variety of different print effects in advertisements produced over the years, together with published comment on their impact, stands as testimony to their role as primary persuasive strategies.

Even the earliest surviving press advertisements deployed certain type effects to call attention to themselves. The most common of these was probably the extension of the first letter over two lines of type (a drop capital) and the use of capital letters for the remainder of the first word. This technique was used in some of the earliest news sheets produced in the 1670s and remained popular throughout the eighteenth and nineteenth centuries. A range of other techniques, including the use of NB, asterisks, pointing hands, as well as some small woodcut illustrations, were also widely deployed to mark the advertisement.

These effects may seem too crude to be considered persuasive strategies. But this is belied by Addison's (1710) description of such devices:

> The great art in writing advertisements, is the finding out a proper method to catch the reader's eye; . . . Asterisks and Hands were formerly of great Use for this Purpose. Of late Years the *NB* has been much in Fashion, as also little Cuts and Figures, . . . I must not here omit the blind *Italian* Character, which being scarce legible, always fixes and detains the Eye, and gives the curious Reader something like the Satisfaction of prying into a secret.

Addison's characterization of italic type, 'the blind Italian', gives some indication of the way mundane type effects were experienced when they were still a relative novelty.

The significance of type effects to advertisers as primary persuasive strategies is well illustrated by what happened to press advertising display in the nineteenth century. As numerous histories will attest, throughout the eighteenth century a variety of display techniques and small illustrations were fairly common features in advertisements (Elliot, 1962; Fleming, 1976; Sampson, 1874). By the nineteenth century, however, the situation in press advertising had altered considerably. Presbrey (1929) describes how, in the United States, illustrations had almost entirely disappeared by 1850 and a rule requiring uniformity in typography effectively prevented display advertising in numerous newspapers. This rule was known as the 'agate only', and whilst it was only ever an informal restriction, the majority of popular papers in the nineteenth century banned large type and allowed only classified agate type with the drop capital in the style of the earliest press advertisements. In the UK, newspapers enforced similar restrictions on type size and format, confined advertisements within single-column rules and generally refused illustrations.

There were a variety of reasons for this. The historian, Presbrey (1929), describes technical difficulties in reproduction and a newspaper culture with a preference for many small, over few large, advertisements fuelled by the belief that numerous, varied advertisements attracted readers. Further, it was considered unfair competition for any advertiser to have a display advantage over others. Any advertising edge should, it was felt, come from copy, not display. These, however, were not the only factors prompting the tight, regulative environment.

Historically, relations between newspapers and advertisers have tended to be difficult and ambivalent. From the earliest years some newspaper publishers regarded advertising as vulgar, dishonest and of dubious value. As newspaper publishing itself became more established and respectable in the nineteenth century, this attitude may well have become more entrenched in some quarters. John and Leigh Hunt's *Examiner*, for instance, refused advertisements in the early nineteenth century on the basis that trade announcements would lower the dignity of the paper (Sala in Sells, 1891). A compositor writing in 1863 is exemplary of the attitude taken to display advertising:

> The rapacity of advertising respects nothing, and the virtue of newspaper proprietors will not be proof against the assaults waged upon it. Already spasmodic typography has appeared in country papers. . . . It is very sad and I would recommend any old compositor who has saved a little money, to retire from his profession.
>
> (Quoted in Presbrey, 1929: 93)

In addition, the stamp duty, which in Britain was levied on every printed sheet of paper until 1855, effectively limited papers to a single sheet folded once. This placed considerable pressure on space and forced newspapers to adopt small type sizes and increase the number of columns per page (Nevett, 1982).

Not all advertisers accepted this regulative environment passively. Figure 8.2 shows examples of the stunts some businesses pulled to evade the restriction. Prior to this, British auctioneers and book publishers in Britain had, since the 1800s, employed repetition as a strategy to gain attention. These advertisers adopted the practice of saving up advertisements so a long eye-catching string could be placed rather than placing fewer advertisements more regularly (Presbrey, 1929). Commonly, a single capped phrase with

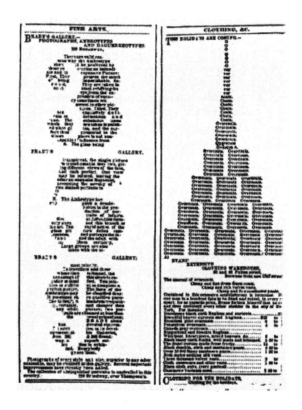

Figure 8.2
Evading the agate-only restriction on press display advertising, 1856

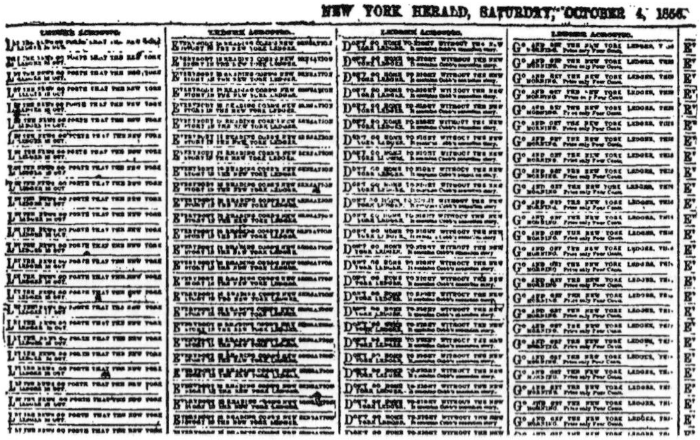

Figure 8.3
Bonner's iteration copy advertisement in the *New York Herald*, 1856

drop capital would be repeated several times down a column, giving the entire column a distinctive appearance from the miscellaneous small ads. This method was also considered to boost prestige by giving an exaggerated impression of the extent of the advertiser's business. Robert Bonner, the publisher of the literary periodical, the *New York Ledger*, developed this technique further in his attempts to promote his paper (Presbrey, 1929). Bonner had attempted to place display advertising in the *New York Herald* but had been refused space. In response he placed 93 identical advertisements in the paper which filled a column (Figure 8.3). He then began placing advertisements using iteration and acrostics which ran across columns. The use of iteration-style copy became widespread at this time and this emphasis on repetition, according to some practitioners, was a direct factor in the later adoption of the advertising slogan.

The relaxation of these restrictions on press advertising display was a slow process. By the turn of the twentieth century newspapers in the UK had begun to admit bold type and allow advertisements to run across more than one column. Display advertising and illustrations were becoming more common but were still only reluctantly admitted by many newspapers. Figure 8.4 shows a 1900 advertisement which, whilst capitalizing on this relaxed environment, sticks closely to the established technique of repetition. The interesting thing about this advertisement is that it demonstrates the role of pre-existing peer practices in producing advertising. By the time this was placed in the *Daily Telegraph*, the regulative environment had relaxed, making the use of agate type repetition as an 'attention-getting-strategy' somewhat redundant. The technique, however, was so widely accepted and understood that it remained a standard practice long after alternative strategies were possible. In this respect, past practices can be seen to pattern future practices. This tendency is made more sensible by the industry practice, typical in agencies like Sells in the UK and J. Walter Thompson and N.W. Ayer in the US, even in the 1890s, of keeping scrapbooks and guardbooks recording both internal and competitors' campaigns. This archive was not for posterity but would be meticulously studied as source material for future campaigns.

The variety of ways in which typography has been used as a persuasive strategy emerge even from this brief review as being formed by a range of concrete, material circumstances prevailing in the field of production. The regulative environment imposed by the government in the form of the stamp and advertisement duties, paper shortages, the technical challenge of reproduction, the detailed restrictions imposed by the press and the weight of example provided by previous advertising practices all shaped the uses to which typography was put. Further, the use of typography did not steadily evolve in sophistication throughout the nineteenth century. Rather, it followed a more convoluted path. In the US the display stunts pulled by

Figure 8.4

Advertisement

combining

repetition and

illustration,

1900

Bonner and his contemporaries, coupled with a more enterprising newspaper culture, resulted in the lifting of display type restrictions in most papers by the end of the 1860s. In the UK, however, the more conservative attitudes of leading newspapers, particularly the *Times*, meant that display restrictions persisted in some parts of the broadsheet press until well into the twentieth century. It was within this historical context that H.G. Wells, in *Tono-Bungay*, his fictional account of the marketing of a proprietary medicine, described the impact of advertising typography:

> That alluring, button-holing, let-me-just-tell-you-quite-soberly-something-you-ought-to-know style of newspaper advertisement, with every now and then a convulsive jump of some attractive phrase into capitals, was then almost a novelty. 'Many people who are MODERATELY well think they are QUITE well,' was one of his early efforts.
>
> (1923 [1909]: 132)

Despite being made two centuries later, Wells' comments are reminiscent of Addison's on the effectiveness of italic type. These type formats may seem quite primitive but their impact is shaped by the media environment in which they appear. What this serves to illustrate is the importance of contextual factors in the style and content of the persuasive appeal which advertisements make. Over a two-hundred-year period a range of display, layout and type effects have been utilized but the dominance of particular styles at particular moments cannot be understood as symptomatic of the best that was currently known or possible. As Treasure remarks of advertising history: 'Conflicting trends and sub-trends emerge and disappear, ideas are expressed which find fulfillment many years later . . .' (1977: 19).

The purpose of this section of the chapter has been to demonstrate that the emergence of advertisement styles and trends is inextricably bound up with the production context. This production context is not simply a matter of what it was technologically, or even epistemologically, possible to do but should also be understood to embrace the cultural, economic and political dimensions of production. These dimensions have played a formative role in the final appearance of advertising throughout history. In this respect production is best understood as a cultural economy in the sense described by du Gay (1997), where the economic practices of advertising production are intrinsically caught up with the cultural understanding of the role, functions and nature of advertisements.

concluding comments   The tendency in recent critical work to attribute to advertising a central, mediative role in the transformation of the cultural and economic basis of contemporary industrialized societies raises problematic issues both theoretically and empirically. Theoretically, this work is generally grounded in an 'epochalist' impulse to situate particular cultural phenomena in an ongoing narrative of historical, industrial transformation. Whilst large-scale processes of industrialization have undoubtedly impacted on the changing forms and practices of advertising, this in itself tells us little about the specific, local forces which have shaped the nature of advertising in any given historical period. Moreover, the cogency of critical work in this vein depends upon the acceptance of very specific, abstracted definitions of key entities like meaning, culture and economy. For these critical accounts to be convincing, meaning has to be understood as either a stable category or at least a category negotiated in a cultural sphere which is entirely separate from the commercial sphere of economic practice. Meaning, however, might be better understood as a contingent category constructed in instances of use and practice where the cultural and economic dimensions are not easily disentangled.

Empirically, critical assertions of this type have often been derived from evidence in the form of historical advertisements which appear to show a gradual shift from simple, informational announcements to symbolic, emotional and persuasive advertising appeals. But, I have argued, decontextualized advertisements are a bit too amenable to this type of assertion. In the absence of any material, contextual information, advertisements can be made to mean just about anything. For this reason I have attempted to foreground the historical context of production to reconstruct a more detailed sense of how it was intended and experienced contemporaneously. In this respect, economic factors, institutional regulations and organizational arrangements emerge as having had a significant impact on the final appearance of advertising. These lower-level operational rules, procedures and practices are more directly implicated in the type of advertising strategy adopted than are more global epistemologies around the production of demand. Such factors are material to, yet are seldom taken into consideration when assessing, the persuasive intent of any given advertisement.

Osborne (1998: 19) has argued that epochal theories have a tendency to over-dramatize and reduce complex changes to a few core elements. This over-dramatization renders crucial contextual details insignificant, unremarkable and ultimately invisible. Much advertising theory renders the development of the industry in terms of fundamental changes in the mode of production, from agrarian to industrial to post-industrial economies or from producer to consumer societies. As significant as these transformations may be, they cannot reveal the specificity of factors which underlie all the swings and sweeps in advertising methods and styles and products featured. What must be guarded against is the desire to observe in these changes both the direct traces of grand epochal shifts and a systematic evolution in sophistication. Rather than a sensible and legible journey through distinct production epochs, an historicized account of practice provides us with an array of contradictions: continuities alongside changes; the appearance, disappearance and re-emergence of conflicting trends; and subtle, incremental and partial examples of changes in practice. Advertising technique over the last three centuries has regressed as well as progressed at particular moments, and an understanding of why this is the case is best achieved through specific reference to the political, economic and institutional context of production.

Despite its obvious attractions, historical description, as Cousins (1988) has ably demonstrated, cannot provide the human sciences with neat and incontrovertible solutions to theoretical problems. Historical investigation has definite conditions and definite consequences and the 'facts' it uncovers should not be expected to reflect exhaustively everything which is sayable about an event (Cousins, 1988). Nevertheless, this does not nullify the validity of the contingent historical 'truths' which an historical investigation of a field of production can yield. Rather it urges caution in regarding the results of historical investigation as privileged above the results of any other method. With this proviso in mind, the contention here is that a contextualized historical investigation of practice can help to enrich and revise the theoretical conception of advertising's role produced through other methods of analyses.

notes

1. This type of usage is increasingly common in many branches of contemporary sociology and cultural studies. See, for example, Hall (1997) for a fuller discussion of competing usages of the term 'culture'.
2. The survey conducted by Leiss et al. (1990) referred to above provides an unusually systematic example.

references

Published sources

1855: 'Advertisements' Art Vii.–1. *Quarterly Review*. Unauthored article.

Addison, J. (1710) *The Tatler*, 224, 14 September.

Appadurai, A. (1986) *The Social Life of Things*. Cambridge: Cambridge University Press.

Barthes, R. (1977) *Image – Music – Text*. London: Fontana.

Baudrillard, J. (1988) 'Consumer society', in M. Poster (ed.), *Selected Writings*. Cambridge: Polity.

Bourdieu, P. (1993) *Sociology in Question*. London: Sage.

Cousins, M. (1988) 'The practice of historical investigation', in D. Attridge (ed.), *Poststructuralism and Questions of History*. Cambridge: Cambridge University Press.

Davidson, M. (1992) *The Consumerist Manifesto*. London: Routledge.

du Gay, P. (1997) 'Introduction', in P. du Gay (ed.), *Production of Culture/Cultures of Production*. London: Sage.

du Gay, P. (1999) 'Cultural economy: an introduction', seminar given at Goldsmiths College, University of London.

Dyer, G. (1982) *Advertising as Communication*. London: Routledge.

Elliot, B. (1962) *A History of English Advertising*. London: Business Publications Limited.

Ewen, S. (1976) *Captains of Consciousness: Advertising and the Social Roots of Consumer Culture*. New York: McGraw-Hill.

Falk, P. (1994) *The Consuming Body*. London: Sage.

Featherstone, M. (1991) *Consumer Culture and Postmodernism*. London: Sage.

Fleming, T. (1976) 'How it was in advertising: 1776–1976', *Advertising Age*, 19 April, pp. 27–35.

Fowles, J. (1996) *Advertising and Popular Culture*. London: Sage.

Goffman, E. (1979) *Gender Advertisements*. London: Macmillan.

Goldman, R. (1992) *Reading Ads Socially*. London: Routledge.

Hall, S. (1997) 'The work of representation', in S. Hall (ed.), *Representation: Cultural Representations and Signifying Practices*. London: Sage.

Harvey, D. (1989) *The Condition of Postmodernity*. Oxford: Blackwell.

Haug, W. (1986) *Critique of Commodity Aesthetics*. Cambridge: Polity.

Hower, R. (1939) *The History of an Advertising Agency*. New York: Arno.

Jameson, F. (1991) *Postmodernism, or, the Cultural Logic of Late Capitalism*. London: Verso.

Jhally, S. (1987) *The Codes of Advertising: Fetishism and the Political Economy of Meaning in Consumer Society*. London: Routledge.

Laclau, E. and Mouffe, C. (1990) 'Post-Marxism without apologies', in E. Laclau, *New Reflections on the Revolution of Our Time*. London: Verso.

Lash, S. and Urry, J. (1994) *Economies of Signs and Space*. London: Sage.

Lears, F.J. (1994) *Fables of Abundance*. New York: Basic Books.

Leiss, W., Kline, S. and Jhally, S. (1990) *Social Communication in Advertising: Persons, Products and Images of Well-Being*. London: Routledge.

Leymore, Varda Langholz (1975) *Hidden Myth: Structure and Symbolism in Advertising*. London: Heinemann.

McKendrick, N, Brauer, J. and Plumb, J.H. (1982) *The Birth of a Consumer Society*. London: Hutchinson.

Miller, D. (ed.) (1995) *Acknowledging Consumption*. London: Routledge.

Miller, D. (1997) *Capitalism: An Ethnographic Approach*. London: Berg.

Morris, M. (1988) 'Banality in cultural studies', *Block*, 14: 15–26.

Myers, G. (1998) *Ad Worlds*. London: Arnold.

Nevett, T. (1977) 'London's early advertising agents', *Journal of Advertising History* 1 (December): 15–18.

Nixon, S. (1996) *Hard Looks: Masculinities, Spectatorship and Contemporary Consumption*. London: UCL Press.

Osborne, T. (1998) *Aspects of Enlightenment*. London: UCL Press.

Pope, D. (1983) *The Making of Modern Advertising*. New York: Basic Books.

Presbrey, F. (1929) *The History and Development of Advertising*. New York: Greenwood.

Sahlins, M. (1976) *Culture and Practical Reason*. Chicago: University of Chicago Press.

Sampson, H. (1874) *History of Advertising*. London: Chatto & Windus.

Turner, C. (1992) *Modernity and Politics in the Work of Max Weber*. London: Routledge.

Turner, E.S. (1952) *The Shocking History of Advertising*. London: Michael Joseph.

Wells, H.G. (1923) [1909] *Tono-Bungay*. London: Collins.

Wernick, A. (1991) *Promotional Culture: Advertising, Ideology and Symbolic Expression*. London: Sage.

Williams, R. (1980) 'Advertising: the magic system', in *Problems in Materialism and Culture*. London: Verso.

Williamson, J. (1978) *Decoding Advertisements*. London: Marion Boyars.

Unpublished sources

R.F. White agency file; History of Advertising Trust Archives, Norwich.

C.E. Raymond memoirs, Officers and Staff Box, J. Walter Thompson Archive, Hartman Center, Duke University.

Sala, George (1891) 'The world's press and what I have known of it', in Sell's Dictionary of the World Press, Sell's Box, History of Advertising Trust Archives, Norwich.

Treasure, J.A.P. (1977) 'A history of British advertising agencies', Edinburgh University Jubilee Lecture, History of Advertising Trust Archive, Norwich.

the unintended political economy

Daniel Miller

introduction: who runs British capitalism, and why?
This chapter is intended to draw attention to a process so basic that it has become something of a cliché in the social sciences, and yet whose implications and consequences are often ignored: that is, the degree to which the political economy that we see around us is the result of the unintended consequence of intentional actions or structural conjunctions. I will suggest that one of the reasons for this relative neglect in recent times is the rise of what has been called 'the cultural turn' and the degree of emphasis upon symbolic systems or systems of meaning. But first I will present some evidence for my contention that the contemporary political economy does indeed remain best characterized as a result of unintended actions and forces. This evidence is presented here in two stages. The first is an argument about who runs British capitalism, and the second an expanded consideration of contemporary historical change based on a summary of an argument about what I will call virtualism, the details of which are published elsewhere (Miller, 1998a). Finally I will turn to the implications of these macro perspectives on historical change for the continued study of agents and their intentions in micro-'scale analysis of particular aspects of the political economy.

My starting points are a couple of recent conversations, one with a senior official in a major management consultancy firm, the other, vicariously, with someone who had recently interviewed a senior figure in the management of pension funds. If we take contemporary British capitalism as a whole and ask 'who runs it?' or 'where is power located?', then two major shifts in recent decades seem evident enough. Around 45 per cent of all the quoted equities in the UK are owned by pension funds and life companies. Given the fragmentation of most of the rest of the ownership of equities, this means that in effect these companies could be said to own most of British capitalism. Taken on a world scale, the *Economist* seems right to note that such institutional investors 'move markets, hold governments to account, sire new companies and dispatch moribund ones' (6 November 1999, p. 129). So, for example, when Britain's Chancellor of the Exchequer wants to lay the blame for what he sees as the low economic growth of the country (which he views as the result of a dearth of investment in small and innovative companies), it is the allocation of funds by pension funds and life insurers that he puts under scrutiny (*Economist*, 20 May 2000, p. 138; see also Clark, 2000; Leyshon and Thrift, 1997: 121).

This change in the balance of power has been gradual. Writing about the US in the seventies, Peter Drucker (1976) described the pension fund control that had taken place, undetected, in the sixties. While prescient about its importance, his concern was mainly with the possibility of a pension fund socialism in that in some sense workers and the elderly seemed to be in control of business. By the time of writing an epilogue to this book in 1995, however, it was evident that the consequences were rather different. Gradually the funds had moved from passive investors to more active players: 'Increasingly, they demand a voice in the companies in which they invest – for instance, a veto over board appointments, executive compensation, and critical corporate charter provisions' (Drucker, 1996: 207). But this control was about boosting share prices, not helping pensioners or workers. As a result the Chief Executive Officers of major companies have increasingly seen their jobs as under the ultimate control of such major shareholding institutions. Since corporations are in effect 'owned' by their shareholders, we have a situation in which it is the managers of pension funds rather than the actual managers of companies who are in a position to determine ultimately the way those companies are run.

There is, however, another candidate for holding the reins of power in contemporary British capitalism. This may be found in the quite astonishing rise of management consultancy firms from a minor aspect of accountancy to probably the major employers of graduates from the university system worldwide. Anderson Consulting (rebranded in 2001 as Accenture), for example, had started as a mere spin-off from accountancy operations in 1989. By 1995 it had an annual income of $4.2 billion, employed 44,000 people and had 152 offices in 47 countries. The scale and speed of this growth could almost be matched by other companies such as McKinsey and Figgie. Individual companies such as AT&T might spend half a billion dollars alone on such consultants. O'Shea and Madigan (1997 – see also surveys by the *Economist* over March 1997), who describe this transformation, have used instructive sources, such as the accounts of court cases where management consultants have been sued, to shed considerable doubt as to what, if anything, firms gain from this vast expenditure on what they call 'dangerous company'.

It seems today that most major decisions by most major companies have to include the involvement of a consultancy firm such as Accenture or McKinsey, and that a great deal of the responsibility, first for decision making and in the last few years also for implementation, now rests with the consultancy firm itself. So if pension funds own the equity, the way management demonstrate to these fundholders that they have carried out their proper responsibilities seems increasingly to depend on evidence that they have called in management consultants to almost do their jobs for them. So here too is a candidate for holding the reins of power within contemporary British capitalism.

The conversations that I report relate, then, to these twin sites of power. The first was a conversation arranged by an anthropological colleague who had herself worked for some years in management consultancy. The woman we were speaking to was a senior figure in one of the largest companies which, as is often the case, had started out as mainly an accountancy firm but was now identified as a full-fledged management consultancy. This individual had over twenty years of service in the firm. The point she reiterated was that the radical changes in circumstance were largely unplanned and their consequences unforeseen. Her own training was in accountancy, which is what she was expected to work in when she joined the firm. But increasingly she found herself being invited in to draw up reports that went well beyond the initial brief of accountancy and involved the larger planning of corporate futures. In effect what started as the auditing of such plans for their financial implications developed gradually into consulting about and then taking over the drawing up of such plans. For her, writing such reports was problematic since this was not something she had originally trained to do, and in effect it meant she was taking over much of the role and responsibility of the indigenous management.

But things did not stop there. Report writing itself does not involve too much responsibility: the consultants could make their case and then exit. It was up to indigenous management to decide whether they followed such proposals. But this became itself a problem. Firms felt they were spending huge sums of money on consultants who had no real responsibility to ensure that these were viable programmes. So increasingly the larger management consultancy firms were asked not only to draw up the proposals but also to implement them, thus taking major responsibility for the outcome of their own suggestions. For example, a firm such as Anderson Consulting, which tended to lay stress on the positive potential of new information systems, became the firm mainly responsible for actually putting such new systems into place. Or if a consultancy firm suggested that a new branch of activity would be lucrative, it became responsible for establishing this additional brief within its client's portfolio.

So if senior executives, such as the one we interviewed, were already feeling a bit out of their depth in writing management reports, they soon appreciated that they had quite considerable challenges to face when they were actually having to manage the consequences of those reports. Of course I am not for a moment trying to suggest that consultancy firms are somehow the passive victims of those they advise. As with most firms, they had always been looking for almost any means possible to expand their business. They saw quite early on that there was money and scale to be gained by consultancy rather than merely accountancy and then in turn by implementation and not just advice. It is precisely this trajectory that has turned them from relatively small and insignificant firms into the commanders of the world economy, where they advise and implement for not only firms, but also governments and transnational institutions.

Merely desiring to expand is, however, clearly not a sufficient explanation for why those responsible for managing firms, and indeed governments, should turn over so much of their responsibilities to such consultants. From the point of view of employees, such as our interviewee, however welcome and rewarding these developments, they are also something of a shock. It was – to say the least – not intuitively obvious to her as an accountant that she would be saddled with such responsibility for the management of contemporary British – or even, today, one might argue, global – capitalism. In general their emoluments have expanded enormously but anecdotes suggest that they have become the vanguard of a new workaholism which does not grant them much in the way of leisure time. Furthermore, as this executive noted, as accountants they had had less training and many fewer qualifications to undertake much of this more extended work than had the people who were calling them in as consultants. This may in part explain why, according to O'Shea and Madigan (1997), their success rates at least during this period of rapid expansion have not on the whole been particularly good.

Before reflecting upon this rather strange turn of events, I would draw attention to the parallel situation with regard to the other seat of power, that is, pension fund management. Here my information is a second-hand conversation, which I intend to follow up in future research, but the logic is the same. Pension funds are, after all, simply the capital accrued by the laudable aim of ensuring that people retiring from their labours have money to live on thereafter. The main other branch of these institutional investors is based on the equally laudable goal of paying insurance claims. Unfortunately they tend to work under a regime which insists that the only criteria allowable to such management is the maximizing of the fund on behalf of those whose capital they represent. Because this is defined so narrowly in terms of the performance of investments, the results can be highly perverse. As Clark's (2000) excellent analysis of these funds demonstrates, this becomes the primary reason why pension funds are hesitant to invest in the infrastructures that are of benefit to actual pensioners, although, with the decline of state investment, it is more important than ever before that they do so. An extreme example of the underlying contradiction was drawn by Davis in his book *City of Quartz* (1990). Davis noted that pension funds were the primary investors in property firms that were making considerable profits by destroying the traditional housing sectors in Los Angeles and replacing them with more profitable forms of commercial building. The result of this was that the pensioners whose money they held were being increasingly stripped of affordable housing. One only has to look at the low rates of return on annuities in the British market to see that the success and profitability of pension funds does not seem to result in major benefits to actual pensioners – pensioner socialism this isn't.

There is, however, another consequence of this increased equity share of institutional investments. Pension funds are managed by trustees, often appointed representatives of the plan's beneficiaries: 'All the evidence from the Anglo-American world is that most trustees begin their term relatively ignorant of investment theory and practice' (Clark, 2000: 272). Clark documents the problems they have knowing which, if any, investment experts to work with in a climate of risk assessment of such complexity that it is hard to know what expertise consists of. This problem is much exacerbated when we turn to the consequence of this new power held by pension funds. Even those trained in maximizing financial returns are almost entirely unprepared for a state in which they have become in effect the controllers of a majority or near majority holding in any given company. Then almost by default they take on the ultimate responsibility for the performance of that company. If that company has any kind of problem or its performance is not entirely satisfactory, then pension fund managers, whose training is largely in terms of finance, may find themselves having to consider the specific workings of the particular firm in question. In short they are suddenly having to think about why a particular retail strategy has not been successful, or whether a merger between an old media and new dot.com company is in the interests of either. So simply by virtue of finding themselves holding the reins of power, they also take on the ultimate responsibility for the management of the firms themselves. This may occur even when the pension funds wish to preserve the illusion that they are merely passive investors and it is not their job to run companies. The conversation I was told about with a particular pension fund manager seemed to echo my own conversation inside the management consultancy firm. Those who had worked in pension funds for a considerable period were finding that their jobs had accrued power and responsibility to such an extent that they could easily find themselves out of their depth at least with regard to their initial training and their own expectations of what their work would or even should entail.

Putting these two conversations together, we come to a rather curious conclusion. The two major powerbrokers in the running of contemporary British capitalism consist of institutions whose officials were neither trained to undertake such powerful roles nor expected or even intended to be placed in such a position. But changes occurred during the two or three decades in which they dutifully performed their work such that they accrued the levers of power that made them increasingly responsible for running British capitalism, sometimes over and above the heads of chief executive officers and their teams of management who were originally supposed and expected to undertake this task. I don't want to exaggerate this movement; obviously much management is done by management. Nevertheless, any reading of the financial press or any perusal of the size of shareholdings or the simple statistics that show the increasing size of management consultancy would indicate that this is anything but fanciful speculation. I believe it is a quite straightforward reading of some of the most evident and incontrovertible changes that have taken place in modern capitalism.

what cultural turn?　　There have been periods within social science studies in which such a conclusion would not have appeared particularly problematic, since most analysis concerned itself with the development of particular structures and the effects of their interaction over time. Furthermore, I suggested a stress upon the unintended consequences of intention is something of a cliché. But changes of various kinds have occurred over this same period which I suspect have made such observations and the obvious conclusions to be drawn from them unpopular and unpalatable, so that this has become a largely disregarded perspective. Much of this relates to what have been called 'the cultural turn' in the social sciences. Recent books such as those by Cook et al. (2000) or Ray and Sayer (1999) clarify the implications of this phrase.

The meaning of the term 'cultural turn' is not at all straightforward. For example, I do not wish to oppose the study of culture *per se* or replace it with an equally problematic concept of 'social relations' in the manner suggested recently by Kuper (1999). There seem to be two main versions of the contemporary 'cultural turn', one of which I embrace and the other I oppose. I do not see any problems arising where authors such as du Gay (1996) note the rise of the study of culture within economic life, such as the norms and values of shop-floor 'culture' or management 'culture'. In working on finance, Clark (2000), Leyshon and Thrift (1997) and McDowell (1997) have demonstrated the absurdity of not treating economic life as a cultural form. There are clear advantages of the new economic geography and sociology over the study of 'technical' economics, precisely because the latter seems to desire to distance itself from issues of cultural contextualization in the search for esoteric abstraction.

Furthermore, the study of culture within such studies is in several respects more sophisticated and encompassing than in previous periods. It seems to include the study of the economic agents themselves, often seen in their broader contexts of, for example, gender relations (McDowell, 1997, 2000), or of personal relationships at work (Leyshon and Thrift, 1997). Increasingly it also includes the materiality of the contexts in which people work and the effect of cultural norms embedded in structures that do not reduce to the intentionality of agents. The rise in reputation of material culture studies and the attraction of actor network theory, both of which give agency to objects as well as subjects (e.g. Gell, 1998; Latour, 1993), combined with the sheer impact of technological developments such as the Internet, have allowed us to develop cultural analysis based on a concept of culture which includes the dialectical relationship between subjects and objects (Miller, 1987).

There is, however, another version of the cultural turn which I find far less compelling. Many of the essays in the two books I have cited – Cook et al. (2000) or Ray and Sayer (1999) – imply a change in the object of analysis rather than the style of analysis. They see a movement away from the emphasis upon political economy in the 1970s and 1980s across the social sciences to a contemporary *rapprochement* with postmodern ideals of self-referential interpretive concerns with identity, difference and the symbolic nature of social and economic life. A concern with culture in some ways replaces that with political economy. Within this version of the cultural turn there exists a wide range of perspectives, but overall there could be said to be an increasing concern with symbolic systems, systems of meaning and the self-reflexive. I am probably most influenced by an anthropological trajectory. Within that discipline the 1970s was dominated by structuralism and Marxism, both of which were seen as conducive to a grand narrative approach and paid scant regard to agency and intentionality. By the 1980s, under the influence of figures such as Bourdieu and Giddens, there arose a complaint that at least situated agency and internationality had been neglected. By the 1990s there was a more full-blooded concern with the task of directly representing the thinking and perspective of informants and writing ethnography in terms of the subject. This included the subjectivity of the anthropologists themselves, leading to an emphasis upon the self-reflexive.

In sociology, cultural studies and more generally across the social and human sciences there arose arguments that critical changes had occurred within the economy itself. Where once the economy was about commodities and capital, now we were moving towards a 'symbolic', a 'knowledge' or an 'information' economy in which the key was the new self-reflexive subjectivity and the manipulation of signs. Where once most studies were directed to topics such as the factory and the firm, now the popular object of study was the advertising industry, and the wide spectrum of 'culture industries' which not surprisingly feature particularly strongly within cultural studies itself. The implication was no longer just that these had been neglected; rather, it was that they were now the heart and core of the modern economy and should take centre-stage. Not only the protagonists of such studies but also their opponents (in particular see the introduction to Ray and Sayer, 1999) tend to a dualist position on economy and culture that in some respects reflects the formalist versus substantivist debates that were prompted by the work of Polanyi in the 1950s (see also the introduction to this volume).

This version of the cultural turn I would strongly oppose. It seems to me to be a sleight of hand through which a shift in academic emphasis is pre-supposed to reflect a shift in the world that these academics are describing, that is, an assertion that the economy itself is more 'cultural' than it was. Do the two transformations I have just described suggest either this cultural turn or its opposite? Neither the shift to institutional equity nor the rise of man-agement consultancy seems to me to reflect any particular ideology. I can't see that these changes make British capitalism a better or clearer example of capitalism whether the model of capitalism used is either that of neo-classical economists or indeed that of Marxism. They don't seem have any particular postmodern aspect to do with the changing nature of symbolic representa-tion. Nor do they suggest any greater power for the media or what might be called the 'culture industries'. Indeed if anything it is remarkable how far such major changes have gone unremarked and unreflected upon. Apart from Peter Miller's (1998) fine work on the rise of accountancy, there has been remarkably little attention paid to either of these vast changes until quite recently. Indeed, if we start from these two case studies considered in this chapter, it seems quite absurd to suggest that we live within some new self-conscious, self-reflexive information economy (e.g. Lash and Urry, 1994; Leadbeater, 1999). Not even a consideration of the information industries themselves appears to lend much support for the idea of a self-reflexive, 'intelligent' new economy. Witness the unedifying spectacle of a colossal bout of crude 'market testing' where e-commerce ventures are launched at great expense by new dot.coms with little idea of their consequences except to see whether they sink or swim. Compared to most aspects of the econo-my, e-commerce seems better characterized as crass and unreflective. Certainly there are powerful marketing discourses today, but advertising and Hollywood were extraordinarily important in the US of half a century ago, and, as Miller and Rose (1997) note, these made as much use as they could of the then current psychological theories about how to create subjects.

On the other hand the economy was just as cultural at the time when most academics saw themselves as Marxist. I will argue below – using the concept of virtualism – that the economy is radically affected by the attempt to make it accord with neo-classical theory. But would this be any less true of the prior attempt to make many national economies accord as closely as possible with the principles espoused in Marxism? It is hard to imagine a more systematic attempt to impose a cultural model upon the global economy. So if anything it was Marxism itself, not the move away from it, that should be called the cultural turn. Nor would I credit the opposite contention, which might argue that rather than becoming more cultural (where this is opposed to instrumental, as, for example, in Ray and Sayer, 1999), instead there are more areas of cultural life, including symbolic systems of taste, that can now be incorporated within a largely instrumentalist and economistic science. Fine (1998) has argued that the present period has seen at least as strong an attempt by economists to colonize the rest of the social sciences under the leadership of Gary Becker through concepts such as social capital. From Fine's perspective, we are actually in the midst of an 'economic turn' in academic fashion. But I see no alternative scenario that would see a 'real' instrumental set of economic forces exerting ever more pressure to express their authority beneath the mere froth of cultural change. I am not too sure what economists mean by the term 'rational', or, for that matter, 'instrumental' and 'functional', but I can hardly think of three terms that seem less appropriate to the description of the two major changes that I have just outlined. What form of rational agency would replace those best trained and equipped to manage British capitalism with two forces neither of which was trained and both of which would privately admit to being sometimes rather ill equipped to take on this task? Have these two changes made British capitalism or the state more efficient? That is certainly not O'Shea and Madigan's (1997) conclusion about the impact of management consultants. Drucker (1996: 203–27) notes that the main effect in the US of pension fund control has been a riot of aggressive mergers and leveraged buy-outs (LBOs) that have largely failed to boost performance (1996: 203–27), while Hutton notes for the UK that equity holders have tended to encourage an extraordinary short-termism when new controllers of companies get about six months to lift share prices, often artificially, instead of being able to engage in long-term planning (1995: 154–65).

So, to conclude this section, while there is no denying the existence of a cultural turn as an approach to the study of economic institutions within social science, there is no reason to assume that this reflects changes in the political economy itself. I assume that the economy, now as before, consists of institutions that, and agents who, can be studied in terms of cultural norms and values and in terms of constraints and structural causes, and that these are inseparable elements of the whole. So 'cultural' here, as in other chapters in this book, does not separate out into aspects of instrumentality as against symbolism, but rather stands for processes in which these are integral and often indistinguishable components of economic life. (See the

Introduction and the chapters by Law, Slater and Heelas). Having established this point for the two case studies considered here, I now want to reconsider them from within a still broader perspective.

virtualism: the unintended consequences of history

In the previous section of this chapter I tried to demonstrate that macro changes do not simply follow from the more micro changes in agents and their intentions. In this section I want to ascend to a still higher plain, one that comes close to the much-derided ambition of 'grand narrative', to suggest that there are congruencies in the development of discourse and its powers that are best understood not so much as the unintended consequences of intentional action, but rather as the unintended consequences of history. The philosophical implications of such a position defeat me – I am quite unsure of whether history without purpose still counts as teleology, a point I return to in the conclusion. The trajectories described here have been characterized in more detail elsewhere (Miller, 1998a) under the term 'virtualism'.

The same two decades that have witnessed a prodigious expansion of management consultancy have in the public sector seen an equally astonishing rise in the size and scale of audits. As Power (1994, 1997) has argued, the effect on institutions such as the higher education sphere within which I work has been demonstrably paradoxical, in that academics may reduce their actual teaching quality in order to spend time demonstrating to managers that their teaching quality has improved. Small managerial auditing units have mushroomed to become amongst the largest components of educational establishments. Much of this has been accomplished in the name of students as consumers of educational services – just as people who used to be patients are now consumers of state health services. It is clear in Power's account of this revolution that time and again actual consumers have been replaced in this process by managers who take the form of 'virtual' consumers, in the sense that they stand in the stead of actual consumers. It is the managerial models of consumption that are used to adjudicate how state services should perform.

As well as fetishizing the consumer, the audit explosion also conforms to the second characteristic of virtualism, which is that it gives power and authority to abstract modelling. Power notes that '[o]ne of the paradoxes of the audit explosion is that it does not correspond to more surveillance and more direct inspection. Instead, audits generally act indirectly upon systems of control' (1994: 19), so the National Audit Office is really the control of control, that is, legitimacy now depends more on being seen to be audited than in the actual outcomes of audit. 'By abstracting from local organisational diversity it has enabled audit to assume the status of an almost irresistible cultural logic' (1994: 20). Instead of making organizations more transparent, audits tend to make them more opaque, adding another layer of control. Strathern (1997) provides an anthropological perspective as participant observer of the audit process. She observes that under the strictures of audit, measures become reduced to targets (1997: 308), research quality is conflated with research departments (1997: 310), descriptions become prescriptions (1997: 312), any sense of contradiction or ambiguity is replaced by canons of clarity and itemization (1997: 315), and quality of teaching becomes reduced to a measure of usage of new information technologies (1997: 318).

These observations about the public sector put my earlier case study of the rise of management consultancy in a new light. While one might want to explain the rise of audit in terms of the politics of the public sector, and the rise of management consultancy in terms of changes in commerce, the two parallel each other in ways that seem to demand some wider account. There are strong similarities between them. One of the effects of management consultancy has been a halt in the previous tendency by a wide range of firms and service providers to try to come closer to understanding the consumers of their goods and services. Instead companies increasingly listen to consultants, who come to 'stand for' the voice of consumers and users. An example is in retail, where, as in many companies, the knowledge of workers and management about their own customers tends to be replaced by abstract consultancy models such as 'category management' (Cook et al., 2000b; du Gay, 1996). The development of category management is suggestive of the way consultants tend to apply fashionable general solutions such as outsourcing and downsizing to a diverse range of more specific business problems. It may also reflect the degree to which consultants tend to 'learn' from their experience in one company they are consulting for and then apply this to the next company (see O'Shea and Madigan, 1997). This might not have mattered so much were it not for the sheer scale of modern management consultancy. This means that increasingly the character we observe in empirical studies of the way contemporary business operates is an outcome of the use of these consultancies across all sectors, such that terms such as 'outsourcing', 'downsizing' and 'category management' become the daily life of ordinary companies.

The rise in parallel of these two forces can be placed in a still broader context when we turn to an institutional form already regarded as virtual by the Frankfurt School in the 1930s, that is, the rise of economics. As predicted by these theorists, the economists' conception of government as efficient managers has increasingly replaced other criteria of good politics. Institutions established at Bretton Woods that were supposed to embody Keynesian criteria and work for the benefit of humankind have evolved to become the World Trade Organization, the International Monetary Fund and the World Bank, institutions commonly blamed for exacerbating the poverty of the developing world and in the first case promulgating a strictly ideological call to free trade at whoever's expense this may be. The 'virtual' nature of these institutions was evident in the case study of Trinidad (Miller, 1997). In many respects the major capitalist institutions, such as oil and grocery companies, that had developed in order to exploit that island had been fought back – though more through nationalism than socialism – and there had followed a degree of taming of the more negative effects of capitalist development, thanks in large measure to the local authority invested in the island by an oil boom. Capitalism in contemporary Trinidad is surprisingly localized, including some powerful local transnationals that were starting to become incorporated within state-based welfare politics. Trinidad was no ideal society, but this was a clear step up from colonialism, let alone from slavery.

Into this situation came a programme of structural adjustment almost identical to that found in many other countries. Structural adjustment comprises a series of procedures and models that were devised by groups of economists working within some of the key institutions that were set up following the epochal meeting at Bretton Woods. These models, fostered by the IMF, the World Bank and their ilk, are purely academic in the sense that they seem to pay no attention whatsoever to local context. These sometimes fitted the interests of capitalist corporations, but surprisingly often they did not. This is because they are not the product of capitalism as an institutional practice of firms, or of regional interests (e.g. the US), as has often been claimed. Rather they are simply idealized and abstract models that are characteristic of the university departments of economics engaged in academic modelling. This rise of academic authority runs parallel to my first two cases in that it seems to represent a largely unintended shift in capitalism that leaves sometimes quite inexperienced theoretical economists in effect running actual governments and the details of dismantling welfare and other programmes.

Once again the same sleight of hand operates. The theoretical argument found most clearly in contemporary neo-liberal economics is that under conditions of pure free trade all goods are made at the lowest possible costs and come to the market at the lowest possible prices for the ultimate benefit of consumers. But there is almost no relationship at all between flesh-and-blood consumers and the consumer who is represented in economic models. Economists' consumers are individuals working on strict rationalist principles based around price and utility and with perfect knowledge of the conditions under which they make their decisions (Fine, 1998). When it comes to the ethnographic encounter with actual consumption (see Miller, 1998b), the effective units of consumption are rarely individuals, their rationality is likely to be based around concepts of care and style, and most of the precise assumptions of economics as to the knowledge they have and how they use it bears no relation to any observable worlds. By the same token, anthropologists have had a terrible time finding any actual markets that accord with economic models (see Carrier, 1997; Dilley, 1992).

There are acknowledged ties between economics, audit and management consultancy around approaches such as cost–benefit analysis. So in order to keep the spectrum of history as broad as possible I will end on a quite different example of virtualism. With about the same swiftness that audit has expanded, we have seen an expansion in debates over the term 'postmodernism' and the claims that we live in a postmodern world. The initial source of much of this debate was Baudrillard (1975, 1981), and one of the most recent sources is Bauman (1992). What both of these have in common is that they pay a great deal of attention to the rise of the consumer society. For them the new depthlessness, in which people are replaced by the symbolic value of the commodities that stand for them, is simply a manifestation of the commodity world of consumer capitalism. Yet for a hundred books on the topic of postmodernism it would be hard to find one that has actually engaged with consumers, let alone attempted any kind of empathetic ethnography of what consumers actually do. There is very little in this literature that approximates the empathetic account given of consumption as a practice in deVault's *Feeding the Family* (1991), or, for that matter, a host of other feminist writings that have engaged with consumption as mundane practice.

Once again the consumer as a situated being is replaced by model building that purports to represent our world. The debate over postmodernism is simply another example of virtualism and it is no coincidence that it grew at almost the same time as the forces it would never wish to be associated with such as the rise of audit. Heaven knows how the same literature concludes that we have become more self-reflective. It is only by becoming extraordinarily unreflective that we have managed to build vast models of the postmodern and the virtual that reflect not one iota upon what we do in our very own private and working lives. If there is one example of true postmodernism – that is, a world based on an endless cycle of symbolic referents – it is surely the literature on postmodernism itself. It is not difficult to write a scholarly book on postmodernism. There are hundreds if not thousands of papers and books that can be cited, all of which reinforce the conviction that somewhere out there must be a world that this literature describes – since how else could the literature itself exist? So postmodernism based on a largely autonomous world of self-reference may be congratulated upon its triumphant creation of its own object of inquiry.

By finishing with the example of postmodernists, we can see the wider implication of my argument for an unintended political economy. The debate about the cultural turn itself turns out to be not an analysis of what is going on but a symptom of it. The fact that postmodernism may not really exist as an attribute of the world but still manages to dominate academic representations of that world doesn't matter a great deal in that the power of those in the social sciences and humanities who propound these ideas is quite limited. By contrast, the fact that economists have a completely daft model of consumers matters enormously. As a result, models such as structural adjustment have been applied mechanically over two decades to highly diverse economies with devastating results. Both groups of academics have striven on behalf of their particular representations of the world, but one set of esoteric models happens to have hold on those reins of power and the other does not. One in effect becomes the political economy, the other tries to pretend the political economy has gone away. The point is not that economists are more deluded or malign than social scientists proclaiming the postmodern. That is certainly not my experience of the individuals in question. It is that power and its consequences arise out of institutional conjunctures whose effects are often about as predictable as the effect of planetary conjunctions on our behaviour. What we can see, however, are larger trends in history: for example, the tendency to have negated the rising power of actual consumers by replacing them with virtual consumers. This and the tendency for new abstract models to replace processes such as consumption which had previously been the form in which models of capitalism had been grounded in particular social contexts suggests that, put together, these various changes amount to a kind of grand narrative, in the tradition of Hegel and Marx.

Virtualism is clearly not the same as abstraction or modelling *per se*. The last thing I intend is a critique of either process. After all, the very concept of virtualism is itself clearly a model, and a highly abstract one, which I have attempted to create. These are integral to all aspects of modern cultural practice, especially, though by no means exclusively, economic practice. Their benefits are immense, as fully acknowledged by Simmel (1978) [1907] in his study of those abstractions that created and sustained modern forms of money and capital. Equally, inasmuch as bureaucracy requires certain elements of abstraction and anonymity in order effectively to serve as an instrument for creating equality and democracy, I would praise rather than condemn it (du Gay, 2000). The problem is to discriminate between the legitimate use of abstraction and the rise of virtualism, which is destructive to the degree that it incorporates two further factors. The first is that it replaces rather than models the phenomenon it purports to represent. The academic audit is legitimated by consumers of services but actually siphons efforts away from students towards its own managerial bodies. The second is the degree to which such bodies have the power to change the world to make it accord with their abstract representations of it.

The two case studies with which this chapter started would seem to fit quite well within this larger framework. The case is already made for management consultancy, since it was used to exemplify virtualism. The case of pension fund capitalism seems to accord equally well with my primary characterization of virtualism. It is quite clear that the group that could be called the 'consumers' of such funds are actual pensioners, and that it is their interests that legitimate and authorize the existence of such funds. It is equally clear that the rise of pension fund capitalism has seen a sleight of hand by which the actual consumers have been replaced with a body of managers. Although some of these are drawn from the representatives of the beneficiaries, the way these institutions have evolved and been regulated has resulted in a situation in which, far from acting in the interests of pensioners, they have become one of the primary agents in turning capitalism towards short-term shareholder interests which may often result in actions to the detriment of actual pensioners. As Clark (2000) makes clear, there are a whole series of factors in pension fund organization and practice that make the funds quite unlikely to favour the kind of infrastructural investment that pensioners, by virtue of being elderly, benefit from more than almost any other section of the population.

Pension funds form an integral part of the rise of modern financial institutions, which do indeed tend to impose their particular 'model' of the world upon as much of the commercial world as they can. I have recently analysed an example of this in a study of a retail merger (Miller, 2001: Chap. 5).

history and its consequences I have argued that the material discussed in this chapter is better analysed in terms of the un-intended political economy rather than at least the 'strong' version of the cultural turn. During the course of the chapter I have suggested several contributory forces that work within the unintended political economy. These include the unintended consequences of intentional action, the effects of unintended structural conjunctures, and a wider concept of 'history'. I would think the last of these is the most suspect, and I want to conclude with its defence.

Neither of the two case studies is particularly difficult to explain. There are perfectly good reasons why institutional investments such as pensions and insurance premiums should soak up such an amount of capital that they gain a tremendous amount of power. There are also good reasons why, faced with all sorts of new systems of audit and accountability, management might seek to make rather more explicit than in previous times the evidence that it has acted responsibly by conspicuously bringing in external consultants to whom ultimate responsibility can in effect be shifted. In all such cases we can see the unintended consequences of intentionality.

The unintended consequences of structural change is an equally important factor. For example, Clark provides a detailed account of the rise of pension funds (2000: 53–60). First, he shows this is a development that is characteristic of Anglo-American capitalism, but not capitalism in general. In Germany, France and Italy, for example, pension assets amount to a mere 5 per cent of GDP and are not particularly significant powerbrokers. In the UK, pension assets amount to 93 per cent of GDP and dwarf other forms of savings (p. 29). If one compares Germany with the UK, there are four primary reasons for this difference. These are the form by which pension contributions are incrementally collected; the legal requirements to fund private company liabilities; the tendency to centralize assets in pension funds rather than to outsource them to insurance companies; and the right to self-invest by German companies, unlike Anglo-American companies. Clark argues that some of these differences in turn go back to differences in the way financial structures were established in the nineteenth century.

So it is entirely possible to account for even such an extraordinary disparity in the contemporary control of capitalism between different national capitalisms, which have clearly not disappeared under some globalizing juggernaut. But it is highly implausible to suggest that any one of these factors was developed with the intention of making pension funds the controlling stakeholder in most major companies. Rather, structural conjunctures and intentional actions have unintended consequences because the actors themselves are largely concerned with much narrower and more immediate concerns. The consequences that matter most may arise from the larger structural and institutional developments within which these smaller intentions have effects. This is probably as far as we could reasonable push the two case studies that have dominated most of this chapter.

But in addition to these case studies I have added several others in order to subsume them both within a general concept of virtualism, which, it was argued, made them, in addition, exemplars of some still larger and wider changes. I also invoked a further level of causation, termed (with admittedly more than a little hubris) 'history'. There are all sorts of reasons why one should be very cautious about invoking such intangible and presumptuous levels of analysis. Nevertheless I would attempt to justify the concept of virtualism on two grounds. The first arises from the material itself and the second from a commitment that exists irrespective of this material. In the section on virtualism I argued that there were common elements that seemed to link not just pension fund capitalism and management consultancy but also the rise of audit, economic modelling and, most surprisingly, the concept of postmodernism. If these links are at all convincing, then they become academic imperatives in themselves. They imply that the analysis of audit just in terms of debates about the public sector are not enough, that to observe the rise of academic economics is vital, but to account for it we need to look beyond the usual horizons. It implies that merely interviewing those academics involved in developing the concept of postmodernism would not get us very far in understanding why this concept has come to occupy such a mighty role in modern academic discourse.

If these phenomena are connected, then we are looking for some common unifying principles. In my longer study of virtualism (Miller, 1998a), I argued that it was precisely the fetishism of the consumer that was central to them all. I suggested further that this could be best understood in terms of an argument I had made some time ago (Miller, 1987) with respect to the development of modern consumerism as not the manifestation of but rather the negation of capitalism. I argued that capitalism led to an unprecedented abstraction around the rise of capital itself, which originally reduced production workers to mere instruments. Consumption was the means by which humanity fought for the resources to return to the world as consumers in which they used goods to create highly specific worlds that negated the abstractions of the market. So Trinidad turns American popular culture into Trinidadian culture (Miller, 1994), families in North London express their relationships of love by the careful selection of goods for each other out of the plethora of goods available (Miller, 1998b), and so forth. Ordinary mundane consumption was neither hedonistic, materialistic nor individualistic; it was above all the form by which capitalism was negated and through which labour brought its products back into the creation of its humanity.

Furthermore, I argued there was a political manifestation of this rise of consumption in the form of a new ideal of consumer authority (Keat et al. 1994). This was used equally to challenge Marxist regimes in the East and capitalist regimes in the West. This progressive development in consumption is the background to the rise of virtualism. Each of the institutions described as virtualist has developed through a sleight of hand that took the authority of the consumer and appropriated this for the interests of the institution in general and to the detriment of people in their social role of consumers (and in most cases also as workers). If consumption was developing as the negation of capitalism until it was trumped by virtualism, then virtualism could be argued to represent the negation of a negation within a grand narrative. It is at this level that history may be invoked as a player in the development of the unintended political economy. The term 'history' is helpful inasmuch as it removes us from the temptation to reduce these developments to either agents or intentions.

So one legitimation for virtualism comes from the analysis itself. The other, I suggest, arises from the intentions behind the analysis and is irrespective of the material. The reason I focused upon consumption as the foundation of virtualism is because it is the issue that I have been primarily concerned with for most of my academic career. During that time I have argued that the topic of consumption has a particular advantage. It is one that focuses not on the causes of historical change but upon their consequences. Clark makes a similar point in the final chapter of his book, when he notes that it was a philosophical logic central to the development of British political thought that led to a legal requirement that trustees of pension funds were supposed to maximize financial benefits (2000: 275–80). This in turn led to a situation that completely ignores the consequences for society in more general terms. The central irony that the present chapter is based upon is brought out with particular clarity when we reflect upon the degree to which the development of pension fund capitalism acts to the detriment of the specific interests of pensioners. In a similar fashion academics who have suffered from what they consider the undue burden of the rise of audit have little difficulty tracing the logic by which consultancy and management have grown in authority. They have seen a positive ideal of being held responsible lead to a vast paper trail that turns academic attention to the explicit legitimation of action rather than the action itself. But the counter-argument can only come from the sense of the consequences – the detrimental effects on education, especially evident when the student is reappraised as the consumer of educational services.

So virtualism as an approach is justified both because it tackles the broad sweep of what otherwise seem unrelated trajectories and because the focus upon the consumer places emphasis upon the consequences of these trajectories for the population. I have a sense that the present chapter remains a rather unfashionable contribution. To detract from the study of intentionality, agency and subjectivity seems at first a dehumanizing turn. But I would suggest it is more than compensated for if it turns our attention from an emphasis upon origins and causes and balances this with a clear focus upon consequences and effects.

references

Baudrillard, J. (1975) *The Mirror of Production*. St Louis, MO: Telos Press.
Baudrillard, J. (1981) *For a Critique of the Political Economy of the Sign*. St Louis, MO: Telos Press.
Bauman, Z. (1992) *Intimations of Postmodernity*. London: Routledge.
Carrier, J. (1997) *Meanings of the Market*. Oxford: Berg.
Clark, G. (2000) *Pension Fund Capitalism*. Oxford: Oxford University Press.
Cook, I., Crouch, D., Naylor, S. and Ryan, J. (eds) (2000a) *Cultural Turns/ Geographical Turns*. Harlow: Prentice Hall.
Cook, I., Crang, P. and Thorpe, M. (2000b) 'Have you got the customer's permission? Category management and circuits of knowledge in the UK food business', in J. Bryson, P. Daniels, N. Henry and J. Pollard (eds), *Knowledge, Space, Economy*. London: Routledge.

Davis, M. (1990) *City of Quartz*. London: Verso.

Dilley, R. (1992) *Contesting Markets*. Edinburgh: Edinburgh University Press.

Drucker, P. (1976) *The Pension Fund Revolution*. London: Heinemann.

Drucker, P. (1996) *The Pension Fund Revolution*, with a new Introduction and Epilogue by the author. New Brunswick, NJ: Transaction Press.

du Gay, P. (1996) *Consumption and Identity at Work* London: Sage.

du Gay, P. (2000) *In Praise of Bureaucracy: Weber, Organization, Ethics*. London: Sage.

deVault, M. (1991) *Feeding the Family*. Chicago: University of Chicago Press.

Fine, B. (1998) 'The triumph of economics: or "rationality" can be dangerous to your reasoning', in J. Carrier and D. Miller (eds), *Virtualism: A New Political Economy*. Oxford: Berg.

Gell, A. (1998) *Art and Agency: An Anthropological Theory*. Oxford: Oxford University Press.

Hutton, W. (1995) *The State We're In*. London: Jonathan Cape.

Keat, R., Whiteley, N. and Abercrombie, N. (eds) (1994) *The Authority of the Consumer*. London: Routledge.

Kuper, A. (1999) *Culture: The Anthropologist's Account*. Cambridge, MA: Harvard University Press.

Lash, S. and Urry, J. (1994) *Economies of Signs and Space*. London: Sage.

Leadbeater, C. (1999) *Living on Thin Air: The New Economy*. Harmondsworth: Viking.

Latour, B. (1993) *We Have Never Been Modern*. Hemel Hempstead: Harvester Wheatsheaf.

Leyshon, A. and Thrift, N. (1997) *Money/Space*. London: Routledge.

McDowell, L. (1997) *Capital Culture: Gender at Work in the City*. Oxford: Blackwell.

McDowell, L. (2000) 'Economy, culture, difference and justice', in I. Cook, D. Crouch, S. Naylor and J. Ryan (eds), *Cultural Turns/Geographical Turns*. Harlow: Prentice Hall.

Miller, D. (1987) *Material Culture and Mass Consumption*. Oxford: Blackwell.

Miller, D. (1994) *Modernity: an Ethnographic Approach*. Oxford: Berg.

Miller, D. (1997) *Capitalism: an Ethnographic Approach*. Oxford: Berg.

Miller, D. (1998a) 'A theory of virtualism', in J. Carrier and D. Miller (eds), *Virtualism: A New Political Economy*. Oxford: Berg.

Miller, D. (1998b) *A Theory of Shopping*. Cambridge: Polity.

Miller, D. (2001) *The Dialectics of Shopping*. Chicago: University of Chicago Press.

Miller, P. (1998) 'The margins of accountancy', in M. Callon (ed.), *The Laws of the Market*. Oxford and Keele: Blackwell and the Sociological Review.

Miller, P. and Rose, N. (1997) 'Governing economic life', *Economy and Society*, 19 (1): 1–31.

O'Shea, J. and Madigan, C. (1997) *Dangerous Company: The Consulting Powerhouses and the Businesses They Save and Ruin*. London: Nicholas Brearley.

Power, M. (1994) *The Audit Explosion*. London: Demos.

Power, M. (1997) *The Audit Society: Rituals of Verification*. Oxford: Oxford University Press.

Ray, L. and Sayer, A. (eds) (1999) *Culture and Economy After the Cultural Turn*. London: Sage.

Simmel, G. (1978) [1907] *The Philosophy of Money*. London: Routledge and Kegan Paul.

Strathern, M. (1997) ' "Improving ratings": audit in the British university system', *European Review*, 5: 305–21.

production, consumption and 'cultural economy'

Alan Warde

One of the central questions raised in this collection, 'To what extent is it useful, or indeed possible, to claim that contemporary economic relations are more or less "culturalized" than their historical predecessors?', can only be posed on the basis of a clear definition of a relevant notion of the economic and the cultural. Any answer requires an ability to distinguish the economic and the cultural, whether as separate spheres or as different types of practice (leaving open the question of what other spheres or practices, if any, might also exist). This in no way implies that economic activity is other than socially meaningful conduct. The rules, norms and conventions of economic conduct are of the same type, *qua* guides and constraints on action, as those of political conduct, aesthetic conduct, and so on. However, some contemporary accounts conclude that because economic practice is meaningful, it is thereby cultural. In turn, this leads to the suggestion that no conceptual distinction can be sustained between the economic and the cultural. However, to hold such a view entails that there can be no answer to the question 'Is the economy becoming more cultural?', for unless we can distinguish clearly between economic activity and cultural activity, culturalization would be unidentifiable. The problem arises from the profligate use of the term 'cultural' in the recent social scientific literature as synonymous with all of the following: non-material, social, aesthetic, informational, intellectual, normative, communicative, meaningful, human and civilizing. So long as it has such extensive reference, there can be no chance of depicting change in the prominence of the cultural. All we can say is that economic relations have cultural aspects. A sensible and satisfactory answer requires simultaneous conceptual clarification and purposeful empirical observation.

Most recent analyses of the relationship between culture and the economy assume that the boundaries between them are collapsing. Moreover, it is much more widely asserted that there is more culture in the economy than the converse, that there is more economy in the culture. Yet there are two alternative causal claims. The former, 'culturalization', implies that culture has become more central in economic relations, a process usually implicitly considered good because no one is against more culture. The latter suggests that economic relations are now more central to culture and, because this might be the result of commodification or rationalization, this might be bad.

As regards the origins of the idea of culturalization, I surmise that it emerges from reflections on consumption and its relationship to production. Until recently, consumption was largely ignored, deemed superstructural, or considered economic only as an instantiation of demand, necessary for continued accumulation, but of no other interest, because driven by the logic of production. However, once one turns a theoretical axiom of economics, the sovereignty of the consumer, into an empirical postulate, and especially when combined with a post-Fordist view of emergent niche markets wherein successful firms must service consumers who are essentially unpredictable, then consumption becomes a more explicit and complicated problem in the understanding of the economy. I suppose that the problematic of the culturalization of the economy mainly stems from a perception of consumption as increasingly cultural. Such a view is sustained by the notion that consumption is oriented no longer to use values and the satisfaction of needs, but rather to symbolic gains, a position advanced powerfully by Baudrillard (1981). It therefore seems promising to re-examine the concept of consumer culture, which apparently encapsulates a notion that consumption is deeply cultural. This chapter mostly attends to that concept.

culturalization of the economy or economization of culture

Arguably, what we call culture, and how we separate culture from economy, is almost entirely a function of the general models that we use to characterize societies. We might distinguish between economy and society; or base and superstructure; or economy, civil society and the state; or the economic, the political and social. Increasingly we seem to distinguish between economy and culture, only to say that these are scarcely separate spheres any more because they are collapsing into one another. The disadvantages of this are clearly identified by Ray and Sayer (1999: 1–9), and I concur largely with their argument that economic logic is distinctive, economic activity having an irreducible instrumental component which underpins the many and diverse forms of concrete, historical economic practice. No equivalent generic definition of culture is sufficiently uncontentious to adopt as a basis for analysis. Hence, rather than examining general sociological frameworks in the abstract, it is more immediately productive to turn to an operational definition of culture.

Williams identified three modern uses of the term 'culture' (besides the specialized one referring to the tending of nature, as in sugar beet culture or germ culture):

> (i) the independent and abstract noun which describes a general process of intellectual, spiritual and aesthetic development ... (ii) the independent noun, whether used generally or specifically, which indicates a particular way of life, whether of a people, a period or a group, from Herder ... (iii) the independent and abstract noun which describes the works and practices of intellectual and especially artistic activity. This seems often now the most widespread use: culture is music, literature, painting and sculpture, theatre and film. A Ministry of Culture refers to these specific activities, sometimes with the addition of philosophy, scholarship, history.
>
> (Williams, 1976: 80)

Williams notes different emphases for the term in different European societies, and that the three meanings overlap, indicating some problems which are not simply ones of confusion. Culture (ii) is the standard anthropological and sociological usage *par excellence*. Culture (iii) is the more specific contemporary one.

A more economical culture?   If we conduct a rather simplistic exercise on the position that the economy or economic relations are increasingly altering the nature of culture, then using these three dimensions of culture would suggest the following possible themes.

Economic relations might be entering, or promoting, Culture (i) insofar as commercial activity might play a role in a civilizing process. There are a number of arguments to this effect from the New Right, neo-liberals and some others interested in the notion of consumer citizenship. One sense in which economic relations are affecting Culture (ii) is through their role in the rationalization of everyday life. There is a long history of critique of capitalist societies to this effect, with perhaps surprisingly few proponents today, though Ritzer's work (1993) has had remarkable appeal in the last decade. Finally, regarding Culture (iii), people argue that there has been a commodification of culture, as the volume of capital accumulated through the circulation of cultural products through the market has increased rapidly and disproportionately.

There is comparatively little interest in these themes at present, though I consider them of some continued significance. It is the converse argument – that culture has become more central to the operation of the economy – that commands most current attention.

A new, more cultural economy?   Let us consider the implications of the phrase 'the culturalization of the economy' with respect to each of the three meanings in turn. Culture (i) would entail that the forces of 'intellectual, spiritual and aesthetic development' are becoming incorporated in industrial and economic activities. There is a very vague sense in which this might be seen as coterminous with arguments about the information society, with the increasing incorporation of the products of the arts and sciences perhaps, as rather general intellectual properties (or the fruits of 'civilization') become more important inputs to production. The spread of Culture (ii) into the economy might perhaps signify an argument that individual or group ways of life, perhaps their styles of life (or their consumption practices), increasingly impact upon economic relations. I will take this as a central and interesting hypothesis for exploration below. Culture (iii) would imply greater output of cultural products, with a direct impact on industrial structure, but also that products of the culture industries might affect other aspects of economic activity, including some indirect effects on economic processes and relationships (e.g. advertising). There is a very clear set of claims to this effect and there is little doubt that they are of some significance. Thus Lury, in her exposition of consumer culture as a particular instance of material culture, writes that:

> It is widely argued that the art-culture system, a system made up of the set of institutions, practices and beliefs which, historically, has organized the production and consumption of cultural goods (such as visual art, literature, music, radio, film, and television), has influenced the development of consumer culture in a number of ways, particularly following the rapid growth in the so-called culture industry in the twentieth century (Adorno and Horkheimer, 1979). It is argued, for example, that the history of art and the development of popular culture have shaped the production and display of consumer goods. This argument is substantiated by pointing to the pervasive and taken-for-granted use of high art in advertising (Berger, 1972); the ubiquity of commercial design, packaging and display in everyday life (Forty, 1986); the increasing importance attached to imagery in the production and consumption of all material goods and services (Jameson, 1991); and the growth of sectors of the economy concerned with some kind of cultural production (Lash and Urry, 1994).
>
> (1996: 52)

It is not merely the products of the culture industries supplied for final consumption, but their role in affecting advertising, marketing and packaging which are significant in introducing culture to the economy. I will return to this later.

The progress of culture   These considerations offer a weak typology of the potential range of mutual interactions between culture and economic practice generally conceived. Some of the processes that might be affecting the relationship between culture and economy are identified. The typology hints at greater specificity regarding the same empirical effect; a reduction of the differentiating features of cultural and economic practice is observed. It is, however, a remarkably crude exercise, placing much better considered analysis in a rather barren categorial scheme. One obvious weakness is its failure to differentiate adequately within the sphere of economic practice. One might proceed by examining separately elements like the logic and process of production, products and their distribution, purchasing behaviour, and so forth. Pursuit of that line of investigation proved rather tedious, but not without generating some reservations regarding claims that labour processes and corporate organizations have become more cultural.

I find overstated the claim that culture is more important in economic relations of production. I broadly concur with Thompson and Findlay (1999) regarding the organization of companies when they argue that despite much talk about the strategic re-engineering of organizational culture – and indeed as Thrift (in this volume) shows, huge resources are devoted to training managers in the art of manipulating organizational cultures – the effect upon most workers is probably negligible. The most authoritative recent survey of the British workforce as a whole commented on low levels of commitment to organizations:

> One of the most striking findings at the decriptive level was just how limited organizational commitment appeared to be among British employees. While there was little sign of explicit alienation, it was nonetheless notable that only 8 per cent of employees were strongly of the view that their own values and those of their organization were very similar, only 14 per cent that they were proud of their organization, and only 30 per cent that they felt any loyalty to it. Moreover, only 28 per cent felt sufficiently attached to their organization to say that they would turn down another job if offered higher pay.
>
> (Gallie et al., 1998: 306)

My analysis of the contemporary experience of work would be that it is increasingly insecure and stressful, for managers as much as any other group, and that the encouragement of personal commitment to the firm is little other than rhetoric for all except a small proportion of managers.

Nor do I find very plausible the frequently stated claim that interactive service work has increased the role of culture in production and workplaces. The contention that the growth of interactive service work makes economic activity more cultural is somewhat misleading. In the first place, interaction is social rather than 'cultural'. Second, a large amount of interactive service work is so thoroughly imbued with an economizing logic that it begins to undermine the conventions of face-to-face interaction, as Leidner (1993) argues. I recall an illustration of instructions to workers, which she quotes, requiring them to treat every customer as a unique individual, but in no more than 60 seconds. The range of counter-examples to a trend towards cultural, or indeed social, interaction in the field of retailing, for example, is vast. Self-service, e-commerce, discount, catalogue and cash-and-carry stores, and automatic vending machines provide very little personal inter-action. Arguably, the amount of conversation between staff and customer in retail outlets has reduced in absolute and relative terms. The meaning that people take to shopping comes at least as much from social relations of the household as from commercial and artistic artefacts (Miller, 1998). I suspect the extent to which service industries are delivering face-to-face and intangible products has been exaggerated and that the labour processes involved are less distinctive from other kinds of work than is usually implied. But, of course, these are issues amenable to ongoing empirical investigation.

the cultural culture of consumption   If a culturalization of the economy were occurring, it would be most likely to surface in the phases of distribution and consumption. I therefore turn to an examination of two different approaches to consumer culture, ones which put most emphasis, respectively, on Culture (iii) and Culture (ii).

I seek to trace some intellectual threads in the development of the notion of a cultural economy. The idea, as it has subsequently been developed regarding the convergence of economy and culture, can be found in Mike Featherstone's very fine essay 'Lifestyle and consumer culture', first published in *Theory, Culture & Society*, in 1987, where he says, in the course of defining the term 'consumer culture':

> To use the term consumer culture is to emphasize that the world of goods and their principles of structuration are central to the understanding of contemporary society. This involves a dual focus: firstly on the cultural dimension of the economy, the symbolization and use of of material goods as 'communicators' not just utilities; and secondly, on the economy of cultural goods, the market principles of supply, demand, capital accumulation, competition and monopolization which operate within the sphere of lifestyles, cultural goods and commodities.
>
> (1987: 57)

That essay contains a series of themes that came to underpin one dominant understanding of contemporary cultural change. Indeed, perhaps, in retrospect, the journal *Theory, Culture & Society* will come to be seen as the vehicle of one of the key schools of thought in British sociology. In any case, the particular arguments sketched out in 'Lifestyle and consumer culture', and more broadly in Featherstone's collection of essays *Consumer Culture and Postmodernism* (1991), have survived and come to be widely accepted and repeated. Indeed, it might be suggested that the arguments have been repeated without the original rigorous qualifications about the range of their application. What strikes me on rereading those essays, a process which much enhanced my estimation of their importance, is their modest provisional nature, their balance, and a clear sense that they probably have limited application. The tone was of restrained conjecture. The project involved a careful juxtaposition of claims about postmodernism against sociological understandings of economic power and group practices.

What strikes me about Featherstone's position is that it has not developed much; neither he nor his associates have pushed the arguments further. Even more noticeably, they have made no real attempt to substantiate empirically the very many plausible hypotheses about contemporary cultural change contained in those essays. An implicit programme of empirical inquiry seems to have been ignored. The tendency has been, rather, to take the hypotheses and conjectures as fact and to found a more general position on that basis.

Probably unwittingly, I think that the position of Featherstone has most effectively been consolidated and specified in detail by Celia Lury in her excellent book *Consumer Culture* (1996). She takes the view that consumer culture is simply one type of material culture, the one characterizing the present epoch, its many and diverse traits (1996: 29–36) being associated with a rapid increase in consumer demand in modern societies. She maintains that 'the symbolic or cultural aspects of material objects have come to take on a special importance and distinctive organization in contemporary Euro-American societies, so that consumer culture is said to be drenched in meaning' (1996: 226). This drenching in meaning is the most important condition of that 'distinctive organization' namely: 'the increasing impact of the art-culture system and the significance of the use of cultural goods, not only in itself, but as a model of consumption for other goods' (1996: 226). She cites authors who say that contemporary consumption is 'culturally drenched' (Featherstone), 'is not only about images, it is also about play, especially play with meaning' (Abercrombie), and 'no society has ever been saturated with signs and images like this one' (Jameson) (1996: 52). Another way of putting this, after Appadurai, is that aesthetic knowledge is more important than it used to be. Lury claims 'that the art-culture system has provided a context within which an aestheticized mode of involvement with objects has been adopted by many consumers' (1996: 54). In studying the escalation of demand, consumer culture adds the important insight 'that the cultural dimensions of the increase in consumer demand have come to take on a distinctive form and a special importance. As a term, it thus highlights what might be described as the stylization of consumption' (1996: 50–1). It is this, stylization and aestheticization, and not just the existence of a consumer ethic or attitude, that characterizes consumer culture. Thus, in a manner of speaking, Lury emphasizes the *cultural* culture of consumption, indicating the prevalence of items denoted in Williams' Culture (iii).

This position places 'cultural goods' at its core, where cultural goods are ones whose aesthetic features are dominant. Lury then explicitly considers whether cultural goods do set the stage for attitudes towards non-cultural goods, and concludes that probably they do. Thus there is a potential aetheticization of all aspects of consumption. Hence, this account offers both grounds for holding that the economy is more cultural and some means for empirically assessing its extent.

Thus, consumer culture is defined by aestheticization and stylization, as generated through 'the art-culture system', and is illustrated by the dual movement of the increase of cultural goods produced in the economy and of economic forces operating on culture. Very importantly, I think, Lury maintains that the account is of the nature of 'cultural goods' (defined in terms of Culture [iii]), though she speculates that the techniques involved in their circulation might well have effects on the fields of consumption. Lury also supplies one major and essential advance on Featherstone's own work by considering the relationship between social groups other than the new cultural intermediaries and cultural consumption. Thus she considers gender, ethnicity and age as bases of identity shaped by, and shaping, cultural consumption. It is to the process of group formation that she returns in her conclusions:

> Consumer culture provides an important context for the development of novel relationships of individual self-identity and group membership. ... [T]hese relationships do not function in the same way for everyone and, consequently, they do not enable everyone to understand themselves as individuals in possession of themselves. In this sense, social groupings, rather than being displaced, are being reworked in the diverse processes of stylization characteristic of contemporary consumer culture.
>
> (Lury, 1996: 256)

Absolutely. However, I have some reservations regarding the postulate of the aestheticization of everyday life and the suggestion that the logic of cultural goods is extendable to other types of consumer item; indeed I am doubtful whether it is possible to extend this analysis much beyond cultural consumption.

I would suggest that while Lury has isolated those trends and processes relevant to a culturalization of consumption, the effects are, as yet, comparatively limited, with only a small part of all production governed by such imperatives. If the impact described is restricted explicitly to products of the art-culture system, with some additional side-effects in advertising, packaging and design, then the process of culturalization is far from dominant. On the face of it, economic activity (remembering that much economic activity takes place outside the market and commodified sphere) does not seem to concentrate sufficiently within the culture industries and their subsidiary processes when they operate (as in advertising and packaging) in other sectors. Moreover, Lury admits this orientation is probably limited to a fraction of the population. Hence I have doubts about the pervasiveness of consumer culture so defined.

However, to the extent that her claim is true 'that the art-culture system has provided a context within which an aestheticized mode of involvement with objects has been adopted by many consumers', that people now make consumer decisions and judgements with new aesthetic considerations in mind, then the impact might be greater. I am sceptical of this claim because much consumption behaviour seems driven by other than aesthetic considerations. First, much of the activity of consumption is subject to the criteria of economising. One of the more intriguing aspects of Miller's (1998) account is the explicit role of the logic of thrift as a justification for skilful and sacrificial shopping. Classifications of types of shopper (e.g. Lunt and Livingstone, 1992) suggest also that only a minority of people treat shopping as a pleasurable leisure pursuit, and that an equally large minority is primarily concerned with price and value for money. Second, much consumption has as many of the characteristics of work as of passive entertainment. The extensiveness of productive consumption, of hobbies, of cooking, of DIY, and so on, is one discovery of recent research. In such activities the instrumental orientation is uppermost, the moment of consumption subsidiary. If purposive consumption is not especially cultural, nor is its counterpart routine consumption. A good deal of consumption is characterized less by its meaningfulness than by its taken-for-granted ordinariness (Gronow and Warde, 2001).

Consumption is not only, nor even especially, 'cultural'. It is easy to exaggerate the aesthetic component of consumption. Recent work (Warde and Martens, 2000) attempting to explain why people almost universally reported enjoying eating out argued that a meal out offers several types of gratification. These types, applicable to other forms of consumption too, were summarized as sensual, instrumental, contemplative and social. A diner is relieved of hunger, without having to labour, through a meal judged by culinary criteria, taken in congenial company. We reasoned that even if positive gratification was not forthcoming on all counts on a given occasion, at least some would be. Hence the likelihood of abject disappointment was low. Thus, although meals out were subjected to aesthetic judgement in several respects – regarding presentation of food, the surroundings and ambience, the culinary authenticity of dishes, and so on – they were also evaluated in terms of sufficiency of food, value for money and the quality of social interaction and conversation. There is an aesthetic dimension to eating out, but it is not the only, and, we argued, not the most important, dimension in understanding the popularity of the practice.

The extent of aestheticization might be assessed by the frequency with which an aesthetic orientation to practice is adopted. I think it is limited. In the end, my guess would be that most people prefer a comfortable to a beautiful life, and that the heroic consumers of Featherstone's account are indeed restricted to a fraction of the middle class and some youth sub-cultural groupings. The evidence for my belief is hardly overwhelming. Nevertheless, some support emerges from Longhurst et al.'s (2001) study of the Manchester middle classes and from the protests of scholars against the tendency to assume that glamorous youth cultures set the tone of the aspirations of most young people (e.g. Roberts, 1997), in that much consumption is oriented towards passing oneself off as ordinary rather than distinctively stylized. Even though it might be said that it requires the adoption of a certain style to be seen as ordinary, such behaviour seems scarcely to support an aestheticization thesis.

This is not to deny that consumption practices are often expressive – the aesthetic is a dimension of much consumption practice – and even less to deny that they draw increasingly upon items which have cultural properties in Williams' third sense. Almost uniquely, with Lury, we know very clearly where to look to see whether there is a culturalization of the economy, and since the process probably affects consumption most, then the limits of the claims can be clearly identified. Lury offers a robust definition of consumer culture: it is characterized by the distinctively high prominence of the products of the culture industries in the marketplace; as component elements of the lifestyle of an important fraction of the middle class; and in publicity and communication. This could be said to be a feature of the contemporary period; and to identify some possibilities for development in both production and consumption. But it is only a part of the way of life; only part of consumption; and only a minor part of production.

All accounts are one-sided; that is the point of abstract analysis. It is usually a poor criticism of scholarly work to say that things have been missed out because an account comes from a particular perspective. More important is to know what the perspective is, to know what aspect of an account has been thematized and will therefore appear prominently within it.

In this case the central theme is aestheticization, rather than, for instance, communication or commodification. So I do not want to say that this approach to the cultural culture of consumption should do something other than it currently does – though I do confess to a degree of disappointment that there has not been more empirical work specifically addressed to evaluating the position. To the extent that this approach remains within its self-defined parameters of application to the cultural culture of consumption, and does not extend its claims to offer a generalized explanation of economic or everyday life, then it passes the test of a plausible and cogent, though not yet proven, account of the impact of expanded cultural production on social group formation.

consumer culture as a way of life: the societal culture of consumption The second account of the nature of consumption I want to consider draws on Williams' Culture (ii). The central claim, applying at the level of the society as a whole, is that the way of life of entire societies is shaped primarily by the activity of consumption. An exemplar of this position is Bauman (1998). This suggests that the phenomenon to be analysed is a societal culture of consumption. (I think that we should make it a rule that the word culture should always be preceded by a qualifying adjective!)

Bauman has presented the argument for the primacy of consumption in several different forms. He has argued, to my mind convincingly, that the consumer atttitude is pervasive in contemporary societies (1990). He has argued, somewhat less convincingly, that consumption is the principal means of achieving social integration in the contemporary world (1988). And he has presented several versions of the claim that consumption has superseded production as the dominant organizing principle of what he will call 'consumer society'. The most recent version put the case in terms of a parallel with industrial, or producer, society:

> The reason for calling that older type of modern society a 'producer society' was that it engaged its members primarily as producers; the way in which that society shaped up its members was dictated by the need to play this role and the norm that society held up to its members was the ability and the willingness to play it. In its present late-modern, second-modern or post-modern stage, society engages its members – again primarily – in their capacity as consumers. The way present-day society shapes up its members is dictated first and foremost by the need to play the role of the consumer, and the norm our society holds up to its members is that of the ability and willingness to play it.
>
> (1998: 24)

He goes on to insist that 'the difference is one of emphasis, but that emphasis does make an enormous difference to virtually every aspect of society, culture and individual life' (1998: 24).

While accepting that there has been a tendency for the elements of the consumer society, so defined, to become more prominent in recent years, I am less certain that they are sufficient to sustain the claim of primacy. My objections to the use of the term 'consumer society' are as follows:

1. The scope and intensity of the politics of consumption is not great, particularly when compared with the conflicts over material resources in the so-called 'era of the politics of distribution', and unless consumer politics becomes much more central it will remain implausible to define the social formation in terms of consumption.

2. Work still matters enormously to people. There is very little evidence that people are less concerned about, interested in or committed to work. They are, indeed, much more committed to employment than they are to the particular organizations in which they are employed (Gallie et al., 1998).

3. The suggestion that people work now in order to consume (as in the work-and-spend thesis of Cross, 1993, and Schor, 1992) is difficult to substantiate. Financial reward has always been a principal reason for undertaking employment and probably pecuniary gain remains the overriding motive for most – though work means much else besides. However, it does not follow that this is because people prioritize consumption. Commodification makes it imperative that everyone, in order to get by, shall have an income and most people are ethically persuaded that they should put some effort into the obtaining of that money. No active, vital or exceptional desire to consume can be imputed.

That the dominant characteristics of the societal culture of consumption are not especially 'cultural' is captured in Slater's definition of consumer culture:

> [C]onsumer culture denotes a social arrangement in which the relation between lived culture and social resources, between meaningful ways of life and the symbolic and material resources on which they depend, is mediated through markets. Consumer culture marks out a system in which consumption is dominated by the consumption of commodities, and in which cultural reproduction is largely understood to be carried out in the exercise of free personal choice in the private sphere of everyday life.
>
> (1997: 8)

If markets, commodities and individual choice are the defining characteristics of consumer culture, then this seems as much a feature of contemporary economic and social institutions as of distinctively cultural forms *per se*. It might be preferable to call Slater's position a view of consumer *society*, since it is primarily characterized less by its distinctive cultural features than by its system of production and exchange.

I find Slater's approach congenial because it covers a much wider range of consumption practices, being, for instance, not at all dependent upon a claim of progressive aestheticization. Moreover, it makes a direct connection between the principal economic institutions of modern capitalist societies, their techniques of circulation and distribution, and the construction of the activities of consumption as the properties of self-possessed individuals. Economic activity comprises forms of action, founded in norms and values which provide the tacit knowledge, empathy and sentiment sustaining conduct appropriate to context and situation. In that regard it makes little sense to consider economic activity as anything other than meaningful. Contemporary capitalism, in all its varieties, presents us with a strongly formed mode of economic life, with hegemonic conventions of economic practice. The appropriate orientation for individual or collective actors in economic situations is prescribed as entrepreneurial, purposive, calculating, self-regarding and designed to match means to ends efficiently (i.e. with least overall cost and effort). Not all economic action remotely conforms to such a template, and much fails fully to conform with this ideal type. Nevertheless, this orientation probably remains predominant in economic transactions. That this orientation, rather well fitted to behaviour in competitive markets, will spread into other spheres of social life where it is less capable of securing the common good and less effective in coordinating the actions of individuals, a concern of many critics over the years, tends to become lost in accounts which elide meaningfulness and culture. Instrumental rationality remains the bedrock of judgement about the appropriateness of most forms of practice and action. One merit of the societal culture of consumption approach is that it recognizes these normative features of economic practice. Perhaps, however, what this account gains in generality – in understanding structural conditions of long duration and in their widespread application – it loses in specificity when compared with the alternative approach.

discussion   I contend that economic activity is, and always was, meaningful and culturally embedded; that instrumental action is predominant within contemporary capitalist societies; and that economic organizations are more constrained to operate instrumentally than other social actors. I am yet to be convinced that the process of the rationalization of everyday life is not the dominant tendency emanating from economic activity, with ramifications in the fields of domestic and family life, leisure and recreation, as well as in ordinary consumption. Ritzer's (1999) thesis that the spectacular paraphernalia of the distributive apparatus of contemporary society is a rearguard and precarious attempt to re-enchant a disenchanted world contains, in this regard, a basic element of truth.

Nevertheless, the contribution of consumer culture (iii) – the outputs of the culture industries – to the contemporary world is surely greater than in the past. After Lury, we live in a more cultural culture of consumption. There are many associated facets, including the following:

1. Mass mediatization spreads available cultural items of all kinds; and casual acquaintance with a wider range of cultural products must be a consequence (people don't have to be paying attention during very much of their 26 hours per week of watching TV for there to be some impact!).

2. Advertisements are a popular, pervasive, indirect form of cultural transmission – though we might not expect audiences always to make much cultural (iii) sense of their nuances; nonetheless they are of considerable consequence both as art products and as guides to cultural consumption.

3. Selling techniques, the technologies enhancing the role of the symbolic in the process of distribution, have increased their impact.

4. There is a greater volume of cultural capital, of competence in the knowledge and appreciation of the variety of cultural options.

All these things matter. But they imply neither the cultural saturation of everyday life nor the attenuation of the logic of economic practice. The effect may be less all-encompassing than is often inferred. It would seem appropriate to adjudicate on the basis of empirical research. However, it would seem that specifically 'cultural goods' (if we can isolate them properly) comprise a small proportion of household expenditure, sectoral employment and capital investment. (Of course if we were to say that culture includes all communication, all information production, electronic software, etc., then we get a different picture – but I don't see why such items should be considered 'cultural'.) In the specific sense of Culture (iii), even though arguably an increased proportion of consumption is of the products of the culture industries, the vast bulk of household expenditure remains devoted to other categories of item.

Even specifically cultural outputs are not necessarily related to in an aesthetic fashion, and it seems to me that an aesthetic orientation is a necessary attribute of the use of cultural goods if they are to have the predicted effect on everyday life. It is easy to exaggerate the aesthetic component of consumption. Featherstone acknowledged that explicitly. In concluding his review of the nature of aetheticization and its relationship to informalization, he noted that appreciating aspects of the carnivalesque made for better emotional lives for sections of the middle class. 'In effect fractions of the middle class have become more educated into a controlled de-control of the emotions and the sensibilities and tastes that support a greater appreciation of the aestheticization of everyday life' (1991: 81). This is indicative of the likelihood that relatively few people approach many of their consumption decisions with aesthetic considerations in mind. This is because consumption is a multifaceted practice, as implied by the variety of different types of gratification discussed above.

The focus on aestheticization has had the effect of relegating the importance of consumption in the process of sustaining social relationships and defining social membership. Differentiation among groups in their patterns of consumption remains an important feature of behaviour, as studies of everyday life and cultural consumption demonstrate (e.g. Bennett et al., 1999). Patterns of consumption still correspond to social structures of class, age, generation, gender, region, and so on. They are not so hierarchical as they might have been in the past. There is no longer any very simple correspondence between class position and forms of cultural participation, which made it possible to predict class position from cultural taste, or vice versa. But distinction is not yet extinguished.

It is possible, as I hope to have shown, to make a claim 'that contemporary economic relations are more or less "culturalized" than their historical predecessors'. However, whether it is useful remains to be decided empirically. Ultimately it will be the outcome of competition between research programmes as to which reveals more about contemporary social arrangements. Nevertheless, my current, provisional view is that supporting evidence from studies of economic practice, studies of how work is experienced, how labour processes operate, how economic organizations function, is not sufficient to suggest any demotion of the logic of economizing in the face of counter-pressure from cultural (iii) logic. Indeed, as other chapters in this volume demonstrate, the economy has a remarkable capacity to recuperate and discipline the outputs of cultural culture.

references

Baudrillard, J. (1981) *For a Critique of the Political Economy of the Sign*. St Louis, MO: Telos Press.

Bauman, Z. (1988) *Freedom*. Milton Keynes: Open University Press.

Bauman, Z. (1990) *Thinking Sociologically*. Oxford: Blackwell.

Bauman, Z. (1998) *Work, Consumerism and the New Poor.* Buckingham: Open University Press.

Bennett, T., Emmison, M. and Frow, J. (1999) *Accounting for Tastes: Australian Everyday Cultures.* Cambridge: Cambridge University Press.

Berger, J. (1972) *Ways of Seeing.* London: BBC Books.

Cross, G. (1993) *Time and Money: The Making of Consumer Culture.* London: Routledge.

Featherstone, M. (1987) 'Lifestyle and consumer culture', *Theory, Culture & Society* 4 (1): 55–70.

Featherstone, M. (1991) *Consumer Culture and Postmodernism.* London: Sage.

Forty, A. (1986) *Objects of Desire: Design and Society since 1750.* London: Thames and Hudson.

Gallie, D., White, M., Cheng, Y. and Tomlinson, M. (1998) *Restructuring the Employment Relationship.* Oxford: Clarendon Press.

Gronow, J. and Warde, A. (eds) (2001) *Ordinary Consumption.* London: Routledge.

Horkheimer, M. and Adorno, T. (1979) *Dialectic of Enlightenment.* New York: Herder and Herder.

Jameson, F. (1991) *Postmodernism, or, the Cultural Logic of Late Capitalism.* London: Verso.

Lash, S. and Urry, J. (1994) *Economies of Signs and Space.* London: Sage.

Leidner, R. (1993) *Fast Food, Fast Talk: Service Work and the Routinization of Everyday Life.* Berkeley, CA: University of California Press.

Longhurst, B., Bagnall, G. and Savage, M. (2001) 'Ordinary consumption and personal identity: radio and the middle classes in the north west of England', in J. Gronow and A. Warde (eds), *Ordinary Consumption.* London: Routledge.

Lunt, P. and Livingstone, S. (1992) *Mass Consumption and Personal Identity.* Buckingham: Open University Press.

Lury, C. (1996) *Consumer Culture.* Cambridge: Polity.

Miller, D. (1998) *A Theory of Shopping.* Cambridge: Polity.

Ray, L. and Sayer, A. (eds) (1999) *Culture and Economy After the Cultural Turn.* London: Sage.

Ritzer, G. (1993) *The McDonaldization of Society.* Thousand Oaks, CA: Pine Forge Press.

Ritzer, G. (1999) *Enchanting a Disenchanted World: Revolutionizing the Means of Consumption.* Thousand Oaks, CA: Pine Forge Press.

Roberts, K. (1997) 'Same activities, different meanings: British youth cultures in the 1990s', *Leisure Studies* 16 (1): 1–15.

Schor, J. (1992) *The Overworked American: The Unexpected Decline of Leisure.* New York: Basic Books.

Slater, D. (1997) *Consumer Culture and Modernity.* Cambridge: Polity.

Thompson, P. and Findlay, P. (1999) 'Changing the people: social engineering in the contemporary workplace', in L. Ray and A. Sayer (eds), *Culture and Economy After the Cultural Turn.* London: Sage.

Warde, A. and Martens, L. (2000) *Eating Out: Social Differentiation, Consumption and Pleasure.* Cambridge: Cambridge University Press.

Williams, R. (1976) *Keywords: A Vocabulary of Culture and Society.* Glasgow: Fontana.

performing cultures in the new economy

Nigel Thrift

This chapter is intended to provide a symptomatic reading of some of the practices of modern Western business (see also Thrift, 1996, 1997, 1998, 1999). I want to argue that something new is happening to Western capitalism – not as new as some of its more evangelical proponents would argue, no doubt, but not just business as usual either. That something new is preparation for a time that Walter Benjamin once forecast, the time when the emergency becomes the rule.

For, so the stories go, firms now live in a permanent stage of emergency, always bordering on the edge of chaos. So firms must no longer be so concerned to exercise bureaucratic control. Indeed, through a variety of devices – cultivating knowledge workers, valuing teams, organization through projects, better use of information technology, flattened hierarchies – they will generate just enough organizational stability to change in an orderly fashion and sufficient hair-trigger responsiveness to adapt to the expectedly unexpected.[1] Firms will therefore become faster, more agile (e.g. Illinitch et al., 1998). They will be able to live life in a blur of change.

Such a turn towards the rule of emergency demands new disciplines and skills of managers. 'Organization man' is gone. In his stead, new subject positions must be invented. Managers must become 'change agents' able, through the cultivation of new disciplines and skills, to become the fastest and best.

Obviously we need to be careful. For a start, the vast bulk of business consists of the reiterative rollover of practices laid down many centuries ago, practices like double-entry book-keeping, invoicing and filing and the like which have changed much less than those who want to believe that we live in the new would be willing or would want to concede (Thrift, 1998). Then, much of what I have written so far draws on analyses which are, by their nature, rhetorical. 'For all we read about bold companies managing in new ways, most enterprises continue to noodle with functionally organized many-tiered hierarchies, the mechanistic model of a century ago' (Colvin, 2000: F5).[2]

So how has the new discourse of permanent emergency obtained so much grip? I want to argue that the best description of its effectivity is provided by the word 'style', a word which gives the right sense of an intention or a modulation rather than a wholesale changeover of practice, but which, none the less, does not suggest something trivial. Of course, style is one of the key words in the social sciences and humanities at present, suggesting the need to understand a change in the style of engagement governing a repertoire of practices. Generally speaking, style is a means of making different things significant and worthy of notice: 'a style governs how anything can show up as anything' (Spinosa et al., 1997: 20).[3] Style will therefore include the creation of new metaphors, stories, concepts, percepts and affects but will, at the same time, contain considerable ambiguity; indeed this ambiguity is a crucial part of the power of style.

What I want to argue in this chapter is that the new style hails managers in new ways. What we are seeing, in particular, is the gradual unfolding of an attempt to engineer new kinds of 'fast' subject positions which can cope with the disciplines of permanent emergency. This is a project which involves much more direct engineering of the management subject than has heretofore been attempted. Further, and crucially, it involves the production of new spaces of intensity in which the new kind of managerial subject can be both created and affirmed. This is a project, in other words, which relies on the construction of an explicitly *geographical machine*.

The chapter is therefore in three parts. In the first part, I will outline some of the pressures that face contemporary managers, pressures which, I argue, are leading to attempts to institute a new regime of managerial governmentality centred on the creation of a maximally creative 'fast' subject position. In the second part of the chapter, I then move to an examination of some of the spaces of intensity through which the new subject position is being engineered, spaces of visualization, spaces of embodiment and spaces of circulation. The chapter then concludes with a number of speculations about the viability and potential bent of the nascent form of governmentality. Fast subjects, I will argue, may well turn out to be fragile subjects able to be held together only with certain costs.

Before I follow this agenda, however, I want to make a number of methodological points. First, as already stated, this is a synoptic reading. It is not, therefore, intended to be a buttoned-down piece of research. Second, that said, it is not any old story. It is based on a series of different research strategies: reading what managers themselves read, visiting all kinds of business websites, sustained conversations with numerous managers and management consultants over the last five years or so, presentations to audiences which have included managers and management consultants, and so on.[4] Third, the shape and style of the chapter is intended to simulate the fast-moving nature of the new discourse, which is, intended to produce effects through action, not simply reflect on already made possibilities (Bourdieu, 2000).[5] In a sense, I want to push a little way into the future.

practising manager   What is the forcing ground of new ways of doing 'manager'? I think it can be said to be time. Of course, since the industrial revolution, time has been a watchword of capitalism. But modern economies are based upon a particular fine-grained approximation of time, arising out of two linked developments.

The first of these developments is the increasing attention given to the measurement of *short-term financial performance*. For example, the rise of a metric like 'shareholder value', a term introduced in the 1980s by US management consultants, is indicative of both the construction of a broader field of financial visibility and, by increasing still further the pressure to increase returns, a spur to new means of corporate governance (Froud et al., 2000; Lazonick and O'Sullivan, 2000; Williams, 2000).[6] In turn, such measures have bred other measures which make more and more parts of the business organization visible to the financial gaze and so become a means to check that all parts of the business are doing equally well – at least by financial yardsticks. In turn, other measures have come into existence (often, ironically, as attempts to critique and fend off simple financial metrics like shareholder value) which attempt to summarize and often quantify all kinds of non-financial indicators like market share and quality, such as the so-called 'balanced scorecard' approach (Kaplan and Norton, 1996).[7] The net result of the spread of these measures is that not only workers but also managers now find themselves a part of a panoptic (or at least oligoptic) world based on shorter and shorter time horizons. In other words, managers too have become a part of Power's (1997) 'audit explosion', the rise of an orientation to constant checking of performance.[8]

The second development is a general speed-up in the conduct of business, chiefly, although not only, because of the increasing use of information technology.[9] In particular, the increasing speed of production and consumption (which itself seems to problematize these two terms) means that firms are forced to launch new products more frequently. It means that they are forced to compress product development cycles, especially through so-called 'concurrent engineering' – performing historically sequential activities in parallel (see Fine, 1998). And it also means that firms are driven closer to the chief actors in their world – competitors, suppliers and customers – and must react to them more quickly.

The emphasis on constant measurement of all aspects of business performance and the increasing speed of business practice put the business organization – and the manager – under growing pressure to perform as the whole process of reproduction of products and services becomes subject to more and more demanding disciplines in ways which are inevitably self-reinforcing since successful competition between firms seems to depend increasingly upon success in adopting them.

So managers must learn to manage in what is framed as a faster and more uncertain world, one in which all advantage is temporary. In such circumstances, hierarchical organizations based upon long-term strategic planning clearly will not suffice. To use the words of a well-known management guru (Kanter, 1992), giants must learn to dance. And nowhere is this terpsichorean imperative more apparent than in the need to produce rapid and continuous innovation. Under such circumstances, it is therefore no coincidence that *knowledge* has come to be seen as a resource in its own right. Knowledge becomes an asset class that a business must foster, warehouse, manage, constantly work upon, in order to produce a constant stream of innovation (Thrift, 1997, 1999).[10] New positions in the managerial division of labour –like the knowledge officer – have even been produced which are symptomatic of this recognition.

In turn, this increasing pressure to innovate has led to a much greater emphasis on *creativity*. In the rhetoric of the times:

There is more room for creativity than ever. Smaller and smaller groups of smart people can do bigger and bigger things. . . . Now there's sobering news: you're only as good as your last great idea. The half-life of any innovation is shorter than ever. People, teams and companies are feeling the heat to turn up new products, services and business models. What's the reward for one round of successful innovation? Even greater pressure to revisit your success, and to unleash yet another round of innovation.

(Muoio, 2000: 152)

Of course, innovation has always been an important part of a business organization's practice and self-image, but what we now see is much greater attention being paid to fostering the powers of creativity that will lead to innovation, most particularly through models which eschew the black-boxed model of information processing in favour of an emphasis on what Krogh and Roos (1995; Krogh et al., 1998) call 'creative' knowledge. Thus, creativity becomes a value *in itself*.

On the one hand, then, remorseless pressure towards the short term. On the other hand, remorseless pressure to be creative. Managers must somehow learn to manage in this more uncertain world in which all advantage is strictly temporary, whilst also conforming to the rigours of audit.

Against this background what is striking is the efforts to produce new kinds of 'fast' management subject able to swim in this world. They must be calculating subjects able to withstand the exigencies of faster and faster return. Yet, at precisely the same time, they must be subjects who can be creative. It is this project of new managerial subject formation that I want to address in this chapter.

Such a project requires finding a whole variety of different methods of acting upon others in order to produce subject effects. Still the best means of understanding this process are Foucault's brief writings on 'governmentality' (Dean, 1999; Foucault, 1991). In these pieces, Foucault concentrates on the *practices* of power – famously 'the conduct of conduct' – all those endeavours to shape, guide and divert the conduct of others, including the ways in which one might be urged to control one's own passions, to govern oneself. In other words, what he wanted to consider was the formation of theories, programmes, strategies and technologies for the 'conduct of conduct'.

> To govern is to act upon action. This entails trying to understand what mobilizes the domains or entities to be governed: to govern one must act upon these forces, instrumentalize them in order to shape actions, processes and outcomes in desired directions. Hence when it comes to governing human beings, to govern is to pre-suppose the freedom of the governed. To govern human beings is not to crush their capacity to act, but to acknowledge it and to utilize it for one's own objectives.
>
> (Rose, 1999: 4)

If 'governmentality' is taken to be the modern version of rule, then what is being suggested is that increasingly to rule properly means ruling in the light of particular and specific characteristics that are taken to be immanent in that over which rule is exercised. In other words,

> The activity of government is inextricably bound up with the activity of thought. It is thus both made possible by and constrained by what can be thought and what cannot be thought at any particular moment in our history. To analyse the history of government, then, requires attention to the conditions under which it becomes possible to consider certain things to be true – and hence to say and do certain things. . . .
>
> (Rose, 1994: 8)

An important element of governmentality is space. Why? Because to govern it is necessary to render visible the space over which government is to be exercised.[11] And this is not a simple matter of looking: space has to be re-presented, marked out. And these governable spaces are not fabricated counter to experience; they make new kinds of experience possible, produce new modes of perception, invest percepts with affects, with dangers and opportunities, with saliences and attractions. Through certain technical means, a new way of seeing is constructed which will 'raise lived perceptions to the percept and lived affectations to the affect'.

(Rose, 1999: 32)

This stance means that I am interested not in management identity as such (cf. Knights and Willmott, 1999), but rather in the means by which spaces can produce identity effects, the ways in which spaces figure as, to use that well-worn Foucauldian phrase, 'technologies of the self'. I am interested, in other words, in how spaces can be used to produce collective bodies and identifications 'through the inscription of particular ethical formations, vocabularies of self-description and self-mastery, forms of conduct and body techniques' (Rose, 1999: 47). This means that I think not that managers are unrelenting drones but rather that, like all of us, they are the products of (increasingly engineered) circum-stance. Nowadays, this kind of view is often gathered under the sign of 'performativity', understood as the temporalized regulation/constant re-citation of norms (Butler, 1990, 1993).[12] What I want to suggest is that practices have citational force because of the spaces in which they are embedded and through which they do work. As I have argued elsewhere (e.g. Thrift, 2000a), this kind of view runs counter to the predominant model of performativity, which is based on socio-symbolic signification (and on a corresponding politics of recognition) in that it makes more room for non-representational qualities which are a crucial part of spaces of subjectification and which allow some of the more active and positive aspects of citational force to become known and worked upon (e.g. McNay, 1999). Such a move also tracks the move to pastoral models of discipline which are so characteristic of modern societies, models which allow more space for a self-regulating subject. This move can be seen in the world of managers who are being locked down by regimes of perpetual training which also, at the same time, demand an opening up of their imaginative powers. The gendered dimension of this move is, I hope, obvious (cf. Wajcman, 1998).

This brief excursion allows us to sort out the agenda for the rest of the chapter. For what I now want to consider is a series of procedures which both show up and value the new things which are necessary to create 'fast' subjects, the subjects of the new managerial governmentality. I have called these procedures, rather glibly, *sight*, *cite* and *site*. But what I am trying to suggest by deploying these words is precisely how bound up these new procedures are with the productions of *new spaces*, spaces which, by being more active, more performative than those of old, can help to foster creativity (Thrift, 2000a). Thus sight – new spaces of visualization; cite – new spaces of embodiment; and site – new spaces of circulation.

I want to conclude this section by making four extra points. The first is that most of these spaces have only become possible because of the advent of information technology. Information technology is pivotal in numerous ways. To begin with, it is one of the main products of the new economy. Then, it is one of the main signifiers of the new economy. Information technology signifies youth, speed, excitement, buzz, and being appropriately tooled up is therefore essential for a modern manager – Palm Pilot, portable, mobile, favourite software and websites. . . . But there is more to it than this. The very ubiquity of information technology – the burgeoning ecology of everyday computing devices – means that it increasingly becomes background as a means of storing and working with knowledge, as a new expressive medium, as an image of bodily change, and as a means of producing new geographies. For example, in the case of new spaces of visualization, we will see it used – more often than not – through a crude technological determinism which maps the characteristics of technologies on to subjects – as a means of hailing the new management self ('web-ify yourself', 'becoming fast', 'becoming digital', etc.). But we will also see it used as a stylistic glue, holding new kinds of text together. In the case of new spaces of performative embodiment, we will see that computer software is part of the model of embodiment. And in the case of new spaces of business circulation, information technology is a key moment of agency. It has its own voice.[13]

The second point is that it would clearly be ludicrous to suggest that the project of governmentality I describe in more detail below has a total grip. It is quite clearly confined to certain parts of certain Western national economies. It is most prevalent in the United States (and especially states like California, with a long history of constructing of the managerial self [see Kleiner, 1996]), but it is spreading rapidly through all Western economies, usually as a key element of the 'new economy' or 'knowledge economy' package (see, e.g., *Business Week*, 2000). Similarly, this project is more likely to be found in certain industries, especially those that characterize themselves as 'fast'. For example, for manufacturing industry, Fine (1998) has produced a classification of industries based on their 'clockspeeds', which seems a very appropriate indicator. No doubt a similar classification could be produced for service industries with advertising or management consultancy in the van. Then there is firm type. The project is more likely to be found in large firms than small, but with significant exceptions, for example high-technology small firms and small services firms dependent upon project work (cf. Grabher, 2000). And there is also management type. The project of governmentality is most likely to be found where highly educated managers exist, especially those in lines of work (like human resource management) which are intimately connected to fashioning the self (Thrift, 1997, 1998). But it cannot be easily tied down to any managerial specialisation. Indeed this would be to miss the point that this project is concerned with a style of being that many managers often *want* to attain. For example, working as a manager in a top-heavy bureaucracy can be frustrating and the new project gives resources for both critique and action.[14]

Then there is a third point. Managers *are* often cynical and sceptical about the practices I describe below, aided by professional debunkers like Lucy Kellaway or 'Dilbert' (Adams 1996; Kellaway, 2000). There is a saying which managers constantly use to describe their reaction to training – '10 per cent is worth doing but you don't know which 10 per cent' – which summarizes the reaction of all but the most evangelical. However, this does not mean that these practices have no grip. Some of them, indeed, are powerful in their own right (cf. Martin, 1994). But even when their touch is light, they can still be brought to bear. They can be used by frustrated managers to produce change in stodgy organizations. They can be used by ambitious managers as a career platform. They can be used by fractious managers to justify a change of job or setting up a small firm. They can be used by managers going through personal crises to work those crises out. Managers, in other words, can be hailed in many ways.

I end this section with one more point. The project of governmentality I outline here is still nascent, still hesitant. It has not yet precipitated out into general understanding, and it may fail. 'Fast' subjects, as I will argue in the concluding section of this chapter, may well turn out to be fragile subjects only able to be held together with certain costs which ultimately may turn out to be too great to bear.

performing manager

Sight (seeing truth)   To refigure the subject of business, so that it sees new things from new perspectives, requires considerable resources: what is being produced is new means of picturing business power and identity which frames the world in a different way. Business magazines have often been used as a means of undertaking this reframing. When *Fortune* was launched in the United States in 1930, it was as a bullet aimed at the heart of American business's self-image. 'Where', asked Henry R. Luce in the prospectus, 'is the publication that even attempts to portray business in all its heroic present-day proportions, or that succeeds in conveying a sustained sense of the challenging personalities, significant trends, and high excitements of this vastly stirring civilization of Business?' (cited in Hugh, 2000: 8). So Luce's *Fortune* was high price, and included high-quality journalism and photography; the writers and editors even invented new journalistic forms like the 'corporate story' and the history of top companies. *Fortune* set the tone for how business would see itself. This was a world which was serious, masculine, 'business-like'. Pictured in suits, against the background of compact offices and board-rooms, business managers were *in control*. And the control of business was a sober and serious affair. Smartly dressed, arms crossed, photographed face on or from below.

But since the 1980s, this way of framing business has been coming under siege. Beginning, I suspect, with the financial markets of the 1980s, in which were to be found younger business people who wanted to be recognized as cultural and not just business figures, and continuing with the publication of a series of glossy business journals (for example, in the UK, the now defunct journal *Business*), a new means of framing business has gradually come about. A new style of business magazine has come into existence, of which the most visible (in a number of ways) is *Fast Company*. Founded in 1995 in the United States, published out of Boston but with a number of regional offices, the magazine is currently published ten times a year. *Fast Company* is 'the handbook of the business revolution'. 'More than a magazine; it's a movement. . . .' In effect, *Fast Company* is a cultural weapon aimed at changing business's self-image by focusing the insights of the 'new economy', an economy based on constant and unremitting change, high technology and adaptation as a way of life. It is both a material and a semiotic manifesto.[15]

A symptomatic reading of *Fast Company* suggests that it achieves five things. First, it is an attempt to produce a new 'virtual' rhetoric, aimed at visualizing the values of the new economy. To this end, much of its format is based on visual devices which simulate speed and change, for example picture layouts which mimic high technology (through devices like pixelized pages that look like computer screens) and which involve constant adaptation – by, for example, scanning, embedding and mixing images together. Much of the phatic imagery – the name given to signals which maintain discourse or dialogue but have little or no ultimate meaning – such as panels, framing devices, rules and motifs, is clearly intended to simulate computer screens. Thus, one cover designer argues that 'even when I'm not working on a computer, people think that I am because my art is very hard-edged and because I use a lot of bright, simple colours' (*Fast Company*, December 1998: 18). Second, and following on, the magazine is highly pictorial. It is a magazine for browsing – with many articles broken down into segments, which also demand a considerable degree of visual literacy, of the kind associated with computer-intermediated layouts (Cubitt, 1998; Stafford, 1999; Wood, 1998). Third, the magazine is based upon a semi-naturalistic depiction of business people. They are often photographed in casual preppy clothes, in action (although there are also power shoots of people in suits). This democratic depiction of business is enhanced by numerous characteristic biographies which are meant to act as a role model for those working in the new economy. Fourth, the emphasis is on youth. Even when subjects are over 50, they are often dressed and depicted in youthful ways: running, jumping, rarely standing still. Fifth, the magazine assumes an active audience 'like us' which will respond to its articles. It has a large website, which allows participation in online polls. And there is a readers' network, called 'Company of Friends', which has more than 18,000 members. Communication is all.

How might we see *Fast Company* as a cultural project? It is clearly an attempt to produce a new community based around the idea of a new economy which will embody particular values and produce new foundational stories. 'You are already like me' or 'You can become like me.' But it is, I think, more than this simple appeal to simulate. Most of all, I think that it can be seen as an attempt to boost the cultural capital of business. Business becomes funky, youthful, sexy, caring, fun. Business becomes where it's at, not just work but popular culture. In most studies of the distribution of economic, social and cultural capital in developed countries (e.g. Bourdieu, 1984; Lamont, 1992) managers are seen as occupying a high position in terms of economic capital but a much lower position in terms of cultural capital. But now this positioning is changing. In part, it is changing because new generations of better-educated managers brought up with the cultural preoccupations of their class and time – and keen to gain the respect of these cultural preoccupations – have come into existence. In part, it is changing because business is being seen and is seeing itself differently. As a knowledge business, it becomes a major site of cultural intensity with faster turnover times nearer to those of 'creative' industries like, say, popular music or film, which have become some of its chief exemplars. And in part it is changing through the offices of projects like *Fast Company* which provide both rallying points and means of diffusion.[16]

Cite (embodying truth)   It is February 2000. In a marquee in the grounds of Ribby Hall holiday village near Blackpool, managers from Asda, Britain's third largest supermarket chain, are being inducted into the spirit of the squirrel (making work worthwhile), the way of the beaver (control of achieving the goal) and the gift of the goose (cheering others on). It is all part of a proprietary American management training system called Gung Ho! (Blanchard and Bowles, 1998) apparently based on Native American customs and designed to motivate managers.

> Sue Newton of Asda said: 'We have devised a three-day event for managers to put it into practice among all their colleagues. Our aim is to make the event a memorable experience – there are valuable lessons to be learned about motivation, team work and leadership.'
>
> (Steiner and White, 2000: 1)

A little bit unusual perhaps, but no longer remarkable. For in the last ten years, management training – now estimated to be a $250 million business worldwide[17] – has taken a markedly performative turn, one that is based on the much more explicit design of the business of trainings. Take the case of Asda's events:

> The events, involving 40 managers, run twice a week in a marquee made up to look like a woodland scene. Coir matting covers the floor, which is crossed by a stream running to a model of a lake complete with model beavers building dams.
>
> Plastic geese hang from the ceiling in a V-formation, while models of squirrels are dotted among painted trees. Group discussions are held in mock log cabins to create what Adsa calls 'a rough and ready feel'. Staff have to prepare their own evening meals to encourage team working.
>
> As they sit round a mock fire, managers are told stories showing them ways in which Gung Ho! can be implemented when they return to civilization (fire regulations ban the real thing).
>
> (Steiner and White, 2000: 1)

Why such a performance? I think such events have to be seen as another of the means now being used by business of making the invisible visible, in this case the citational force of the body. Where has such a motivation come from? There are two main strands of practice that inform this move (Thrift, 1997, 1998).

First, there is that whole stream of work concerned with management trainings stemming from experiments at the Tavistock Institute in London in the 1940s and 1950s, the National Training League experiments in the United States in the 1950s, various counter-cultural experiments in the 1960s, and so on (cf. Kleiner, 1996), which are now exemplified by a whole series of practices which work on the management body, from encounter groups, through various forms of programming, to outward-bound courses. Then, there is a stream of work produced by those in management studies (and especially human relations) on subjects as diverse as the minutiae of management talk, ambiguity, cultural difference, emotional investments, even humour (Hatch and Ehrlich, 1993), which has made its way into actual management practice in all sorts of ways, but especially through a raft of popularizing books and trainings, as in, for example, the current vogue for 'emotional thinking' (cf. Marcus, 1998).

Arising out of these practices of inscription onto the management body, therefore, have been a whole series of practices which stress citational force and especially the use of the body as a central element of organizational processes of *learning* which can produce 'better' (i.e. more productive, more valuable) business through active participation in heightened practices of *interaction*. Such work on experiential learning dates from the 1970s on (e.g. Argyris and Schon, 1974, 1978) and became very powerful in the 1990s (Argyris, 1991; Senge, 1990, Senge et al., 1999). In other words, what is at stake is unlocking the potential of the management body, and most particularly the potential to innovate.

But to enable this process to happen, the body must be made visible so that it can be worked upon. The key difference with many previous ways of making the body visible is that this cannot happen in an unduly prescriptive way, as in, for example, the various forms of drill often applied to workers, but must be of a participative nature using interaction of a relatively open-ended kind.

> If we believe that people in organizations contribute to organizational goals by participating inventively in practices that can never be fully captured by institutionalized processes, then we will minimise prescription, suspecting that too much of it discourages the very inventiveness that makes practices effective. We will have to make sure that our organizations are contexts within which the communities that develop these practices may prosper. We will have to value the work of community-building and make sure that participants have access to the resources necessary to learn what they need to learn in order to take actions and make decisions that fully engage their own knowledge ability.
>
> (Wenger, 1998: 10)

If this process of community-building is successful, then what will be produced will be an organization which will be committed to innovation. Most particularly, it will be able to unlock its managers' imagination and *creativity*.

Many solutions to the engineering of the managerial imagination (Clegg and Birch, 1999) are on offer. However, nearly all of them involve the production of spaces of 'serious play' (Schrage, 2000) which, through partially engineered processes of inspiration, can produce innovation. The idea is that managers will be 'prepared for surprise', both in their openness and adaptability to unexpected events and in their ability to see productive anomalies.

> Innovation requires improvisation. It . . . isn't about rigorously following 'the rules of the game' but about rigorously challenging and revising them. . . . [I]nnovation is less the production of how innovators think than a by-product of how they behave. . . . The essence of serious play is the challenge and thrill of confronting uncertainties. Serious play is about improvising with the unanticipated in ways that create new value. Any tools, technologies, techniques or toys that let people improve how they play seriously with uncertainty is [sic] guaranteed to improve the quality of innovation.
>
> (Schrage, 200: 1–2)

But being prepared for surprise is not easy. Roughly speaking, we can say that it consists of activating three qualities. The first of these is cultural (Amabile, 1998). All successful learning and creativity needs to engage the passions and senses of the 'whole brain' of the company through what Hamel and Prahalad call the fostering of strategic intent, a sense of mission which is 'as much about the creation of meaning for employees as it is about the establishment of direction' (1994: 134). The second is the establishment of innovative groups which are more than the sum of their parts because they are able to deploy group-generated transactional knowledge through techniques as different as brainstorming a problem, role play, purposeful shifts in metaphors, shock experiences, visits to new environments, developing empathy through detailed observation, benchmarking, and so on (Leonard and Rayport, 1997; Leonard and Strauss, 1997; Leonard and Swap, 1999; Lester et al., 1998). The third is the design of thinking spaces which allow groups to create. This can simply mean highly malleable and adaptative spaces which allow a multitude of options and sensory registers or it can mean spaces which are highly specific means of producing innovation (see Leonard and Swap, 1999: Chap. 5).

Each of these three qualities requires, in effect, the ability *to 'stage' learning through the explicit design of memorable events* (Pine and Gilmore, 1999), events which, above all, generate passion. Given these requirements, it is no surprise that so many business organizations have tended to draw inspiration from the performing arts as a means of giving life to community, creativity and space. The performing arts are a rich archive of knowledge and techniques for making community, tuning creativity and enlivening space (Thrift, 2000a). Four examples of this tendency will suffice.

The first arises out of the increasing desire to generate commitment through 'strategic stories'. The organization is constructed as a community with its own narratives. For example, Nike has a corporate storytelling programme, first launched in the 1970s, and a number of senior executives spend much of their time acting as corporate storytellers. When the programme started it was an hour-long lesson given to all new employees. Now orientation lasts two days and the company envisages the process lasting a week and taking place at 'Nike University'. The storytellers concentrate on innovation and on heritage.

> When Nike's leaders tell the story of how Coach Bowerman, after deciding that his team needed better running shoes, went out to his workshop and poured rubber into the family waffle iron, they're not just talking about how Nike's famous 'waffle sole' was born. They're talking about the spirit of innovation. . . . 'Every company has a history,' says Dave Pearson, 43, a training manager and storyteller. But we have a little bit more than a history. We have a heritage, something that's still relevant today. If we convert people to that, chances are that they won't view Nike as just another place to work.
>
> (Ransdell, 2000: 45–6)

Much of this modern corporate storytelling has been inspired by the 'computers as theatre' movement (Laurel, 1993), and this is emphasized by the vogue for 'digital storytelling'.

> Dana Winslow Atchley III, 57, . . . uses modern tools – computers, scanners, video – to update the ancient craft of telling tales. He helps companies to harvest their artefacts, to surface compelling stories – and to render these stories in ways that are engaging and exciting. . . .
>
> Digital storytelling is more than just a technique. In fact, it's become something of a movement among both artists and business people. One convert is Bill Dauphinois, 53, of PricewaterhouseCoopers (PwC). He's been using it to teach members of the accounting and consultants group about the PwC brand. Dauphinois has collected stories about PwC's founders, patrons, and clients, and he's captured these stories on digital video and housed them on a PC. Now he travels regaling employees with video tales of the firm's core values. 'Brands are built around stories,' says Dauphinois, 'and stories of identity – who we are, where we've come from – are the most effective stories of all. This is a powerful way to bring them to life.'
>
> (Pink, 1999: 32)

The second example is the use of artistic genres which both communicate and create corporate values and strategy by amplifying new thinking. For instance, there is currently much interest in applying different modes of theatre – platform theatre, matching theatre, improvisational theatre and street theatre – to actual business situations (Pine and Gilmore, 1999). Take the case of Barbara Waugh, Hewlett Packard Labs Worldwide Personnel Manager. She has used 'Readers' Theaters' both in the labs and in the company as a whole to present options and explain strategies. For example, in one play put on by employees for an audience of colleagues, the issue was whether to extend benefits to long-term partners of gay and lesbian employees. 'Combined with dramatized evidence of discrimination and hardship, senior management reversed its original (negative) decision. The drama placed managers in the uncomfortable position of experiencing firsthand what colleagues had told them about in general terms before' (Leonard and Swap, 1999: 70). In another play, her interest was to produce a new corporate research style.

> The last thing she wanted was to preach through PowerPoint. So instead of creating bullet point slides, she drew on her experience with street theatre and created a 'play' about HP Labs. She worked passages from the surveys into dialogue and then recruited executives to act as staff members, and junior people to act as executives. The troupe performed for 30 senior managers. 'At the end of the play the managers were very quiet,' Waugh remembers. 'Then they started clapping. It was exciting. They really got it. They finally understood.'
>
> (Mieszkowski, 1998: 152).

The third example is the tendency to use actual artistic groups to enliven trainings and to help the process of thinking creatively about situations. For example, in the UK, there are currently about 80 groups of actors, dancers, artists, musicians, and so on, working in this area, either acting out situations and halting the action at key points to solicit feedback or producing means of thinking more creatively in teams.

> Companies are beginning to wake up to the advantages of a more creative approach to team-building – one that is altogether less threatening and more enjoyable. No more ropes, no more freezing mud. All hail, then, to the arts which is producing the new source of inspiration when it comes to bringing out the best in your employees.
>
> Marks and Spencer, Sainsbury's and Allied Domecq are using the UK companies to embrace this new approach to management training. Oxford Stage Company, based in Warwick, ran a workshop for Sainsbury's showing how much can be communicated through body language alone. Trade Secrets, another touring company, ran a series of communication workshops in Sainsbury's stores to accompany a national tour of *Twelfth Night*. The staff's thrill at undertaking Shakespeare for the first time (no mean feat in itself) was matched by their enthusiasm for the games and exercises.
>
> Body and Soul, based in Gloucestershire, has workers dancing along in harmony – by teaching them Rio Carnival-style salsa percussion. Employees without a musical bone in their body are eventually transformed into rhythmic pulsating beasts. It helps to increase their self-confidence and teaches them to work together. . . .

Clients include City merchant banks, along with companies such as Pfizer and Virgin, Our Price. Mr Brotherton says, 'It's very good for self-confidence and team-work. The barriers come down, people take their shoes and socks off and start dancing. They find out an awful lot about each other . . .'

But it is with the arts that management theory is really coming into its own. . . . Living Arts, based in London, gets participants to stage their own performances with the help of performers and technical staff drawn from opera, theatre, circus and film.

One group of UK business consultants on a 'bonding' trip to Lisbon were given a week in which to create an entire opera – a refreshing variation on the usual team-building games. The effect was exhilarating. One participant said, 'You forget most conferences within two days . . . We will remember this retreat in detail until we are 85.'

Tim Stocki, ABSA's (Association for Business Sponsorship of the Arts) director of programmes, reports steadily rising demand for this approach to training. 'This is a growth area,' he says. 'After years being taught to think logically and focus on the bottom line, employees are now being encouraged to think laterally and creatively. This is where artists are ideal.'

(McKee, 1999: 26–7)[18]

The fourth example, upon which I want to concentrate most of my attention, is the use of dramatic techniques to challenge entrenched ways of proceeding, thereby producing more creative outcomes. Many of these techniques for producing drama, and thereby creativity, are now used in business trainings. Just a few instances will suffice. There is, to begin with, the chief exemplar of the creative company, the London-based advertising agency St Luke's (Law, 1999; Lewin and Regine, 1999). St Luke's set out to break the mould by operating as a cooperative, locating outside the main London advertising cluster, and organizing itself in order to promote maximum creativity. For example, there is a carefully designed calendar of events (Monday Meetings, Flag Meetings, Shareholders' Day, St Luke's Day) intended to provide a structure of motivation and celebration. St Luke's has become so successful that special business tours now take place around the office space (Gernot Grabher, personal communication, 2000). Or take the Richmond, Virginia-based marketing agency Play, a small firm which delivers 'creative concepts'. In turn, about 30 per cent of the agency's revenue comes from teaching other companies to be more creative.

The 20 or so staff members in the room are instructed to invent their own super-heroes, create circumstances for them, figure out their superpowers, and invent Clark Kent-like alter egos. . . . These folks aren't goofing off. They aren't fooling

> around. They're not even acting strangely. They're actively engaged in real work for an important client with a tight deadline. But they are trying to be creative – which means, they insist, that they can't sit in boring meetings, in boring conference rooms, and expect to guarantee much beyond boring ideas.
>
> Play's undeniably playful workplace affects the company's overall approach to the hard work of creativity. . . . When you turn work into a place that encourages people to be themselves, have fun and take risks, you unleash their creativity.
>
> (Dahle, 2000: 170)

Or take Rolf Smith's 'Thinking Expeditions', run from Estes Park, Colorado.

> A Thinking Expedition combines creative problem solving with challenging outdoor experimental learning – similar to an Outward Bound boot camp for the mind. 'It's an accelerated unlearning process,' Smith explains. 'The days are intense, full, and demanding. There are no scheduled meals, no scheduled breaks. We deliberately design the expedition to put people out of their "stupid zone" – a place of mental and physical normalcy – so that they can start to think differently, explore what they don't know, and discover answers to mission-critical problems.'
>
> (Muoio, 2000: 152)

Or take the Ehama Institute, the province of a Native American tribe which teaches 'creative development' through ritual and ceremony. The Institute mixes the 'earth wisdom' of Native American spiritual traditions and the tenets of the learning organization as a means of producing 'sustainable cultural change'.

But the instance I want to concentrate on is the work of a firm called Business Development Associates, a $30 million consultancy established in 1989 which now has 150 associates, working from offices in Alameda in California, Santiago in Chile, Colonia Polanco in Mexico and Frankfurt in Germany. It has carried out consultancy in the United States, Canada, Mexico, Chile, Ireland, Italy and Switzerland. The company is, in a certain sense, idiosyncratic but it is also exemplary of a certain performative means of proceeding, and fascinating because of its strong allegiances to transferring certain kinds of academic theory into practice.

The company is based around the charismatic and intensely interesting figure of Fernando Flores. At a very early age, Flores was placed in charge of Chilean state-owned corporations by Salvador Allende. In rapid succession he then became Minister of Economics and then Minister of Finance. During this time, he was instrumental in the large-scale project to apply cybernetic theory to practical economic management problems (Beer, 1975).

After the fall of the Allende government, he was imprisoned for a number of years. On release, he moved in 1976 to the United States, where he began a Ph.D. programme at the University of California, Berkeley, drawing together several fields – philosophy, computing, operations research and management. In particular, he drew on the work of Heidegger and speech act theorists like Austin and Searle to understand language as a constitutive medium and communication as a structure of commitments to act (Flores, 1998). From Heidegger, Flores learned that language conveys not only information – such as 'send message', 'make report' and 'make promise' (Winograd and Flores, 1987: 179) – 'but also *commitment*, and that people act by comparing assessments and promises. Computers, he concluded, would be more effective if they recorded and traded commitments, rather than simply moving information' (Rubin, 1999: 199, my emphasis). Using this kind of insight, Flores finished his dissertation in 1979 and proceeded on a chequered career which has included the setting up of a number of software and consultancy firms. He also completed an important and influential book on software design which argued that computers were essentially concerned with communication rather than computation: 'Computers are not only designed in language but are themselves equipment for language. They will not just reflect our understanding of language, but will at the same time create new possibilities for the speaking and listening that we do – for creating ourselves in language' (Winograd and Flores, 1986: 79). It is clear that Flores already regarded training as a complementary element of this approach to design since 'it is impossible to completely avoid breakdown by means of design. What can be designed are aids for those who live in a particular domain of breakdowns. These aids include training . . .' (Winograd and Flores, 1986: 165).[19] The trainings were devoted to teaching the fulfilment of promises and commitments in day-to-day work operation: 'how to train people to improve their effectiveness in working with others. This training in "communication for action" reveals for people how their language acts participate in a network of human commitment' (Winograd and Flores, 1986: 179).

Flores' ideas are set down most fully in a recent book with Charles Spinosa, a Shakespeare scholar and Vice-President of Business Development Associates, and Hubert Dreyfus, the renowned philosopher (Spinosa et al., 1997). For these authors, innovation cannot be reduced to a series of stable and regular procedures; a systematic means of dealing with the facts of the world. Instead, it is about opening up new spaces for human action by cultivating *sensitivity to anomaly*, that is, purposely attempting to change the way we see and understand things so that what counts as a fact is changed. The approach, then, is 'attempting to develop sensitivities, not knowledge' (Spinosa et al., 1997: 39).

In turn, the book also provides a 'composite' account of Flores' turn to this approach:

Our representative . . . started out as an executive-level director of national economic planning. He thought that the primary concern of a person in his position was to ensure that his office produced the best possible model of the economy, which could then be used as a guide to improve the efficiency and functioning of every economic institution in society. Though he was trained both to develop such models and to evaluate the models others developed, he seldom found time to do this work. Instead he was constantly talking, he explained this and that, to that and this person, put person A in touch with person B, held press conferences, and so forth. It seemed to him that he was doing nothing substantial. And if we think of work as a matter of performing certain tasks to produce certain products, little, indeed, was being done. This entrepreneur, however, did not simply inure himself to the fact that what he was doing was different from what he thought ought to be done. Rather, he retained the oddity in his life as an anomaly.

Holding on to an anomaly as an anomaly is not an easy matter to describe. It is a matter of constantly being sensitive to the anomaly as happening in one's life. In our case, the entrepreneur remained sensitive to the fact that his work was not producing any concrete or abstract theory but that he was working nonetheless. Because he was sensitive to the anomaly, it eventually led him to take a course on the theory of speech acts and in that course he found a key to the anomaly. He came to realize that this anomalous aspect of his work was actually its central feature. He saw that work no longer made any sense as the craftsmanship of writing this or that sentence or the skilled labour of bringing this or that widget into shape but that currently work was becoming a matter of co-ordinating human activity – opening up conversations about one thing or another to produce a binding promise to perform an act.

(Spinosa et al., 1997: 45–6)

In turn, this notion of conversation and promise as central components of work has led to the practices of Business Development Associates, which are aimed at redescribing the nature of particular businesses, and then, through trainings, the implementation of changes of identity that will produce this redescription – a shift in the ingrained domain, in other words. They aim, that is, to increase sensitivity to anomaly, and therefore foster creativity by changing the status of things within the community through the production of speech acts which confer 'new identities, duties, rights, affects and values' (Flores, 1998: 21).[20] The practices are intended to produce trust through total commitment to speech as embodied action, which can create new values and new worlds.

Talk all you want to, Flores says, but if you want to act powerfully you need to master 'speech acts': language rituals that build trust between colleagues and customers, word practices that open your eyes to new possibilities. Speech acts are powerful because most of the actions that people engage in – in business, in marriage, in parenting – are carried out through conversation. But most people speak without intention; they simply say whatever comes to mind. Speak with intention and your actions take on new purpose. Speak with power, and you act with power.

(Rubin, 1999: 144)

To this end, Flores uses scripts which are aimed at conjuring up moments of truth and trust in which transformation can occur. Speech becomes a kind of weapon to batter down prejudices and preconceptions. 'To speak in language that practices action, you must practice *assessments* (to work on truth) and generate *commitment* (to work on trust)' (Rubin, 1999: 149). Assessments are often brutal because 'if we are asked to give conditions under which we would give up being who we are, we tend to fight rather than switch' (Flores, 1998: 23). They are aimed, in effect, at ridding speech acts of the taint of defeat through scripted call and response. Commitment involves making bold promises which drive action by asking more of managers, and ultimately build trust:[21] '[V]alue is produced by a story. Value lies in creating a new possibility' (Flores in Rubin, 1999: 151). And these stories require body.

In a flash, Flores becomes Ryan. He rounds his shoulders into his chest, recedes into himself, and says in a wimpy voice, 'I think it will give us advantages.' Then he shouts, 'There is no energy in that story. You need to put your body into it, there is no truth. And without that you can't sell the idea, not even to yourself.' Flores is standing. Spit is flying from his mouth. He conveys the message with his whole body. 'Ryan, you are a Dilbert leader. You never take a stand. And here you are listening to Felix, who is resignation personified. You know what mood you are in? The life-is-tough mood. "Don't be too optimistic. Next year, we'll lose a little less than this year." If you live in a mood, you are blind to it. The last time I made that mistake, I was in prison for three years.'

(Rubin, 1999: 151)[22]

What can we say about the new means of embodying fast subjects, then? That bodies can be trained to *act* their way out of the new management dilemmas through new techniques of the self based, especially, in the lore of the humanities. Activity becomes a means of making the fictive fact. It is imagination reincarnated. It is a citational force.

Site (geographies of truth)   Let me now move to the final set of procedures I want to discuss: locational practices. For new means of producing creativity and innovation are bound up with new geographies of circulation which are intended to produce situations in which creativity and innovation can, quite literally, take place. I will mention three of these geographies of circulation as currently being particularly important.

The first of these is the constant quartering of the globe by executive travellers. For some time, it was assumed by many commentators that the volume of business travel would ultimately begin to decline as the effects of information technology bit. Yet, in fact, this does not seem to be happening: business travel volume continues to increase as workforces become more and more mobile.

> Personnel [are spending] less of their time working in offices. It may be necessary for them to attend corporate premises for meetings with colleagues but, increasingly, more time will be spent working on projects at home and spending time away from the office with customers and business partners. In the United States roughly 25 per cent of the labour force is mobile in this sense. In the United Kingdom the figure is 35 per cent and growing. By 2010 this [may] reach over 60 per cent – a staggering change in the patterns and culture of work.
>
> (Scase, 1999: 7)

In part at least, this increase in the volume of business travel seems to be the result of attempts to engineer knowledge creation. This process of engineering is oriented toward settings which privilege face-to-face interaction on the grounds that

> All the technology in the world does not – at least yet, and maybe never – replace face-to-face contact when it comes to brainstorming, inspiring passion, or enabling many kinds of serendipitous discovery. A study of geographically dispersed product development has found that team members conducting complex tasks *always* would have preferred to have a 'richer' medium (that is, one supporting more channels and more interaction) than they actually had to use. Fax is fine for one-way communication; e-mail for two-way, a synchronous and relatively emotionless communication; telephone for communications that require no visual aids; and video conferencing if no subtlety in body language is necessary. But face-to-face communication is the richest multi-channel medium because it enables use of all the senses, is interactive and immediate.
>
> (Leonard and Swap, 1999: 160)

But, increasingly, information technology allows these kinds of creative interactions to take place because it enables managers to be in on more face-to-face meetings and the organization whilst still keeping in touch with home base, rather than being a means for the home base to control the periphery. The home base comes visiting. Control, or, more accurately, modulation, is executed through *the circulation itself* (Latour, 1993). For example, take the case of the Chief Knowledge Officer of PricewaterhouseCoopers, Ellen Knapp.

The life requires dedication and organization. The resolutely cheerful Ms Knapp says that her blessings involve a constitution immune to jet-lag, two children who are grown up and two extremely efficient assistants, whom she compares to Mission Control at NASA. She grabs exercise whenever she can and sticks to activities and hotels she knows well (London's Ritz wins points for having rewired its rooms). PricewaterhouseCoopers (PwC) tries to make life easier for her, scheduling meetings at hubs (all the west American partners, for instance, meet in Los Angeles); it has also started a 'hotelling policy' at its offices, where itinerants like Ms Knapp are given a desk and telephone connection when they arrive. 'My place of work', she says 'is simply where I am.'

This sounds endearingly modern. All the same, it is hard not to feel tired just listening to Ms Knapp describe her week. With all this endless flitting around, no wonder that executives are increasingly complaining about stress. The overworked American is, in truth, often an overtravelled American.

All of which prompts the question: are these journeys really necessary? Ms Knapp is, after all, a chief information officer. Surely one of the points of all the computer hardware that PwC has bought (not to mention the even bigger pile it has encouraged clients to buy) is to make big companies seem smaller. Company intranets are supposed to be ways to swap knowledge. Cheaper telecoms are meant to be killing distance. Why go to Frankfurt to talk to colleagues who could read an e-mail or join a video conference?

The answer seems to be that technology is more help as a way of keeping the peregrinating Ms Knapp in touch with home than in getting far-flung offices to collaborate. As Ms Knapp points out, technology depends on trust. PwC has nearly 150,000 people in 152 countries: a bossy e-mail from somebody you had never met could put you off. . . . Ms Knapp thinks that you have to meet people first: 'it is important to gesticulate'. A bubbly lady, her powers of persuasion would indeed be diminished by e-mail. . . .

Merely knowing other people and persuading them to share knowledge is only half the battle. If juggernauts such as PwC are to be more than the sum of their parts they must get people to spark off ideas from each other – and that seems to depend on direct contact. Anecdotal evidence suggests that for every heralded example of something designed 'virtually' by two people in different locations, a lot of other new products are dreamt up during idle banter by the coffee machines. . . .

(*Economist*, 1999: 76)

And this brings us to the second geography of circulation: the construction of office spaces which can promote creativity through carefully designed patterns of circulation (Duffy, 1997; Worthington, 1996). Office space is organized in such a way that it 'can maximize learning through providing the apparatus for much more face-to-face interaction' (Duffy, 1997: 50) and can be saturated with prodigious amounts of information technology, which both enable and expand the opportunities for this interaction: 'the conventions that determine office layout, predating the punch card, have little relevance in a world of work' (Duffy, 1997: 51). The design logic of the new office therefore moves from the old 'hive' and 'cell' spaces, based on institutionalized clerical processes and individualized enclaves which demonstrate the incremental rewards of career longevity, towards 'den' spaces and 'club' spaces, integrative spaces generating transactional knowledge via interactive group work and connected team projects on an as-need basis. Thus the space requirements of offices are increasingly engineered. For example, increasingly explicit information technology strategies are used to break down the barriers between formal and informal working by enforcing mobility. Fixed offices become rarer and instead managers have 'touchdown' areas. At the extreme are offices like those of Accenture (formerly Andersen Consulting) in Paris, which have no fixed abode space: consultants book space as and when they need it; their possessions are kept on a trolley. Moreover, the space requirements of offices increasingly include all manner of meeting spaces: conference rooms, meeting rooms, play spaces, kitchens, and so on. It is even possible to build indoor streets with cafés, restaurants, indoor pubs or even, in the case of one Canadian company, a Zen garden. And the engineering of office space can go even further, down to the smallest of spaces. For example, ranges of high-interaction furniture have been designed, from furniture for meeting rooms which can be rapidly moved about, to break-area furniture which, based on careful observation, enables people to interact.

There are many examples of these new office spaces (see Duffy, 1997). Here, I will fix on just one. This is the new British Airways headquarters designed by Neils Torp and opened in 1998.

When BA decided to abandon the ancient office building beside Heathrow's runways, Bob Ayling, its boss, made up his mind to 'move his office, change the culture'. Mr Ayling . . . has long believed that the airline retains a bureaucratic hangover from its days in the public sector. He wants to use the new offices to make a decisive break with the past. Step inside BA's front door and you soon understand that things have changed. After passing the receptionists, lined up like check-in desks, you walk between two giant wheels from the undercarriage of a jumbo jet. The main corridor, linking six small office blocks within the complex, is a village street, complete with cobbles and wayside trees. The core of the building deliberately tries to ape an English village square. Workers arriving from the basement car park have to walk across the square to get to their office space. The aim is to ensure that people's paths cross, easy informal communications.

John Wood is the airline's director for the Pacific Rim market. Like other BA employees, he does not have his own office. In the two weeks a month that he is not travelling he has a touch-down area next to the team area where his staff work. Previously, BA clung to old bureaucratic norms, with bosses on a floor to themselves far away from their staff. Mr Ayling says that when he wants to talk to one of his directors, he is forced to walk through the building, meeting people on the way and exchanging a few words. 'I learn more in a couple of days than I used to in month,' he says.

The building is more than a traditional corporate headquarters; it also houses a training department right by the village square, complete with a mock-up of a jumbo jet's first class cabin. On any day, 100 front-line cabin crew or ground staff are there on a course. Mr Ayling hopes this too will break down barriers between head office and staff in the field.

It takes more than a world-class architect . . . to make such an idea work. BA has invested £10m ($16m) in fancy IT; staff wander round with digital cordless telephones that double as their desk phones. Employees can even order groceries electronically from a local store and have them delivered to their car in the garage before they go home.

(*Economist*, 1998: 88)

Then there is one more geography of circulation, the increasing move towards constructing new institutions which can promote knowledge exchange and sharing by bringing different actors together via information technology. There are now a multitude of these institutions of exchange, both intra-company (such as Arthur Andersen's Knowledge X-Change, intended, via information technology, to promote continuous exchange of knowledge between partners) and inter-company (such as the numerous 'thinking studios' which have been set up on the Internet, some of which feature spectacular attempts to create virtual simulations of landscapes of information exchange, as in the Strategic Horizons web page). An attempt is thereby being made to produce a 'flocking' of business organizations and people around particular creative intensities on the principle that innovation often comes from taking ideas across boundaries. For example,

To facilitate 'productive flocking' the Marketing Council and London Business School have created an Innovation Exchange, a network of companies keen to foster creativity by swapping ideas and sharing experience. Launched on Tuesday by Stephen Byers, trade and industry secretary, the exchange provides a web site for member companies, access to search on innovation and a programme of workshops and seminars.

(Willman, 1999: 19)

The construction of these institutions is heavily dependent upon technical issues like speed and interoperability but also demands outline human skills like facilitation (Senge et al., 1999). The goal is to provide virtual clustering, the clusters being intellectual 'stages' through which creativity can be unleashed.

conclusions   I have tried to outline a new style of doing business, one in which certain things that were previously invisible are now made visible and so available to be operated on. This creation of visibility is, I hope I have shown, intimately bound up with the construction of new spaces of action in which the previously unremarked becomes marked and objectified, and a new fast subject position can be formed.

This, then, is the first conclusion. What we can see is a new set of embodied resources being brought into the world for capitalist firms to operate on and with, resources that might well prove to be on a par with, say, the invention of perspective, double-entry book-keeping, filing, various means of production management, and so on. These resources are both new business practices and means of creating new kinds of previously unavailable products. We are, if you like, witness to the birth of a new ecology of business.

And the rhetoric of this new business ecology is all nice. This is a world where business is smart and fast but it also has values and reaches out to the community. This is, if you like, a kind of Land's End capitalism, dressed down and tasteful, participative and community-oriented, responsible. Or maybe it is something else, and this is my second conclusion. Maybe what we are seeing is a new phase of imperialism.[23] In the nineteenth century, a great map of mankind was developed by the ideologues of Western nations based upon the distinguishing characteristics of race. The peoples of the world were able to be distributed in order of priority according to racial characteristics. Now, perhaps, a new great map of personkind is coming into existence, a map based upon other attributes of personhood and, most specifically, potential for innovation and creativity. On the border of this map we would see a frieze of particular creative types, no doubt with *Homo Silicon Valleycus* in the evolutionary lead. And instead of maps of climate or characteristics like skull type, there would be major airports and educational systems. Yet the net result might, I suspect, be surprisingly similar to the old map – with a few exceptions made for new entrants like the Japanese and overseas Chinese.[24]

And this downside is accompanied by another, which is my third conclusion. That is, that for there to be faster subjects, there have to be slower ones. Not just in the sense that the new geographies of circulation depend upon a large, static workforce, from Ellen Knapp's 'mission control' to all the people servicing the information technology and the aeroplanes, but also in the sense of all those workers who, living in this marginal world of perpetual training and forced team working, have been shorn of a vocabulary of protest (Crang, 1999; Sennett, 1998).[25] But then, and this is the fourth conclusion, this fast world may not last. It is critically dependent upon an American business model of short-term returns which may well have its limits.[26] Maybe the emphasis on a permanent state of emergency is the most successful one at this conjuncture in time (McKenna, 1997), but it has its problems. For example, by 2000 *Fast Company* was expressing concern over the increasing prevalence of 'built to flip' rather than 'built to last' companies, based on the practice of selling up 'quick companies' that realize instant profits.

> The hard truth is that we're dangerously close to killing the soul of the new economy. Even worse, we're in danger of becoming the very thing we defined ourselves in opposition to. Those who kindled the spirit of the new economy rejected the notion of working just for money; today, we seem to think that it's fine to work just for money – as long as it's a lot of money.
>
> (Collins, 2000: 132)

In other words, managers now more often see themselves as *entitled* to make money; a sure sign of a boom in decay.

But more than this, and this is my final conclusion, there is no guarantee that the process of producing fast subjects that are capable of functioning in this fast world can or will succeed. This is an unfinished project and a legitimate language and body of knowledge is still being created. Indeed, what is interesting about current management literature, from the popular to the academic, is the amount of space given over to the stresses and strains of being a member of the new economy – sometimes it seems as if all that managers have found are ways to oppress themselves as well as workers (Schor, 1993). Is it possible for a manager to achieve 'balance', to 'live lightly', to be a 'sustainable person' – and be a change agent? Or is it the case that 'the more you get the less you feel you have. The faster I go, the faster I feel I need to go' (Barlow, 1999: 84)? There could hardly be a better description of capitalism. And 'how thin can I spread myself before I'm no longer there' (Barlow, 1999: 84)? Could there be a better description of the perils of the new subject position and the parallel necessity to act into it.

notes

I would like to acknowledge the thinking space provided by the Swedish Collegium for Advanced Study in the Social Sciences (SCASSS) and the stimulation from audiences at the Cultural Economy Seminar at the Open University, University of Liverpool, University of Lund, the University of Reading, the University of Uppsala and CRICT at Brunel University. I received particularly helpful comments from Gordon Clark, Paul du Gay, Kevin Hetherington, Orvar Löfgren, Greg McLennan, Tom Osborne, Chris Philo, Maryvonne Plessis-Fraissard, Mike Pryke, Nikolas Rose, Edgar Whitley and Steve Woolgar.

A seminar by Jared Diamond at SCASSS gave me the inspiration to write about imperialism.

1. Thus the constant use of tables of binaries in the literature, such as: bureaucratic/entrepreneurial, management/leadership, individuals/teams, information/intelligence, strategy/uncertainty, etc. (cf. Clarke and Clegg, 1998).

2. Exaggeration is a constant. For example, the notion of most managers flitting from one assignment to another is clearly ludicrous. Thus, in the United States,

> research by Income Data Services found that in 1993, 36 per cent of men had been with the same employer for ten years or more. This was at the peak of the downsizing mania. Interestingly – and surprisingly given the hysterical talk of the emerging promiscuous work force – in 1968 exactly the same proportion (37.7 per cent) of men had been with the same employer for ten years or more. More research from Business Strategies forecast that 79.2 per cent of all employees would be in full-time permanent jobs in 2005 – compared with 83.9 per cent in 1986. The revolution has been postponed.
>
> (Crainer, 2000: 219)

3. 'Paul Klee described the act of painting in similar terms: "not to render the visible, but to render visible" – that is, to render visible forces that are not visible in themselves' (Smith, 1997: xxxv).

4. The chapter therefore represents a kind of empiricism but one that is closer to the transversal empiricism founded by Deleuze when he compares his work in part to a detective novel. Deleuze's emphasis on a method of inventiveness (the invention of concepts as objects of here-and-now encounter) and, accordingly, on small differences and weak generalities is surely appropriate. As Rose adds, it also 'seems closest to the most instructive studies of governmentality [since it escapes] the banal grandiosity of so many sociological proclamations about our "post"-enlightenment, "post"-modern, "post-traditional" epoch . . .' (1999: 13). The chapter can also be seen as the beginnings of a contribution towards 'the anthropology of the contemporary' sketched out in the epilogue of Rabinow (1999), which fixes on local analyses of a relatively small number of objects in order to construct provisional diagrams.

5. The chapter therefore lies appropriately in the midst of my attempts to establish a body of non-representational theory in the social sciences and humanities, especially by emphasizing performance (e.g. Thrift, 2000a, 2000b; Thrift and Dewsbury, 2000).

6. The upshot, as described by Froud et al. (1999: 109) is

> a general cheapening of the work of management, as managers resort to an endless series of cheap financial dodges; this year's target is met by ending the defined benefit pension scheme, which saves labour costs, and next year's dodge is leasing the trucks so the capital appears on somebody else's balance sheet. This work is punctuated by major restructuring and changes of owner- ship where it is the financial engineering which is crucial. . . .
>
> (2000: 109)

Compare this with the rhetoric of the new economy.

7. This approach retains financial measures such as return-on-capital employed and economic value, but supplements these with new measures of value creation for customers and enhancement of processes internal to the firm (such as inno- vation levels and the creation of capital in employees and systems).

8. There is no space here to go into the whole question of accounting, and especi- ally the arguments made by writers like Baruch Lev for new accounting meas- ures that can value newly visible elements of the economy.

9. This has now gone beyond a simple emphasis on 'flexibility' and the like.

10. This knowledge is of two kinds. There is codified knowledge as set down in handbooks and procedures. And, increasingly, there is tacit knowledge, whose importance has been noted since the rediscovery of the writings of Michael Polanyi (1996), but has been most famously set down in Nonaka and Takeuchi's *The Knowledge-Creating Company* (1995).

11. I wholeheartedly agree with Rose (1999: 32) that standard oppositions of the kind – lived and represented, experiment and conceptualized, abstract and con- crete – are unhelpful, even actively misleading (see Thrift, 2000c). Also like him, I am interested not in grandiose statements about 'spatiality' but rather in how spaces are constructed as practical ensembles (cf. Thrift, 1996).

12. This heightened emphasis on performativity can also, of course, be seen as part of a more general cultural turn towards a performative subject (Abercrombie and Longhurst, 1998).

13. Information technology, in other words, is a causal element of almost everything described in this chapter, but as a moment in networks of new practices, not as the new practices themselves.

14. This may be why the project of governmentality also holds out so much attrac- tion for so many Western national governments.

15. Interestingly, many older business magazines have taken on elements of *Fast Company*'s style and layout.

16. As if signifying these new allegiances, a number of British cultural institutions have begun to produce exhibitions of business representation. For example, in Britain in 2000 the National Portrait Gallery had an exhibition on managers and business people, while the Victoria and Albert Museum held an exhibition on brands.

17. The global executive education market has been calculated to be worth more than $12 billion per annum with business schools calculated take at $3 bil- lion of this total. However, if the millions spent on management and business

education at degree level are added in, then this figure is arrived at (Crainer, 2000).

18. The examples can be multiplied. Cranfield Management School, for example, now runs an entire training syllabus around Shakespeare's plays (McKee, 1999).

19. Flores also flirted, not unusually for the time and the place, with EST (Erhard Seminars Training). In certain senses, the origins of much of what is now regarded as writ in modern management can be found in 1960s counter-cultural practice (see Kleiner, 1996)

20. '[I]n large part we live in the as-yet-unknown assessment of others – chiefs, bosses, market analysts, friends, spouses, students, colleagues, anonymous professional evaluators – whose effects we will only come to know later. These judgements themselves live within changing general understandings of the meaning of evaluation terms' (Flores, 1998: 63). In other words, 'we are who we are because of the response we have made to the way we have been recognized' (Flores, 1998: 64).

21. Thus, commitment consists of four basic speech acts: request, promise, declaration, assessment. In turn, focusing on commitments makes it possible to identify mis-coordination (e.g. tiresome meetings or missed engagements), identify possible new institutions, and actively develop them.

> The basic organizing skill is forming and managing a commitment to deal with a concern. On the basis of one commitment many others can be grown. Frequently people who do not see this basic law about commitment end up paralysing themselves by thinking that they need a great deal of money or a large social network to start a new organization. Consequently, we tend to depend upon established parties and organization to take political action and overlook our own organizational powers.
>
> (Flores, 1998: 21)

22. Interestingly the article on Flores in *Fast Company* prompted letters accusing him of using an unnecessarily macho style.

23. The fact that much of the thinking on which this chapter is based comes from the United States and is practised in US corporations may lend some force to this conclusion (cf. Furusten, 1999), but I think this is too easy a step. I am struck by how cosmopolitan some management thinking is now becoming, leaving writers like Beck (1998) to argue that business managers may even be the role model for a new cosmopolitan citizen. What is clear is that the links between academia and business are closer than ever before, which must lead academics to feel some unease about their part in this project (see the chapters in Marcus, 1998).

24. This is an uncomfortable map for academics, I might add. See Bourdieu and Wacquant (1999) and the subsequent reactions in *Theory, Culture & Society*.

25. One of the things that struck me in my constant reading of management magazines is how rarely workers figure. The problems on display are nearly all those of the management self.

26. It should be noted that for some fast is triumphal. Thus McKenna (1997), for example, argues that

> American companies are actually evidence that emphasis on short-term considerations is the best guarantor of longer-term strengths and competitiveness. For this seeming paradox there is a parallel in long-distance running. You do not train for marathons by running marathons every day but by running shorter distances and sprints.
>
> (1997: 83)

I think that this statement will soon look very dated.

references

Abercrombie, N. and Longhurst, B. (1998) *Audiences*. London: Sage.

Adams, S. (1996) *The Dilbert Principle*. New York: HarperCollins.

Amabile, T. (1998) 'How to kill creativity', *Harvard Business Review*, September–October: 83–101.

Argyris, C. (1991) 'Teaching smart people how to learn', *Harvard Business Review*, May–June: 68–93.

Argyris, C. and Schon, D. (1974) *Theory in Practice*. New York: Wiley.

Argyris, C. and Schon, D. (1978) *Organizational Learning*. New York: Wiley.

Barlow, J.P. (1999) Balancing acts, *Fast Company*, February: 84.

Beck, U. (1998) 'Cosmopolitics', *Dissent*, 43: 87–98.

Beer, S. (1975) *Platform for Change*. New York: Wiley.

Blanchard, G. and Bowles, M. (1998) *Gung Ho!* New York: William Morrow.

Bourdieu, P. (1984) *Distinction*. London: Routledge and Kegan Paul.

Bourdieu, P. (2000) *Pascalian Meditations*. Cambridge: Polity.

Bourdieu, P. and Wacquant, L. (1999) 'On the cunning of imperialist reason', *Theory, Culture & Society*, 16: 41–58.

Business Week (2000) 'The New Economy', *Business Week*, 31 January, pp. 34–49.

Butler, J. (1990) *Gender Trouble*. New York: Routledge.

Butler, J. (1993) *Bodies That Matter*. New York: Routledge.

Clarke, T. and Clegg, S. (1998) *Changing Paradigms: The Transformation of Management Knowledges for the 21st Century*. London: HarperCollins.

Clegg, B. and Birch, P. (1999) *Imagination Engineering*. London: Financial Times.

Collins, J. (2000) 'Built to flip', *Fast Company*, 32: 131–43.

Colvin, G. (2000) 'Managing in the Info Era', *Fortune*, 14 (5): F2–F5.

Crainer, S. (2000) *The Management Century. A Critical Review of 20th Century Thought and Practice*. San Francisco: Jossey Bass.

Crang, P. (1999) 'Organizational geographies: surveillance display and the spaces of power in business organisations, in J. Sharp, P. Routledge, C. Philo and R. Paddison (eds), *Entanglements of Power: Geographies of Domination/ Resistance*. London: Routledge.

Cubitt, S. (1998) *Digital Aesthetics*. London: Sage.

Dahle, C. (2000) 'Mind games', *Fast Company*, 31: 168–80.

Dean, M. (1999) *Governmentality*. London: Sage.

Duffy, F. (1997) *The New Office*. London: Conran Octopus.

Economist (1998) 'Corporate head offices: plans to linger', *The Economist*, 1 August, p. 88.

Economist (1999) 'On a wing and a hotel room', *The Economist*, 9 January, p. 76.

Fine, H. (1998) *Clockspeed*. Boston: Harvard Business School Press.

Flores, F. (1998) 'Information technology and the institution of identity: reflections since *Understanding Computers and Cognition*, *Information Technology and People*, 7: 28–42.

Foucault, M. (1991) 'Governmentality', in G. Burchell, C. Gordon and P. Miller (eds), *The Foucault Effect*. Hemel Hempstead: Harvester Wheatsheaf.

Froud, J., Haslan, C., Johal, S. and Williams, K. (2000) 'Shareholder value and financialization: consultancy promises, management moves', *Economy and Society*, 29 (1): 80–110.

Furusten, S. (1999) *Popular Management Books*. London: Routledge.

Grabher, G. (2000) 'Ecologies of creativity: the village, the group and the heterarchic organization of the British advertising industry', *Environment and Planning A*, 33 (2): 351–74.

Hamel, G. and Prahalad, C.K. (1994) *Competing for the Future*. Boston: Harvard Business School Press.

Hatch, M.J. and Ehrlich, S.B. (1993) 'Spontaneous humour as an indicator of paradox and ambiguity in organisations', *Organizational Studies*, 14: 505–26.

Hugh, J.W. (2000) 'We're 70!', *Fortune*, 13 March, pp. 7–9.

Illinitch, A.Y., Lewin, A.Y. and D'Aveni, R. (eds) (1998) *Managing in Times of Disorder: Hypercompetitive Organizational Responses*. Thousand Oaks, CA: Sage.

Kanter, R.M. (1992) *When Giants Learn to Dance: Mastering the Challenges of Strategy Management and Careers in the 1990s*. London: Business Press.

Kaplan, R.S. and Norton, D.P. (1996) *The Balanced Scorecard: Translating Strategy into Action*. Boston: Harvard Business School Press.

Kellaway, L. (2000) *Sense and Nonsense in the Office*. London: Financial Times Books.

Kleiner, A. (1996) *The Age of Heretics: Heroes, Outlaws and the Forerunners of Corporate Change*. New York: Doubleday.

Knights, D. and Willmott, H. (1999) *Management Lives: Power and Identity in Work Organizations*. London: Sage.

Krogh, G. von and Roos, J. (1996) *Managing Knowledge: Perspectives on Co-operation and Competition*. London: Sage.

Krogh, G. von, Roos, J. and Kleine, D. (eds) (1998) *Knowing in Firms: Understanding, Managing and Meaning Knowledge*. London: Sage.

Lamont, M. (1992) *Money, Morals and Manners: The Culture of the French and American Upper Middle Class*. Chicago: University of Chicago Press.

Latour, B. (1993) *We Have Never Been Modern*. Hemel Hempstead: Harvester Wheatsheaf.

Laurel, B. (1993) *Computers as Theatre*. Reading, MA: Addison Wesley.

Law, A. (1999) *Creative Company: How St Luke's Became the Ad Agency to End all Ad Agencies*. New York: Wiley.

Lazonick, W. and O'Sullivan, M. (2000) 'Maximizing shareholder value: a new ideology for corporate governance', *Economy and Society*, 29 (1): 13–35.

Leonard, D.F. and Rayport, J.F. (1997) 'Spark innovation through empathic design', *Harvard Business Review*, November–December: 163–75.

Leonard, D. and Strauss, S. (1997) 'Putting your company's whole brain to work', *Harvard Business Review*, July–August: 65–86.

Leonard, D. and Swap, W. (1999) *When Sparks Fly: Igniting Creativity in Groups*. Boston: Harvard Business School Press.

Lester, R., Piore, M.J. and Malek, K.M. (1988) 'Interpretative management: what general managers can learn from design', *Harvard Business Review*, March–April: 44–57.

Lewin, R. and Regine, B. (1999) *The Soul at Work*. London: Orion.

McKee, V. (1999) 'Dramatic challenge to art of team building', *The Times*, 6 February, pp. 26–7.

McKenna, R. (1997) *Real Time: Preparing for the Age of the Never Satisfied Customer*. Boston: Harvard Business School Press.

McNay, L. (1999) 'Subject, psyche and agency: the work of Judith Butler', *Theory, Culture & Society*, 16 (1): 175–94.

Marcus, G. (ed.) (1998) *Corporate Futures: The Diffusion of the Culturally Sensitive Corporate Form*. Chicago: University of Chicago Press.

Martin, E. (1994) *Flexible Bodies*. Boston: Beacon Press.

Mieszkowski, K. (1998) 'Barbara Waugh', *Fast Company*, December: 146–54.

Muoio, A. (2000) 'Idea summit', *Fast Company*, 31: 150–94.

Nonaka, I. and Takeuchi, H. (1995) *The Knowledge-Creating Company*. New York: Oxford University Press.

Pine, B.J. and Gilmore, J.H. (1999) *The Experience Economy: Work is Theatre and Every Business a Stage*. Boston: Harvard Business School Press.

Pink, P.H. (1999) 'What's your story?', *Fast Company*, January: 32–4.

Polanyi, M. (1996) *The Tacit Dimension*. London: Routledge and Kegan Paul.

Power, M. (1997) *The Audit Society: Rituals of Verification*. Oxford: Oxford University Press.

Rabinow, P. (1999) *French DNA: Trouble in Purgatory*. Chicago: University of Chicago Press.

Ransdell, E. (2000) 'The Nike Story? Just tell it!', *Fast Company*, 31: 44–52.

Rose, N. (1996) *Inventing Ourselves*. Cambridge: Cambridge University Press.

Rose, N. (1999) *Powers of Freedom: Reframing Political Thought*. Cambridge: Cambridge University Press.

Rubin, H. (1999) 'The power of words', *Fast Company*, January: 142–51.

Scase, R. (1999) *Towards the Virtual Corporation and Beyond: Trends and Changes in Mobile Working*. Reading: Oracle.

Schor, J . (1993) *The Overworked American: The Unexpected Decline of Leisure*. New York: Basic Books.

Schrage, M. *Serious Play*. Boston: Harvard Business School Press.

Senge, P. (1990) *The Fifth Discipline*. New York: Domesday.

Senge, P., Kleiner, A., Roberts, R., Roth, G. and Smith, B. (1999) *The Dance of Change: The Challenges of Sustaining Momentum in Learning Organizations*. London: Nicholas Brearley.

Sennett, R. (1998) *The Corrosion of Character: The Personal Consequences of Work in the New Capitalism*. New York: Norton.

Smith, D.W. (1997) 'Introduction: A life of pure immanence. Deleuze's "critique et clinique" project', in G. Deleuze, *Essays Critical and Clinical*. Minneapolis: University of Minnesota Press.

Spinosa, C., Flores, F. and Dreyfus, J.L. (1997) *Entrepreneurship, Democratic Action and the Cultivation of Solidarity*. Cambridge MA: MIT Press.

Stafford, B.M. (1999) *Artificial Sciences: Enlightenment, Entertainment and the Eclipse of Visual Education*. Cambridge MA: MIT Press.

Steiner, M. and White, J. (2000) 'Training the Asda way', *Sunday Times*, 16 March, B1–B2.

Thrift, N. (1996) *Spatial Formations*. London: Sage.

Thrift, N. (1997) 'The rise of soft capitalism', *Cultural Values*, 1 (1): 29–57.

Thrift, N. (1998) 'Virtual capitalism: the globalisation of business knowledge', in J. Carrier and D. Miller (eds), *Virtualism. A New Political Economy*. Oxford: Berg.

Thrift, N. (1999) 'The place of complexity', *Theory, Culture & Society*, 16 (1): 31–69.

Thrift, N. (2000a) 'Afterwords', *Environment and Planning D: Society and Space*, 18 (2): 213–55.

Thrift, N. (2000b) 'Still life in nearly present time: the object of nature', *Body and Society*, 6 (3): 34–57.

Thrift, N. (2000c) 'Spaces of everyday life in the city', in G. Bridge and S. Watson (eds), *The Urban Companion*. Oxford: Blackwell.

Thrift, N. and Dewsbury, J-D. (2000) 'Dead geographies – and how to make them live', *Environment and Planning D: Society and Space*, 18 (4): 411–32.

Wajcman, J. (1998) *Managing Like a Man*. Cambridge: Polity.

Wenger, E. (1998) *Communities of Practice: Learning, Meaning and Identity*. Cambridge: Cambridge University Press.

Williams, K. (2000) 'From shareholder value to present-day capitalism', *Economy and Society*, 29 (1): 1–12.

Willman, J. (1999) 'Knowledge Swap-Shop', *Financial Times*, 22 January, p. 19.

Winograd, T. and Flores, F. (1987) *Understanding Computers and Cognition: A New Foundation for Design*. San Francisco: Addison Wesley.

Wood, J. (ed.) (1998) *The Virtual Embodied: Presence/Practice/Technology*. London: Routledge.

Worthington, J. (ed.) (1996) *Reinventing the Work Place*. London: Butterworth Heinemann.

Websites

Fast Company. www.fastcompany.com

Business Development Associates. www.bda.com

Strategic Horizons. LLP www.customization.com

Play. www.lookatmorestuff.com

Virtual Thinking Expedition Co. www.thinking-expedition.com

St Luke's. www.stlukes.co.uk

The Ehama Institute. www.ehama.org

index

Abolafia 4
abstraction 43, 197, 182
Accenture (formerly Andersen Consulting) 167, 168, 223
accountancy, rise of 173
accounting tools 12–13
actor network theory 132, 172
Addison, J. 156
administrative accounting 33
advertising 7, 15, 51, 74, 75, 148–63, 188
    approach to products 73
    conception of goods and markets in terms of use value 74–5
    cultural economy and persuasive 150–4
    'culturalizing' role 15
    differences between contemporary and pre-twentieth century 150, 154, 155
    Energen crispbread 66–7
    epochalist accounts of 149–50, 154, 161
    as indirect form of cultural transmission 198
    Johnson's Baby Oil 62–5
    links between economic and cultural categories 3, 61
    and newspapers 157, 159
    treatment of as an ideological effort 61–2
    use of typography 149, 154–61
advertising agencies 13
    articulation of economic relations through cultural practices 145, 146
    Bartle Bogle Hegarty (BBH) 134, 141–5
    and changes in advertising media 137
    client/agency relationship 134–5, 143–4, 145–6
    and commission-based payments 139, 140–1, 144, 146
    competition from management consultants and 'media independents' 136–7
    contemporary challenges and changes 134–8

criticism of commercial practices by clients 135
    cultural and commercial calculation in 61–7
    move towards multi-disciplinary project team working 138
    problems 136
    relationship with clients dependent on cultural practices 133, 138
    remuneration models and contract of agreement 15, 133–4, 138–41, 144–5, 146
    and royalty payments 139–40
    scrutiny of by clients and demands for greater accountability 135–6
    segmentation of 136
aesthetic economies
    cultural formation of 115–29
aesthetic knowledge 42, 50, 191–2
aesthetic reflexivity 41–2
aestheticization 195, 197, 199
    and consumer culture 192–3
    and consumption 193–4, 198–9
'agate only' rule
    and advertising 157, 158
Amerco 86, 87–8
Andersen, Arthur 224
Anderson Consulting see Accenture
Anodyne Necklace advertisement 155
anti-economism 133
Appadurai, Arjun 116, 117, 152, 153, 191
art-culture system 188, 191–2, 193
artistic genres
    creation of corporate values and strategy 214–15
artistic groups
    use of to enliven training and creativity 215–16
Asda 210–11
AT&T 167
Atchley, Dana Winslow 214

audits 175–6, 178, 179, 181, 183, 203
Ayling, Bob 223, 224

'balanced scorecard' approach 203
Barthes, Roland 56
    Mythologies 51
Bartle Bogle Hegarty (BBH) 134, 141–5
Baudrillard, Jean 60, 75, 117, 151, 178, 186
Bauman, Zygmunt 34, 178, 195–6
Beck, U. 111
    The Brave New World of Work 102, 104–6
    Risk Society 102
Becker, Gary 174
Bell, Daniel 56, 84, 85
Berger, Peter 84
Berger, Peter et al. 92
blacks
    and music industry 121, 122–3, 126
Blair, Tony 100, 107
Blur 122
body
    use of as central element of
        organizational processes of learning
        212
Body and Soul 215
Bonner, Robert 158, 159
Boughton, I. 112
Bourdieu, Pierre 117, 119, 172
Bowerman, Coach 214
branding 51
Brave New World of Work (Beck) 102, 104–6
Bretton Woods 176, 177
British Airways headquarters 223–4
British Fashion Design (McRobbie) 109
British Film Institute (BFI)
    tracking study (1999) 109, 110, 112
British Rhythm and Blues Association 122
Brown, Arnold 140
BST NBDDP 141
Burkitt, Hugh 140–1
Business Development Associates 217–20
Business (journal) 209
business magazines 17, 208–10
business practice, speed up of 203
business travel 221
Byers, Stephen 224

calculation, forms of 32–3
calculative agency 23, 28
calculative subjectivity 29

Callon, Michel 4, 6, 12, 13, 17, 76
    The Laws of the Markets 24–5
Campaign 134–5, 140
Campbell, Matthew 82
Canclini, Nestor García 117
capitalism 16, 177, 178, 182
    owning of 166–71
Capitol Records 126
Cassirer, Ernst 13, 48–52, 53, 54
category management 176
Cheston, Dr Ian 134
Chief Executive Officers 167
cite 206, 207, 210–20
Clark, G. 169–70, 171, 180, 181, 183
cognitive
    prioritizing of in economic knowledge
        13, 39, 40, 42, 46
cognitive reflexivity 41
Collins, J. 226
commission-based payments
    and advertising agencies 139, 140–1, 144, 146
commodification 116, 196
competition 69–70
complementarity 69–70
computing/computers 40, 45–6, 218
concurrent engineering 203
'conduct of conduct' 205
    consultancy firms *see* management
        consultancy
consumer, representations of 133
consumer citizenship 187
consumer culture 188, 190, 191–2, 194, 198
    and aestheticization and stylization
        192–3
    and the societal culture of consumption
        195–7
consumer fetishism 182
consumption 179, 182
    aesthetic component of 193–4, 198–9
    cultural culture of 190–5, 198
    as foundation of virtualism 182–3
    orientated towards symbolic gains 186
    perception of as increasingly cultural
        186
    societal culture of 195–7
    subject to the criteria of economising
        193
contingency 5
contracts of agreement
    and advertising agencies 15, 134, 138–41

Cook, I. et al. 171, 172
'Cool Britannia' episode 100
corporate culture 2, 8
corporate ownership
    impinging on cultural production
        117–18
cost-benefit analysis 178
country music 127–8
Cousins, M. 163
Coyle, Diane
    *The Weightless World: Thriving in the
        Digital Age* 44
Crainer, S. 227
creative industries 14, 97–112
    and Beck 104–6
    and enforced youthfulness 110
    gap between high and low earners 111
    inequities in 111–12
    and Leadbeater 106–8
    and Sennett 102–4
creativity 109, 207, 212, 213
    construction of office spaces and
        promotion of 222–3
    corrupting of by commerce 115
    increase in emphasis on 204
critical theory 148, 150
'cultural economics' 116
cultural goods 7, 192, 198
'cultural intermediaries' 7, 60, 119
cultural modes of knowing 48–9
'cultural turn' 16, 21, 98, 166, 171–5, 179
    versions of 171–3
cultural turn to life 90–4
culturalization 21
    of economic knowledge 39–55
    of the economy 6–12, 16, 185-6,
        186–90
culture
    commodification of 187
    conception of as 'whole way of life'
        119
    distinction between economy and 9–10
    economization of 185, 186–90
    marriage of culture with 97
    modern uses of the term 186–7
    production of industry 118–19
culture industries 7, 15, 21, 60, 108, 173,
    188, 198
'culture of production' 15
'culture wars' 91

Dahle, C. 217
D'Angelo 126

Daresbury SERC Laboratory 13, 22–33
    integration of manpower booking system
        with cost-accounting apparatus 32
    and management accounting 33
    manpower 25–6
    need for apparatus for calculating 'real
        costs' 29–31
    office of the Director 22–3
    and ordering mode of vocation 33–4
    and standard administrative accounting
        32–3
Dauphinois, Bill 214
Davis, M.
    City of Quartz 170
Davis, Mike 139
Department of Culture, Media and Science
    (DCMS)
    Mapping Document (1998) 97
design process 41
designers 60
desk 22–3
determination, models of 132, 133
deVault, M.
    Feeding the Family 178
di Maggio, Paul 8
digital storytelling 214
Donzelot, J. 109
downsizing 176
dramatic techniques
    use of to challenge entrenched ways of
        proceeding 216–17
Dress for Success campaign 100
Dreyfus, Hubert 218
Drucker, Peter 167, 174
du Gay, Paul 132, 161, 171

e-commerce 173
eating out 193–4
economic agency 23
economic knowledge 39–55
    handing back of to codification by
        disavowal of aesthetic realm 42–3
    and Leadbeater 44–6
    limitation of cognitive view of 48
    prioritizing the cognitive 13, 39, 40, 42,
        46
    and Reich 43–4
    symbolic basis 39–40, 46–54
economic modelling 179, 181
economic theory 14, 25
economics 176–8, 182
Economies of Signs and Space (Lash and
    Urry) 6–7, 40–1

Economist 166–7
economists 179
economy 2
　culturalization of 6–12, 16, 185–6,
　　186–90
　and neo-classical theory 174
Eddie Stobart haulage empire 83
Ehama Institute 217
emergency
　turn towards the rule of 201–2
EMI 124–6
Emin, Tracey 100
emotional thinking 212
Energen crispbread 66–7
engineering 40
Enlightenment 42, 80
epochal theorists 8–9
equities
　ownership of 166, 173, 174
ethics *see* work ethics
ethnography 61
'etho-politics' 100
Evans, Chris 101
Examiner 157
exchange value 117
expressive symbolism 49–50

face-to-face communication 221
fashion designers/design 109, 110, 111
fashion industry 47, 112
Fast Company (magazine) 209–10, 226
'fast' managerial subjects 17
Featherstone, Mike 151, 199
　Consumer Culture and Postmodernism
　　191
　'Lifestyle and consumer culture' essay
　　190–1
Figgie 167
film industry 47
　co-existence of technical and aesthetic
　　53
finance 3–4
finance services 40
Fine, B. 174, 207
Fish, Stanley 5
Fiske, John 116, 117
Flores, Fernando 217–20, 229–31
formal justice 11
Fortune 208–9
Foucault, Michel 8, 24
　writings on governmentality 205
Frankfurt School 176
Franks, T. 112–13

Frears, Stephen 108
freelancers 105, 112
Frith, Simon 129
Full Monty, The 108

Gallie, D. et al. 189
Gap 98
Garcia, Marie-France 24
Gehlen, Arnold 92
George, Nelson 126
Germany
　and pension funds 181
Giddens 172
Goodman, Nelson
　Ways of Worldmaking 53
government regulation 117
governmentality 205–6, 207–8
Green Day 123–4
Gung Ho! management training system
　210–11

habitus 119
Hall, Stuart 99, 119
Hamel, G. and Prahalad, C.K. 213
Harrison, Roger
　*Organization Culture and Quality of
　　Service* 89
Hayden, Ray 122
Heinz 135
Herzberg, Frederick 89
Heuberger, Frank 89–90
Hickman, Craig and Silva, Michael
　Creating Excellence 89
High Fidelity (Hornby) 108
Hirschman, Albert 11
Hirst, Damien 100
history
　and its consequences 180–3
Hochschild, Arlie 86–7
　*Time Bind: When Work Becomes Home
　　and Home Becomes Work,
　　The* 87–8
home
　and workplace 87
Hornby, Nick
　High Fidelity 108
Hunter, Ian 10, 11
Hunter, J.D. 85
Hutton, W. 174

'identification' problem 69
Ienner, Don 123–4
improvisation 213

Incorporated Society of British Advertisers (ISBA) 134, 135
industry
    production of by culture 118–19
information society 188
information technology 207, 221, 223
information-based services 40, 45–6
Inglehart, R. 94
innovation 204, 212, 213
Innovation Exchange 224
Institute of Practitioners in Advertising (IPA) 146
institutions of exchange 224–5
instrumentalized work ethic 79, 80, 85–6, 93
interaction 212
interactive service work 3, 189–90
international financial centres 4
International Monetary Fund 177
Internet 224
Island Records 121

J. Walter Thompson 159
Johnson's Baby Oil 62–3
journalists 110

Kant, I. 10
    Critique of Judgement 55
Kellaway, Lucy 208
Kellner, Hansfried and Heuberger, Frank 89–90
Knapp, Ellen 222, 226
Knight, Beverley 122–3
knowledge 13, 39
    economic see economic knowledge
    exchange of 224
    as a resource in its own right 204
knowledge officer 204
Knowledge X-Change 224
Koppelman, Charles 125
Krogh, G. and Roos, J. 204
Krois, John 49, 52
Kuper, A. 171

labour markets
    and demand for cultural goods 98
Laclau, E. and Mouffe, C. 152
Laclau, Ernesto 133
Lancaster, Kelvin 69, 71, 72
language
    as system of representation 51
Lasch, Christopher 80
    Haven in a Heartless World 86–7

Lash, Scott 13, 39, 54, 111
    Another Modernity: A Different Rationality 40, 42
Lash, Scott and Urry, John 51, 151
    Economies of Signs and Space 6–7, 40–1
Latour, Bruno 28
Leadbeater, C. and Oakley, K. 109, 112
Leadbeater, Charles 13, 46, 52, 54
    Living on Thin Air: The New Economy 39, 44–5, 102, 106–8
Leidner, R. 190
leisure 100
Leonard, D. and Swap, W. 221
Lewin, Roger and Regine, Biute
    The Soul at Work 93
Leyshon, A. and Thrift, N. 171
life, cultural turn to 90–4
lived processes 14
Living Arts 216
Longhurst, B. et al. 194
LSDA agency 139
Luckmann, Thomas 92
Lury, Celia 193, 194
    Consumer Culture 188, 191–2

McDowell, L. 171
McGregor, Douglas 89
McKee, V. 216
McKinsey & Co. 136, 167, 168
McQueen, Alexander 107
McRobbie, A.
    British Fashion Design 109
magazines, business 17, 208–10
Mahesh, V.S.
    Thresholds of Motivation 89
Maister, David 135–6
management accounting 33
management consultancy 167–9, 171, 173, 174, 176, 178, 180–1, 183
management training 210–12
managers 93, 189, 201, 202, 203–8
    being prepared for surprise 212–13
    and cultural capital 210
    pressures facing contemporary 202, 203–5
    as products of circumstance 206
manpower booking system 26, 27, 29
    integration with regular accounting system 29–30, 32
manufacturing industry 207
market(s) 13, 59–77
    and advertising example 63

market(s), *cont.*
  bracketing of 69–71
  constitution of 24–5
  cultural studies in the 74–6
  different product definitions and
    different 67–8
  and Energen crispbread example 66–7
  and identification problem 69
  importance of economic theory 25
  interdependence of economic and
    cultural categories 13, 59–60
  marketing strategy as competition over
    structure of 68, 71
  treating as lived realities rather than
    formal categories 76–7
marketing 7
  and redefining products 68
marketing industry
  links between economic and cultural
    categories 3
marketing people 60
marketing strategy
  as competition over structure of markets
    68
Marxism 172, 174
Mary Kay Cosmetics 88
Maslow, Abraham 81, 89
'material culture' 22
material practices 24
materially heterogeneous relations 23, 25
mathematics 52
meaning 1, 152, 154, 162
media independents 136–7
Mellors Reay & Partners 139
merchant banking 3–4
Merlis, Bob 124
Mieszkowski, K. 215
Miller, D. 153, 193
Miller, P. and Rose, N. 173
Miller, Peter 12, 173
minimum wage 99
mobility of management 17
modernism 42
Mol, Annemarie 33
Morris, M. 153
Mosco, Vincent 117
Muoio, A. 204, 217
Murdoch, Rupert 107
Murdock, Graham 117
Music of Black Origin (MOBO) Awards
  122
music industry 15, 115
  aesthetic hierarchies 120–3

and blacks 121, 122–3, 126
country music 127–8
criteria for repertoire acquisition and
  levels of financial investment 120–2
factor of roster of artists signed to a
  label in attracting artists 124
factor of working conditions in
  attracting artists 123–4
importance of culture issue to executives
  in 123
intersection of US recording industry
  with cultural identities and social
  divisions 127–9
introduction of 'cultural changes' to
  attract talent to labels 124–6
sexist approach to gender relations by
  rock 121
music industry executives 120
Myers, G. 75

National Audit Office 175
National Training League 211
neo-classical utility theory 72
Nestlé 135
'network sociality' 111
network society 6
networking 13
New Age 89
New Deal 99
New Labour 99, 100–1, 102, 107
New York Ledger 158, 159
Newspaper Proprietors' Association (NPA)
  139
newspapers
  and advertising 157, 159
Newton, Sue 211
Nicholson McBride 142
Nike 98
  corporate storytelling programme
    213–14
N.W. Ayer 159

Oasis 122
office spaces
  construction of to promote creativity
    222–3
organizational cultures 16–17, 189
organizational performance 1
organizational work ethic 79, 80, 85, 88
Osborne, T. 150, 162
O'Shea, J. and Madigan, C. 167, 169, 174
outsourcing 105, 176
Oxford Stage Company 215

part-time work 104
Pearson, Dave 214
Pedler, Mike et al.
  Learning Company Project 89
pension fund managers 170
pension funds 166–7, 168, 169–70, 174,
    180, 181, 183
performance 23
Performance and Innovation Unit 1
performativity 206
performing arts 17
  drawing of inspiration from by business
    organizations 213, 215–16
persuasiveness 15
Peters, Tom 106
'phenomenology' of knowledge 49
Philosophy of Symbolic Forms, The
    (Cassirer) 49
Phoenix University 107
Pink 214
Play (marketing agency) 216–17
Polanyi, K. 173
political economy 16
'portfolio careers' 111
'portfolio management' 127
postmodernism 178–9, 181–2, 191
post-structuralism 22
Power, Michael 34, 175
practices
  need to be understood as materially
    heterogeneous relations 12, 23
  reasons for uncertainty in use of
    'culture' in analysing of 21–2
Presbrey, F. 157
PricewaterhouseCoopers (PwC) 214, 222
private
  and public 84, 85
products 71–4
  approach of advertising to 73
  definitions 67–8, 69, 71, 73
  economics 72
  reducing to sign value by culturalist
    accounts 72–3
Protestant work ethic 79, 80, 93
public
  and private 84, 85
public sector
  devaluing of 99

R & B 121, 123, 126
Ransdell, E. 214
Ray, Larry and Sayer, Andrew 8–10, 11,
    81, 82, 171, 172, 186

'Readers' Theaters 214–15
real costs 29–31
Reay, Carol 139–40
recording industry *see* music industry
Reed International 100
Reich, Robert 13, 39
  The Work of Nations 40, 43–4
religion 91
remuneration deals
  and advertising agencies 15, 138–41,
    144–5, 146
repetition
  used as advertising strategy 158–9
representation
  and symbolic function 51–2
retail service work 3
retailing 190
Reynolds, J.R. 126
'risk work' 104
Ritzer, G. 187, 198
Rose, N. 100, 205, 206
Ross, Andrew 111
Rowling, J.K. 101
royalty payments
  and advertising agencies 139–40
Rubin, H. 220

Sahlins, M. 152, 153
Sainsbury's 215
St Luke's advertising agency 216
Salaman, Graeme 1
'salary concept'
  and BBH 144–5
Sanjek, David 128
Scase, R. 221
Schrage, M. 213
Schumacher, E.F. 81
Science Research Council (SRC) 30
Science, Technology and Society *see* STS
self-employment 112
self-expressive work 101
self-reflexive 172, 173, 178
self-work ethics 14, 78, 79–80, 80–1, 83,
    88, 89, 93
Sells 159
semiotics 22, 27
Sennett, R.
  The Corrosion of Character 102–4, 111
service sector 100, 190
Shakespeare, William
  used in teaching modern management
    techniques 82
shareholder value 203

Sharkey, John 141
shopping 193
short-term financial performance 203
Shusterman, R. 49
Sigerson, Davitt 125, 126–7
sight 206, 207, 208–10
signification
    as symbolic function 52–3
signs 40–1
Silicon Valley 106
Simmel, Georg 13, 91, 92, 179
site 206, 207, 220–5
Slater, D. 196, 197
'small groups' 91
Smith, Delia 107
Smith, Martin 142–3
Smith, Rolf 217
societal culture of consumption 195–7
Society of Authors 109, 110
soft capitalism 14, 78, 81–3
    and cultural turn to life 90–4
    as a response to 'problem of work' 84,
        86–9
'soft' knowledge intensive industry 7
space
    and governmentality 205–6
space, office 222–4
speech acts 219
Spinosa, Charles 218
spreadsheet 26, 27–8
stamp duty 157
Steiner, M. and White, J. 211
Stocki, Tim 216
storytelling
    digital 214
    Nike and corporate 213–14
'strategic stories' 213–14
Strategy Selection Outline
    Johnson's Baby Oil 62, 63, 64–5t
Strathern, M. 176
structural adjustment 177, 179
structural change
    unintended consequences of 181
structuralism 172
STS (Science, Technology and Society) 22,
    23, 27
style 202
substantive rationality 10, 11
'support groups' 91
symbolic(s) 40–1, 44–54
    combination of variety of registers of
        within industry 13, 47–8, 54
    and representation 51–2

restricted to certain areas of economy
    47
    and signification 52–3
symbolic abstraction 52
symbolic analysts 43
symbolic expression 49, 52
symbolic function
    cognitive and aesthetic forms 41
symbolic knowledge 48–9
symbolic systems 166, 172
symbols
    manipulation of 43–4, 53

talent-led economy 14, 101–2,103–4, 107,
    111
taste community 42
Tavistock Institute (London) 211
technological culture 42
'technologies of the self' 109, 204, 206
telecommunications 40, 45–6
teleology 175
telephone work 82–3
television advertising 137
television production 98, 109–10
Thatcher, Margaret 34, 99
theatre
    interest in applying modes of to business
        situations 214–15
Theory, Culture & Society 190–1
Thinking Expeditions 217
'thinking studios' 224
Thompson, P. and Findlay, P. 189
Thrift, Nigel 4, 49
Tilley, Andy 139
time 203
Tipton, Steven 79–80
Torp, Neils 223
Trade Secrets 215
tradition-informed workethic 79, 80, 85
training 93
    management 210–12
    use of artistic groups and dramatic
        techniques 215–17
travel, business 221
Treasure, J.A.P. 161
Trinidad 177, 182
Turner, E.S. 153
typography
    and advertising 149, 154–61

under-employment 105
Unilever 137
unintended political economy 166–83

Unity 139
Urry, John 13, 39 *see also* Lash, Scott and
     Urry, John
Ursell, G. 98, 109–10, 111, 112
use value 71, 72, 74, 117

value-rational behaviour 10
virtualism 16, 166, 173–4, 175–80, 181–3

Warner Brothers 124
Waugh, Barbara 214–15
WCRS Healthcare 140
Weber, Max 5, 10, 85, 153
     Economy and Society 10–11
     *The Protestant Ethic and the Spirit of
     Capitalism* 79
'welfare to work' programmes 99
Wells, H.G.
     Tono-Bungay 160–1
Wenger, E. 212
Wernick, A. 151
Who Wants To Be a Millionaire? 102
Williams, Raymond 16, 98, 119, 148,
     186–7
Williamson, Judith
     Decoding Advertisements 75
Wood, John 224
work 196
     Beck's narrative of risk and transition
     104–6
     bringing life back to 89–94
     Leadbeater's narrative of self invention,
     stardom and success 106–8
     and leisure 100

move from welfare to 100–1
     problem of 83–6, 90, 94
     replacing of 'the social' 99–100
     and Sennett's narrative of loss 102–4
     as site of government activity 99, 100
work ethics 14, 78–94
     connection between economic activity
     and cultural values 78–9
     disenchantment with in 1960s/70s 85–6
     economic activities associated with 78
     growth of capitalism due to ability in
     dealing with problems associated with
     79
     instrumentalized 79, 80, 85–6, 93
     organizational 79, 80, 85, 88
     and 'problem of work' 85–6
     self-work ethic 14, 78, 79–80, 80–1, 83,
     88, 89, 93
     and soft capitalism 81, 82–3, 86
     tradition-informed 79, 80, 85
     and value to work 78
     varieties of 79–81
Work of Nations, The (Reich) 40, 43–4
work-and-spend thesis 196
World Bank 177
World Trade Organization 177
writers 111
Wuthnow, Robert 91, 93

youth 101
'youth stalkers' 98

Zukin, Sharon 39
     The Culture of Cities 46–7